"This is as important a book as you are likely to read this year or any year ... a book of marvels, a guided tour of a jaw-dropping future, a travel through time to the world as it might be made.... I urge everyone who cares about the future to read it carefully. Prehoda's world is a world we could make. It could happen. We need only see the vision and grasp it.

"I fervently hope we will do so while there is yet time."

—J. E. Pournelle, Ph.D.
From his *Foreword*

Turn the page now, and enter

YOUR NEXT FIFTY YEARS

This book
is dedicated to

ALINE

A loyal wife, exotic mistress and steadfast friend for a
journey through the next fifty years.

YOUR NEXT FIFTY YEARS

by

Robert W. Prehoda, Ph.D.

Foreword by J.E. Pournelle, Ph.D.

SF
ace books

A Division of Charter Communications Inc.
A GROSSET & DUNLAP COMPANY
360 Park Avenue South
New York, New York 10010

YOUR NEXT FIFTY YEARS

An ACE Book

First Ace printing: January 1980

Printed in U.S.A.

FOREWORD:
The World as It Might Be Made
by
J. E. Pournelle, Ph.D.

Predicting the future is an old game whose origins are lost in the mists of time; doubtless the first "futurist" was some toothless old soothsayer who undertook to tell his clan where to find a new source of wooly mammoths. It can also be a dangerous game. One supposes those early soothsayers found the clan inviting them to make large contributions to the family stewpot when the mammoths were not found.

Over the centuries the art was refined. Futurists learned to keep thir predictions vague, and to leave carefully unspecified the precise time when their prognostications would come true. Strangely, the more vague the prediction, the more important it became, at least for those well versed in the art of obfuscation. This practice may have reached its highest point of development with Karl Marx, whose influence does not seem much to have waned even though almost none of the social trends he foresaw have in fact occurred. Of course his failure was inevitable; Marx wrote before anyone on the planet truly understood the impact science and technology would have on man's history.

In more recent times the art changed again. When historians at last realized how powerful a driving force technology could be, it seemed reasonable to try to predict what the new technologies might be. Technological forecasting was born, and was followed closely by the "futurists" who take the technology forecast and try to deduce how the new technology will change the social order. Alas, most "futurists" know little of real technology, and few with "hard" scientific qualifications have the experience and learning to understand society and economics; but certainly we have had a recent spate of books telling us what our future will be like. (I've written a couple of them myself.)

Visions of the future run in cycles: we foresee utopia or doom. This is hardly a new trend, of course; our oldest literature contains both visions of a bright new world and longing for the Golden Age. Just lately, though, doom has been popular, and most prognosticators prophesy disaster. We shall pollute ourselves to death, or run out of energy, or use up a number of increasingly scarce resources; failing any of these, we shall die of overcrowding.

This book has a different message. Bob Prehoda thinks we have a future, and in the following pages paints a glowing picture of it: a world in which we are all healthier, wealthier, and wiser; a world without war or the possibility of war, without want, without overcrowding, without pollution, and with near-infinite resources; in a word, Utopia.

Has Prehoda a right to make such predictions? Certainly. His qualifications as a "hard scientist" are impeccable, and he already has a good track record in technological forecasting.

Is the world he pictures a possible one?

Certainly the technology is. Although some of Bob Prehoda's predictions may seem a bit far out, the fact is that he has been rather conservative in his estimates of future capabilities. It is almost certain that we can build all the marvels Prehoda describes.

But will we?

Alas, I think not. This is not to place myself among the doomsters. I hope and believe that we in the United States will realize before it is too late that we cannot indefinitely consume without investing; that we are even now eating the seed corn, and without self-denial and investment in new science and technology, particularly in space research, we will hand our children a world stark and joyless indeed. I often think we will realize all this in time to do something about it.

Before we do, though, things are likely to get rather bad here. Already there is a thriving industry built around the concept of "survival". There are experts who teach survival skills: ways to stay alive after the coming collapse of American society, and there are compelling reasons to take such people seriously. Western civilization *could* collapse; as Roberto Vacca has shown so brilliantly in his *The Coming Dark Age*, our complex society is more vulnerable and brittle than most suppose. War could bring us down, but even without war a massive depression with simultaneous runaway inflation could start a worldwide catastrophe from which it would be very difficult to recover.

But though many experts believe collapse to be the most probable course of events, it need not happen. We have the time, talent, technology, and resources to take a different path, a road that leads to Prehoda's bright future.

For that reason, this is as important a book as you are likely to read this year or any year; but please do not groan and return the book to the shelf because of that. I well know that most "important" books are deadly dull. This one is not. It is instead a book of marvels, a guided tour of a jaw-dropping future, a travel through time to the world as it might be made. Yet it remains important.

Important because we must see the vision before we can work toward it. This *now*-oriented society will hardly make sacrifices and costly investments in a future not clearly seen; yet without investment and sacrifice, we will never reach Prehoda's bright future.

In truth, I doubt we will reach Prehoda's world no matter what we do; his vision is too bright for that. I cannot believe that wealth for all will melt away every human conflict; there will remain, in my judgment, a number of unsatisfactory people: paranoids, the greedy, the slothful, the stupid, and they will create problems enough. Still, Prehoda's world remains one to shoot for; and I for one would far rather have the problems that come with affluence than those arising from poverty and disorder.

I would like to think that everyone would prefer a world of wealth to one of want, but I know better. There are many in positions of power and influence who opt for poverty. Of course they don't want to be poor themselves; but they would like the world to have poor people in it. Wealthy people tend to be intractable, to resent regulation and control; the poor have little choice but to submit. Moreover, a world made wealthy is a world with few exclusive places. The comparative affluence of the past ten years has demonstrated that: now almost anyone in the United States can afford access to beaches. Bend over to tie your shoelace on the John Muir Trail and you are likely to be trampled to death by teen-agers wearing inexpensive mountain boots and carrying inexpensive pack frames with Dacron sleeping bags: gear that only the wealthy could buy when I was a Boy Scout.

A wealthy world is a world with colossal servant problems.

I have other reasons to doubt that Prehoda's bright vision will ever come true. He dismisses crime with a single paragraph; by 1989, he says, "a combination of advanced psychological treatment and comparatively severe sentences" will have reduced the high crime rate of the '70's. I doubt that will happen. The number of psychologists and psychiatrists in this country has grown enormously in the past few years, precisely during the decades when the crime rate skyrocketed; and as for severity of sentences, we haven't the jails to detain all the criminals, nor will we have built them in the next decade.

Studies have shown that severity of punishment has far less efficacy in deterring future actions than does *inevitability* of punishment: and even were we to build hundreds of new jails, aye and restore the cat o' nine tails in the bargain, lawyers have far too much to gain by keeping the criminal justice system complex and unsure ever to allow inevitable punishment even for criminals most obviously guilty of the most egregious crimes.

Nor, alas, do I delude myself into believing that nearly unlimited wealth will eliminate crime by eliminating poverty; for if modern psychology has proved one thing, it is that poverty is not the cause of all, or even most, crimes.

In short, I am prepared to believe Prehoda when he tells me that within a century we can eliminate poverty. I am not prepared to believe that we will thereby eliminate crime.

Finally, I cannot accept the casual way that Prehoda has the world turn sensible: by 1989 "the antiscientism which has dominated certain intellectual circles during the 1970's seemed as distant as Naziism and other mental aberrations of times gone by." Hatred of science and engineering and technology is deeply imbedded into many American universities, and it will not easily be rooted out. Indeed, antiscientism has assumed the role of religion for many intellectual leaders, and the antiscientific movement with its mindless slogans and blind opposition to technological innovation is the primary problem of the world. Eliminate antiscientism and you can indeed have the marvellous world Prehoda describes —and it won't take any fifty years to get there, either.

But although I have some reservations about parts of this book, I urge everyone who cares about the future to read it carefully. Prehoda's world is a world we could make. It could happen. We need only see the vision and grasp it.

I fervently hope we will do so while there is yet time.

ACKNOWLEDGEMENTS

Frequently the literary contributions of one author serve as the inspiration for a book written by someone else. Robert A. Heinlein's amazingly accurate forecasts during the past four decades, most of them incorporated in fictional works, have convinced me that outlining a reasonably precise picture of the shape of things fifty years from now is not an impossible task. Behind almost every great man there stands an equally outstanding woman, so my grateful appreciation is extended to both Bob and Ginny Heinlein.

Profound thanks to my good friend Jerry Pournelle for his insightful Foreword to this book. This contemporary Renaissance man shares my vision of a technological Utopia co-existing in complete harmony with nature.

Several paragraphs in Chapter Two were contained in a 1969 essay which was co-authored with William S. Sprague. Neil P. Ruzic's Book, *Where the Winds Sleep* (Doubleday, 1970), was a projected history of lunar development in the 1970-2040 time period, and it is the only book on the future that is similar to *Your Next Fifty Years*. Recent suggestions from Bill and Neil are very much appreciated.

Other good friends who have made useful recommendations include Donald K. Bjelke, Larry Niven, Jerry Pournelle, Vsevolod N. Shmelev and Kurt G. Toppel. My editor, James Patrick Baen, has been extremely generous with both his time and his sage advice which have greatly improved this book in many ways.

Appendix A contains an essay, "The Principle of Optimization," which was first published in the July-August 1977 issue of the *World Future Society Bulletin*. This is an appropriate time to say "thanks" to a friend who shares my dream of a better tomorrow, Edward S. Cornish, the President of the World Future Society.

Appreciation is also extended to Robert C. Dille for permission to include the *Buck Rogers* art work on page 139 which originally appeared in 1938.

My thanks to John Billingham, Vera Buescher and Mark A. Stull of the Ames Research Center for illustrations and data on Project Cyclops (which is not now a NASA funded program).

I affectionately acknowledge the unwavering good disposition of LOBO, my constant companion for thirteen years who has lain next to my desk almost every minute while this book was being written. The deep devotion of this incomparable German Shepherd dog serves as a constant reminder that terrestrial species other than *homo sapiens* must be preserved if the world of the future is to be a worthwhile habitat.

I would like to thank Audrey Assal for her splendid work in typing various drafts of the manuscript from my undecipherable writing and impossible spelling. And most important of all, an expression of appreciation and love far beyond my command of the English language to my wife Aline.

PREFACE

Your Next Fifty Years is a projected history. It is not science fiction, but extrapolated science describing the practical developments that will grow out of research in the physical and biological sciences. This data, when integrated with social and political trends, permits a realistic projection of what we can expect during the next half century.

Fictional devices have been used in several chapters as a means of dramatising the central themes of those chapters; overall, the writing style is one that Arthur C. Clarke has termed "technofictional forecasting." By starting within the confines of the near future and proceeding in five year increments toward 2029, you will see how our future history can evolve toward a dramatically different civilization from today's.

Everything described in this book *presently exists* at some stage in its evolution from theoretical conception to research and development hardware. Projected breakthroughs are not random guesses; they are the predictions of recognized specialists in the relevant disciplines, based on theory or on direct observation. The most "far out" future realities predicted herein are regarded as both possible and likely by leading scientists I have associated with over the years.

R. Buckminster Fuller says that the future is a "choice between utopia or oblivion." But what *kind* of utopia? The following pages describe a high-technology civilization where wildlife conservation and biospheric protection receive the highest priorities—a utopia that is likely to be your tomorrow.

Robert W. Prehoda
Studio City, California
January, 1979

CONTENTS

Foreword by J.E. Pournelle.......................... V
Acknowledgements................................. XI
Preface..XIII
1. 2029: A Transformed World.............. 1
2. On Forecasting the Future................... 22
3. 1989: The Post-Orwellian Era.............. 47
4. 1994: Year of the Malthusian Crisis................. 72
5. 1999: Visit to Micropolis.................... 100
6. 2004: Robots and the Intelligence-Amplifier. 124
7. 2009: The World Set Free.................... 157
8. 2014: Methuselah's Children.............. 185
9. 2019: Project Cyclops....................... 200
10. 2024: The Third Industrial Revolution............ 224
11. 2029: Technological Shangri-La....................... 256
12. Tomorrow and Tomorrow and Tomorrow...279
Appendix A: The Principle of Optimization. 307
Footnotes...332
Index...344

CHAPTER ONE
2029: A TRANSFORMED WORLD

Let me take you on a flight of fantasy which may be the reality of tomorrow. The wings of imagination project us fifty years into the future. It is now the year 2029. A dramatic adventure is about to begin. The central figure is *you*—one of the present readers of this book.

Some readers will be surprised to still be alive fifty years from now; the earlier explosive pattern of breakthroughs in fundamental biological knowledge were translated into a cornucopia of revolutionary medical treatments during the 1980s and following decades. By the year 2029, diabetes, cancer and heart disease are banished into the limbo of history. Also, scientists have discovered the fundamental causes of aging and have perfected aging-retardation treatments that at first slowed down the rate of aging—sometimes to an apparent standstill. Furthermore, during the past few years rejuvenation has become contemporary reality.

1

The rejuvenated *you* of 2029 looks younger, enjoys better health and vigor than the "you" of 1979—unless you are presently an athletic teenager in perfect health. Men and women of this third decade of Century 21 have more energy and virility than they did fifty years ago. Robots do almost all of the tedious work, providing additional time for humans to engage in sports and physical fitness programs. Optimum exercise is supplemented by health-promoting diets individually tailored for each person.

As dawn breaks on March 1, you are sleeping soundly on a bed with a mattress comprised of tubes of memory-gel. Galvanic feedback sensors inside the tubes cause them to form a perfect fit around the portions of your head, torso, arms and legs in contact with the bed. As your scheduled hours of slumber near the end, a signal from the household computer causes the surface of your memory-gel bed to gradually firm up. Quiet music rouses you from your night's sleep in the bedchamber. The ceiling light-panel slowly and gently increases the room's illumination. Waiting patiently beside the bed is your household robot with a tray of juice, coffee, eggs, toast and an array of nutritional supplement and rejuvenation pills. The caloric content of your breakfast is based on your weight level during the past few days.

While you eat breakfast, the news is presented on a wall-sized, 3-D TV screen, a "Tri Vee." But no one else is watching exactly the same news presentation. During the night, your household computer has stored on videotape just those segments of the news of interest to you—based on a personalized interest-profile that you can modify at any time. The computer has scanned several hours of broadcast news, and the interest-profile weeding-out process now allows you to see a 17-minute condensation of events that holds your rapt attention.

After an invigorating swim in your indoor Jacuzzi pool, you walk to a nearby building containing a holographic conference room. Attending meetings can be expensive, time-consuming, energy-consuming and, if travel to a distant site is required, disruptive to home life. By applying holography, it is now possible to send three-dimensional images to a meeting instead of going there in person. The conference room is fitted with a multicolor laser illuminator—a TV-type camera that picks up a holographic image and relays it via satellite to a set of laser projectors in other identical conference rooms in nearby cities and around the world.

The reconstructed images of other conference participants appear completely lifelike, in color, in true three-dimensional depth and perspective. They move around, speak and otherwise function—to your eyes—as almost perfect replicas. Solid models can be examined from different angles. Holographic teleprojection allows every normal conference activity—except shaking hands. (Holographic teleprojection has also revolutionized entertainment, bringing theatrical productions into the home in an incredibly lifelike format.)

The world of 2029 has been completely transformed and you are planning a trip that will show you the complete panorama of changes that have occurred during the past fifty years. The purpose of this morning's holographic conference is to select the places to be visited and the modes of transportation to be employed on the protracted journey. You are a member of the organizing committee selected to plan an itinerary that will be both educational and entertaining.

Some of the other conference attendees live thousands of miles away, but all appear as lifelike as if they were in the room with you. Facsimile reproduction machines permit maps, printed pages and handwritten notes to change hands within a few seconds. The magic of holographic teleportation serves as a catalyst: the itinerary is finalized within four hours.

With business completed, you all decide to have a late lunch. Beverages and food are served by robot waiters in each of the conference rooms. Toasts are made, jokes exchanged, and the luncheon proceeds as if everyone were together in one room. Your mind wanders as you recall past inefficiencies in attempting to conduct business by letter and telephone.

The departure date arrives and you get into your car. Your robot has already put your bags in the trunk and wishes you "bon voyage" as it closes the door.

Your electric car is radically different from those you drove in the past. It has no steering wheel! You press a few buttons on the dash, programming your airport destination into the car's advanced computer. The garage door opens and your car automatically drives out into the street. Aluminum strips beneath the concrete road keep the automatic car in the proper lane, and radar maintains it at a safe distance from other vehicles. Your robot has placed a breakfast tray in front of you, and you eat leisurely as a news summary flashes on the dashboard TV set.

A few miles from your home, your car enters a special lane. The front wheels lock in a straight-ahead position. Beneath the car are four metal flanged wheels of smaller diameter than the car's tires. They are attached to the inside rim of each big wheel. A small side-hatch door slides back and an electric third-rail shoe folds out. It makes contact with a power rail at the same time the flanged wheels roll onto the rails of a track. The rails go down an incline and you enter a narrow subsurface tunnel. Your car accelerates at a controlled rate until an optimum speed for safety is maintained. Computer control maintains the proper distance between vehicles, and since traffic is light, a speed of 75 m.p.h. is maintained. Following breakfast you open the morning's paper and scan the printed news.

Egress from the subsurface electric guideway brings you to the local airport, where your robotized car slows to a gentle stop at the main entrance. You give your luggage to a porter-robot, then punch buttons on the dashboard to automatically return your car to your residence.

At the airport you board a nuclear-powered zeppelin with staterooms, promenade decks and most of the other luxuries of an ocean liner. Boasting an energy consumption ratio only one-twentieth of a comparable jet airplane, this graceful dirigible cruises slowly at a low altitude, permitting passengers to see everything below in intimate detail. On the ground are ethereal cities of optimum size—few exceeding the 300,000 population level.

Over half of the private homes below cannot be seen. They are constructed underground with many soundproofing and energy-conserving features. Many large commercial and industrial buildings are also underground structures—a construction technique

THE WORLD OF 2029 A.D.

MIKE ROYER

that eliminates aesthetic pollution.

More than 75 percent of all heavy industry has been moved to floating platforms connected to off-shore fusion power plants. All forms of radiation and other pollutants are encompassed in closed-cycle technological operations, which means the waste from one process becomes the raw material for another. Thanks to new breakthroughs in chemistry, many metals dissolved in seawater are economically extracted at these zero-pollution bases. The offshore platforms also produce finished goods and process seafood.

The superzeppelin which serves as your temporary home is largely constructed of exceedingly light, ultra-high-strength materials produced in zero-gravity space factories. The entire Solar System has now been explored by man, and each year increasing quantities of finished products are sent to Earth from the Moon, Mars, the asteroid belt and other extraterrestrial sites.

Much of North America has been (or is being) converted into parks and wildlife-preserve territory. Your graceful dirigible cruises slowly at a low altitude over the great Western game ranches where eland and other African animals thrive in scrub areas. These commercial game ranches blend into wildlife reserves where all forms of domestic and foreign flora and fauna are safe from human predation.

Each evening the airship is moored near one of the huge open zoos where captive breeding programs have saved almost all of the birds, mammals, and reptiles on the endangered list 50 years ago. This trip is partly a camera safari, and you take films of rhinos and other exotic creatures roaming freely in natural habitats. Your fellow passengers are enchanted by the nearness of rare birds flying inside huge geodesic domes.

Creatures are now seen that did not exist a century ago. Revolutionary advances in genetic engineering, cloning and other biological techniques have inspired zoologists to create new subspecies of many birds and mammals with unique, sometimes startling characteristics. These "new animals" are kept in open zoos until their commercial viability and potential ecological impact have been properly evaluated.

Flying over the Pacific Coast you can see whales and other cetacean species—again plentiful throughout the world's oceans. An overnight stop is made at a large island north of Vancouver that has been turned into a sanctuary for Siberian tigers. The same area serves as a preserve for the American bald eagle, no longer a rare bird.

The next few days are spent at an enormous open zoo in Alaska which contains one of the most unusual wildlife exhibits on Earth. In 2019, an oil prospecting crew found a well-preserved frozen mammoth at a remote site in Northern Siberia. When she was frozen, the mammoth was pregnant. The story of how that frozen tissue was transformed into living mammoths is one of the most dramatic scientific adventures of the third decade of the 21st Century. Transplant of mammoth embryos into the uteri of Indian elephants is steadily increasing the number of these prehistoric pachyderms.

Children are taken for rides on the backs of the easily domesticated mammoths. The intelligent creatures can perform useful tasks, but their primary importance lies in their symbolic value: their well-publicized existence has helped galvanize support for a global conservation effort to save all known and potential forms of non-human life. That successful program has made wildlife tourism the dominant form of leisure activity—*and* the most important factor in the balance of payments of many non-industrialized nations.

Game ranches, nature preserves and open zoos are by no means restricted to North America; eventually these wildlife areas will cover about 60 percent of Earth's land surface. Hydroponic food production has eliminated the need to farm marginal land. Agriculture is no longer allowed in fragile tropical ecosystems which have become carefully protected state parks of great value in competing for the tourist dollar (yen, ruble, etc.). Forty percent of Earth's total land surface provides ample room for a reduced human population in equilibrium with accessible supplies of both the necessities and luxuries of life.

Population control has been a resounding success and the total number of humans on this planet is slowly declining. Consequently, all forms of Hitlerian insanity have now been totally vanquished. Each of Earth's diverse creatures is allowed to survive in its unique ecological niche without the danger of being ruthlessly driven to extinction by the "master species" that almost destroyed our world during the last century. A comprehensive knowledge of ecology and the other biological sciences has eliminated the "human chauvinism" that prevented man from recognizing how closely he is linked to all forms of life.

Following visits to the transformed cities of Japan and Micronesia, the superzeppelin lands in Hawaii. The remainder of your trip is to be made on a sailing ship—a windjammer! But this vessel only bears a surface resemblance to 19th Century windjammers.

Automated windjammers—called "DynaShips"—were developed during the 1980s as one answer to escalating oil prices.[1] The most striking feature of a DynaShip is the absence of conventional sailing-ship rigging. There are no stays or shrouds. Nobody has to go aloft to handle the sails. The sail area and angle of attack to the wind are controlled servomechanically from the bridge: the sails are automatically set, reefed and furled by these servomechanisms.

The DynaShip has four hollow-pole masts, elliptical in cross section. They are unstayed and turnably pivoted to the hull. To take full advantage of the wind, the masts can be rotated. Thus the ship can be switched to the opposite tack very quickly: it can even sail backwards.

The sails are carried on aerodynamically curved yards, providing an unbroken airfoil from top to bottom of each mast. Each single sail of this efficient airfoil may be drawn separately in or out of the hollow mast to reduce or increase the sail area exposed to the wind.

Moving between the yards, DynaShip sails work something like draw curtains; furled, they are contained in the hollow mast. All control elements, winches and other equipment for actuating the sails and masts are down in the hull. Sails may be set, reefed or furled in a matter of seconds.

The DynaShip cruises at 12 to 15 knots in normal weather conditions, though its top speed is around 20 knots. Gas turbines are used for harbor maneuvering and for auxiliary power when there is no wind. DynaShips consume less than 10 percent as much fuel as the conventional ships they displaced in the 1980s.

Unmanned DynaShips tended by advanced robots are still used in large numbers to transport cargo on the world's oceans. Their success as luxury cruise ships stems from the romance long associated with sailing vessels. DynaShips—clean, quiet and pollution free—also reflect the fundamental design ethic of the 21st Century: "Technology should be developed in harmony with Earth's biosphere."

Cruising at 15 knots, your 45,000-ton DynaShip has all the luxuries of 2029 society. An unusually large human crew is supplemented by a robot servant for each passenger. Swimming pools, promenade decks, holographic theaters, intimate cafes serving gourmet meals, all are accessible 24 hours a day.

Whales can again be seen cavorting below as the cruise ship reaches a site off the Mexican coast in Baja California. This will be the last stop before sailing to a major port near your home city. Here the passengers can visit an undersea community similar to others now located in all the continental shelf regions.

Small submarines allow you and your friends to see marine robots extracting ore from mines on the ocean floor. Other marine robots tend huge farms of seaweed attached to floats which in turn are anchored to the sea floor. This seaweed is converted into a variety of useful chemicals and food products in nearby floating factories.

Your submarine docks at an undersea hotel in the center of this unique community. Here you are able to talk to people whose professional careers cause them to live 600 feet beneath the ocean's surface. They explain their diverse research and commercial activities, which are greatly expanding the productivity of the seas without adverse ecological impact.

The last leg of your journey allows you to reflect on how the wise use of science has permitted the creation of a utopian world. The "energy crisis" and similar patterns of global disruption during your lifetime have all been solved through the magic alchemy of well-funded research. Looking up, you suddenly realize that the graceful sails of the DynaShip demonstrate a vitally important energy-use dictum: *There is no shortage of energy; there is energy all around us—we must only learn how to use it.*

Returning home, you enter your luxurious living room with its "universal information system" console which gives direct access to the contents of all publications and filmed documentaries. You decide to view a series of special programs on space industrialization and other revolutionary changes that have so greatly transformed the world during the past fifty years.

Your 3-D TV screen shows advanced single-stage-to-orbit shuttles providing inexpensive access to orbital factories producing a bewildering array of products. Some of them can only be manufactured in a zero-gravity vacuum environment while others can be produced at less cost in space. Also, orbital manufacture is required for many products because of severe pollution constraints on Earth.

You view mining activities on the Moon that are so extensive that it is difficult to believe that the first lunar landing occurred less than 60 years ago. Nuclear explosives shatter rich veins of lunar ore which are then fed into fusion-powered plasma torches which allow effective separation of the various chemical ele-

ments. Refined metals are put into containers which are then sent to factories circling the Moon by an electromagnetic surface catapult over 15 miles long.

All orbit-to-orbit transfers are now made by huge spacecraft propelled by thermonuclear fusion rockets. These efficient propulsion systems have greatly reduced the costs of deep-space operations. The low cost of 21st Century space flight has allowed a small research city to be built on Mars, a planet with many unexpected surprises for human explorers.

You are fascinated by 3-D films showing astronauts being placed in hibernation chambers prior to a 19-month voyage to the new mining complexes sited in the planetoid belt between Mars and Jupiter. Their temperatures will be reduced to four degrees above the freezing point, halting the aging process as these hibernauts are transferred to a region unbelievably rich in the elements required by an advanced technological civilization.

The first refined metals from the planetoid belt were brought to Earth less than ten years ago. In the decades and centuries ahead, a "space pipe line" will tap this vast source of resources. The raw materials dilemma of the last century has been resolved by the collective breakthroughs of astronautics. Already, eight percent of our supply of scarce elements comes from extraterrestrial sites. Within the next hundred years, this source of material wealth will be greatly increased as potentially polluting industrial functions are moved away from the fragile biosphere of our home planet.

Radio telescopes have detected signals carrying complex technological data from an advanced civilization 134 light-years away from our own Sun.

Man has begun to communicate with alien beings so far advanced that many of their accomplishments will seem to us indistinguishable from magic. Looking toward the more distant future, the most exciting thing expected from space is information from our new-found alien friends—intelligent beings who have reached the "supercivilization" stage of development.

Your TV screen does not show scenes of marching armies. Historic patterns of superstition, prejudice and ignorance that held us in thrall were shattered before the year 2000. Yours is an era in which the arms race is a long-abandoned anachronism, and population control has restored the entire biosphere to a state of ecological balance. Applied science developed in compliance with ecological principles has allowed man to be the master of his technology rather than its slave.

The passing panorama on your TV screen depicts a utopian society destined to survive and thrive. It is a society that has adopted a new ethic concerning the purpose of human life on Earth. That ethic: *Our ultimate goal is to promote the greatest happiness and progressive development for an optimum number of individual humans on a planet with a diverse variety of stable ecosystems—supported by a Solar-System-wide civilization.* This is a "live and let live society," a tolerant society. People are now allowed to do almost anything they wish to do, so long as their acts do not harm other humans or interfere with the rights of another individual.

Your world of 2029 is a society in which *homo sapiens* has reached the full capacity of his genetic potential—living a life free from toil, dependency and

cruelty under conditions which fully liberate imagination, intellect and the capacity to enjoy the fruits of his labor. The new ethic has allowed you and your fellow humans to develop a society which optimizes the desirable qualities of life.

What you now accept as everyday reality would have been profoundly disturbing to many persons fifty years ago. Sixteen percent of all new births are "test tube babies"—about half of them brought to term in the uteri of "host" mothers. This procedure also allows the sex of a child to be predetermined, since male-producing and female-producing human sperm can now be separated in the laboratory. Wealthy women are thereby freed from the physical burden and trauma of pregnancy. Women scientists and other female professionals are increasingly turning to host mothers as a means of optimizing their own productivity.

Some children have only one biological parent. Ova are removed, stimulated into beginning embryonic development, and then brought to term in host mothers—a procedure called "parthenogenesis." The maternal chromosomes are removed from a human ovum, and a sperm cell is inserted into the ovum. Embryonic development then proceeds with only the father's chromosomes. This is called "androgenesis," a procedure that can now theoretically permit one man to be the sole parent of millions of children.

Human clones are also born with increasing frequency. Unlike fertilization in-vitro, cloning is a different form of reproduction. Every cell in an organism carries all the genetic information needed to create the whole organism. The nuclei of unfertilized ova can be removed and replaced with nuclei taken from appropriate human or animal cells. They then proceed to develop into normal animals and humans in the uteri of host mothers.

"Ectogenesis," so-called "test-tube" pregnancy, has recently been achieved with humans. Developing ova are now placed in a plastic womb supplied with essential nutrients and oxygen. Nine months later normal babies are taken from these ectogenesis chambers.

Parthenogenesis, androgenesis, cloning and now ectogenesis! The revolutionary realities of human reproduction have resulted in profound "future shock" for many of your contemporary citizens in 2029. But these techniques have saved many rare species of animals from extinction ... and resurrected some. Ectogenesis may soon permit a profound modification of the human being in the course of embryonic formation—perhaps a larger brain with a greatly increased potential for human intelligence.

The best pedigreed domestic animals are now literally mass-produced. This biological breakthrough is causing a marked increase in our food supply.

Your TV screen now shows how success was achieved in growing new hair on bald men. A new drug without adverse side effects causes dark hair to turn blond—a development considered a boon by many men and women. You view scenes of super-cosmetic surgery that allow even radical alterations in racial characteristics. Any affluent person can now be "handsome" or "beautiful" by his or her standards. There is a fad for this in the Scandinavian countries this year, the announcer tells you.

The scenes showing these exotic biological developments are now followed by an hour-long TV documentary showing the all-encompassing role of intelligent robots in the world of 2029. There are now eight robots—intelligent mobile machines—for every single human adult. They are everywhere, working without fatigue or complaint, performing both dangerous and boring jobs—working 24 hours a day, week in and week out. Their productivity has increased the economic wealth of the advanced nations far beyond the wildest hopes of 1979. And you now live in a world that conforms to the predictions contained in Norbert Wiener's *The Human Use of Human Beings*, first published 75 years ago.

These advanced robots come in a variety of shapes and sizes. Some have multiple extensions permitting them to perform a great variety of dexterous tasks. They work in factories, deep mines, on the depths of the ocean floor and in the freezing polar regions. In space they will soon fill the entire Solar System. Already they are mining the Moon, Mars and the planetoid belt. They can survive the intense radiation environment of Jupiter's moons, as well as the high pressure and high gravity of the gas giant's upper atmosphere. Barring accidents, the self-repairing cybernetic machines are immortal, and they will enable us to reach the stars.

Like many of your neighbors, you have a household robot that performs many mundane functions. He (robots are usually called "he"), can also keep you company and converse with you on virtually any subject. This intellectual capability owes to his connection, via cable and radio waves, to IAN, the supercomputer who controls all of the other robots on Earth. IAN has the complete repository of human knowledge stored in his vast memory banks and is the primary motivating force behind the present explosive expansion of basic scientific knowledge, as man and supercomputer in partnership push back the barriers to the hidden secrets of nature.

The last program you have selected ends, and you shut off your "universal information system." Your long trip has been fatiguing, and it is time for sleep. Since you are feeling rather worn, you decide not to sleep on your memory-gel bed in the master bedroom. Instead you enter another room and get into a cylindrical tank filled with warm saline water a few degrees above normal body temperature. You float face up. The effects of warm saline water enhance the quality of sleep and reduce the time required for the body to obtain optimum rest and physiological restoration. The perforations in the contoured bottom of the tank permit a therapeutic "bubble massage" of varying intensity. Also built into the system is a very low intensity ultrasonic unit which cleanses the body in addition to providing other healthful effects.

A heavy metal cover slides over your Aquarest tank, converting it into an "equalizing pressure chamber" which permits the complete cessation of breathing (normally a continuous activity from birth until death). Oxygen enters the lungs and carbon dioxide is expelled through up-and-down cycling of pressures within the unit. The air density within your lungs changes, but the volume remains constant, permitting a complete cessation of movement in the muscles used for breathing. The changing pressures are equally applied to all parts of the body and lungs.

You find the nonbreathing state to be an extremely pleasant, soothing sensation. Your heart action is decreased and the cessation of breathing also has a beneficial effect on the central nervous system. The impulse to move the limbs diminishes and you lie still for hours.

This night you have difficulty falling asleep. You push a button which causes an 80-percent xenon gas, 20-percent oxygen mixture to enter your lungs—producing unconsciousness within 3 to 5 minutes. Unlike the sleeping pills of fifty years ago, there are no after-effects from xenon narcosis and you could use it every day if you needed it.

You now drift into a very deep sleep. The sleep of a person completely satisfied with the contemporary world of 2029.

Many if not most readers may have by now concluded that this chapter is describing an unobtainable utopia. The next ten chapters will explain how our home planet can be transformed into a utopian paradise over the next five decades. A transformed world you will live to see.

CHAPTER TWO
ON FORECASTING THE FUTURE

This is a book about the future—your future—a book that surveys and describes the probable shape of the next 18,261 days which, taken altogether, make up the full sweep of what I have herein chosen to call "your tomorrow." As such it can be called a book of *prediction*, but not, however, one of *prophecy*. And if the distinction appears to be a semantic one, it is that and much more.

(NOTE: when the word "man" is used throughout this book, it is intended to be a contraction of the word "human" and does not cannote any form of sexual chauvinism. When "man" is used as a part of certain generic words—in "chairman" or "mankind" and elsewhere—it still means and, etymologically, always has meant "person." As far back as the Sanskrit *manus*, the root *man* means *human being*, with no implication of sex.)

Traditionally, the man who made predictions arrived at them through careful study and calculation, if only, as in ancient times, through the study and calculation of occult signs and omens. The prophet, on the other hand, was always held to be a person who received his futuristic visions full-blown and directly from the gods or through some form of religious revelation. In short, the one was an interpreter of more or less natural phenomena; the other, a messenger of the divine.

The distinction must not be dismissed as "merely semantic," for it is also a functional distinction. It marks the difference between two fundamental approaches mankind has always used in dealing with the problem with which this book is concerned—the uncertain future.

Homo sapiens is, it would seem, the only terrestrial species possessed of an unmistakable "sense of future." Other animals prepare for the future. The bear overeats to fatten himself for the onset of hibernation; the squirrel, for similar reasons, stores away nuts and seeds. But each acts instinctively. The preparations of instinct are short-term things. Triggered by the angle of the Sun or by subtle temperature cues, they act to ready themselves for the *coming* winter, but remain unconcerned with the *many* winters beyond. Man alone is fully and consciously exposed to the terror—and the promise—of all his tomorrows. *Homo sapiens* appears to be the only animal capable of worrying.

Your ancestors worried about local problems. But you are a member of a well-educated society with a communications technology that presents both global crises and the problems confronting even the most distant land before us each night in vivid color. Consequently, our worries have multiplied in number, kind and consequence, until today we live in constant fret that, through nuclear miscalculation, through conflicting international ideologies, through a population explosion that may culminate in ecological armageddon, through a technology that has far outstripped our psychological development, through growing internecine racial warfare—through all of this and more, we may soon end *all* of our worries by self-obliteration and the destruction of our planet's biosphere. Thus the story of man continues to be, to a very large degree, the story of his ongoing and ever widening struggle to somehow see beyond the next sunrise, the next year, the next decade, the next era; to somehow discern and avoid tomorrow's tragedies, to isolate and insure its potential joys; to somehow find a basis for all of our plans, hopes and dreams.

In times gone by, there was little that anyone could do to alleviate the perplexities inherent in our "sense of future," little we could do to resolve the questions raised by our unique capacity for worry. Until the Renaissance, the problems of the future were left to the benign aspects of fate, or through prayer and supplication, to Providence and temporal rulers.

The first significant change began with the revolutionary philosophy developed in the early years of the 17th Century by Sir Francis Bacon. He preached simply that the proper function of science was to search for truth and to benefit people. Central to his grand vision was the maxim, "knowledge is power," and this also suggested solutions to the foreseeable problems of the future. Science could allow humans to develop various technologies that would solve these problems.

Oddly enough, as true science flowered, it developed a rigid discipline which, while it warmly embraced objective observations, analysis, experimentation, and interpretation (hypothesizing and theorizing, that is), tended to exclude prognostication, except as it concerned postulations and extrapolations of further scientific discovery based on current research. Prediction, more or less by default, tended to become a literary art, exemplified at length by such giants as Jules Verne (1828-1905) and H. G. Wells (1866-1946). About fifty years ago this kind of prognostication evolved into the distinct literary form called science fiction (hereafter abbreviated as SF). And, while some of its practitioners have been scientists or engineers, most SF authors are professional writers with little or no formal education in the various branches of science.

Critics of SF claim that it is only another kind of escape literature, and indeed much of what is offered to the public on page or screen is little else than some standard adventure yarn set in space, beneath the ocean or in some future time. In order to qualify as genuine and not simply fantasy, every technological aspect of an SF story must be not only possible, but probable. In this puristic view, SF is the heir to prediction and still serves—as did the Cro-Magnon shaman, the Roman augur, and the alchemist-astrologer of the Middle Ages—to alleviate anxieties and reinforce hopes bred in us by our sense of future, by our distinctively human capacity for worry.

The contemporary role of SF in forecasting the future has been summarized by Ben Bova, former editor of *Analog*: "To begin with, science fiction stories do not predict THE future because there is no such thing. Unless you believe in a totally fixed and immutable timestream (in which case it doesn't matter what you do, everything's frozen in cement already), then the future *must be* a series of events that have not yet happened, and therefore can be altered, changed, diverted, moved, shaped by myriads of individual decisions. There is no one certain future; there are countless possible futures, with every moment bringing new opportunities to hand.

"Science fiction writers explore those many possible futures. Each SF story is an exploration of a potential future. If human history can be thought of as a migration of billions of people across the vast landscape of time, then the science fiction writers are the scouts who range far ahead and bring back occasional reports on what the territory up ahead is like, so that the main body of the people can choose their course more intelligently, avoiding the badlands and picking out the sunny, well-watered meadows and cool, green hills."[1]

SF is not the only medium of predictions. The last three decades have witnessed a steady series of forecasts by scientists—characterized by ever-increasing accuracy—of changes, innovations, discoveries and inventions that will shape the years ahead. Indeed, many of the earlier predictions of Verne, Wells and other pioneer forecasters already have come to pass, particularly in the space program. In part, this rise of accurate prediction is owing to the fact that only in our time have scientists come to a better and more complete understanding of the basic laws regulating our universe, and scientific discovery usually is followed by the accurate measurement, and then the gradual control, of new forces. In those areas of technology already enjoying strong financial support, accurate prediction is becoming easier, while in poorly supported areas, such as the biological sciences, future developments still are seen as so many hazy shadows.

In 1966, Edward S. Cornish founded the World Future Society (WFS) to serve as an impartial clearinghouse for a variety of different non-fiction studies of alternate futures (address: Box 30369, Bethesda Branch, Washington, D.C. 20014). Under his inspired guidance, this nonprofit educational and scientific organization has expanded into the largest futurist organization in the world with over 56,000 members in 86 countries. *The Futurist* and other WFS publications now influence America's most powerful leaders in industry, the media, academia and government.

Cornish observes: "If anything is important, it is the future. The past is gone, and the present exists only as a fleeting moment. Everything that we think and do from this moment on can affect only the future. And it is in the future that we shall spend the rest of our lives ... The study of the future is the most exciting intellectual enterprise of today.

"The peoples of the world do not share a common past, but they do share a common future ... Forecasting is not some new and strange activity. It is as natural and necessary as breathing. Forecasting the future is fundamental to humans ... Without forecasting the future, there is no freedom to choose a future: The future is simply thrust upon us. By studying future possibilities, we begin to realize new possibilities that are open to us. We are not locked into our present situation ... We have it within our power to create a civilization incomparably superior to any in human history."[2]

Perhaps the most important discovery of our century is the power of well-organized, well-financed research and development, at both the applied and basic levels, conducted with a minimum of constraint. From our explosive growth of investment in science and related development has come the demand for more and more accurate methods of predicting the probable results of this costly program of investigation. In recent years a new discipline called *technological forecasting* has emerged as a vitally important long-range planning tool. It was originally refined to meet military and space planning needs after the Soviet Union launched the first Sputnik in 1957. Billions of dollars were suddenly allotted to space and advanced weapons systems, and there was a pressing need to determine in great detail what could be accomplished by a certain time period in specific programs. During the past few years many of us who pioneered the use of technological forecasting to meet NASA and DOD requirements have been using it to refine planning data in other fields. This is proving to be a good example of "beating the sword into a plowshare."

In my 1967 book on the subject, technological forecasting was defined as: *"The description or prediction of a foreseeable invention, specific scientific refinement, or likely scientific discovery promising some useful function, including better health and longer life."*[3] These are functions that meet the requirements of industry, government agencies and general societal needs including ecological reform. (In the remainder of this book, "technological forecasting" will be abbreviated as "TF.")

Fundamentally, TF is based on an understanding

of the current limitations of scientific knowledge which were accurately defined by the late Sir George Thomson (1892-1975) in *The Foreseeable Future*. This 1955 book remains a work of stunning brilliance offering insight into the favorable options open to humanity through selective refinement made possible by science. He began with the assumption that ... "Technology is governed by scientific principles, some of which are understood, and there is accordingly a basis for prediction ... I have supposed that developments which do not contradict known principles and which have an obvious utility will in fact be made, probably in the next hundred years. No doubt there will be discoveries which will transcend what now appear major impossibilities, but these are unpredictable, and so are the practical developments which will follow for them."[4]

The reason Sir George restricted his forecast chiefly to the future of technology was his conclusion that "sociology has still to find its Newton, let alone its Planck, and prediction is guesswork." Remarkably accurate projections of the social consequences of technology, however, were included in *The Foreseeable Future*.

The remarkable accuracy of Thomson's technological forecasts can be explained by the fact that he devised a systematic approach to replace, or at least improve, the "educated guess" intuition of traditional prognostication. In making future projections, he observed: "It is because major discoveries are likely to be based on scientific principles rather than on mechanical ingenuity, and because these principles have limitations, that it is reasonable to hope to be able to predict in a general way the trend which these discoveries will have. For this reason it may not be too rash to regard certain kinds of technical progress as foreseeable, though one will certainly miss a great deal."[5]

Sir George pointed out that scientific principles are frequently "principles of impotence." They say that certain things *cannot* be done, but they do not say that everything else *can*, for that would imply that there are no more fundamental principles to discover. From the discoveries of the past 300 years, he identified eight principles based on our current understanding of the laws of nature which can aptly be called "principles of impotence." They include restrictions such as the speed-of-light barrier, the second law of thermodynamics and the conservation of mass and energy.

The validity of this forecasting methodology is demonstrated by the fact that only one of these eight principles of impotence has been seriously challenged by experimental evidence since 1955. In August 1975, a team of scientists reported the discovery of a "magnetic monopole," but the interpretation of physical evidence in their experiment has become the center of continuing scientific controversy. If the existence of the magnetic monopole is independently confirmed by other scientists, this would mean that magnetic charges need not be inseparable north and south poles on the same body. The monopole would be the magnetic equivalent to the positive proton or negative electron that exist independently in nature.

If any principle of impotence is added or discarded, or even radically changed, the unforeseen— and a new scientific era—will be upon us. For example, confirmation of the now uncertain discovery of the magnetic monopole would suggest the possible realization of revolutionary developments in electronic systems, allowing new medical therapies in the fight against cancer, new sources of energy, extremely small and efficient motors and generators and new particle accelerators of much higher energy than any yet built. The monopole might allow the development of unbelievably strong structural materials along with a quantum jump in computer technology.

In other words, reliable forecasts can only be made of technological possibilities that already exist at some stage of what one might call their "scientific evolution." Near-term forecasts can be made of crude prototype devices not yet economically practical. Long-term TF possibilities must presently exist at some stage of their genesis in the form of repeatable laboratory experiments, or as a sound theory, or at least as a coherent and logically consistent idea which does not go against the grain of known scientific laws. And, clearly, just how reliable a given prediction is will relate to the "evolutionary" stage of its present development.

TREND CURVES

The first systematic approach to forecasting future events predated Sir George Thomson's book by several years. In 1949, science fiction author Robert A. Heinlein wrote an article in which he attempted to describe the important changes that were likely to occur during the subsequent half century—a preview of the world in the year 2000. In that exercise, he arrived at the trend curve by observing how people predict the future (see Figure 1, below, which first appeared in Heinlein's 1949 forecast). Trend curves provide a very useful tool in making TF long-range projections beyond twenty years.

Heinlein pointed out that the most that laymen usually anticipated was very little change or progress (Trend Line "1"). People who do not anticipate an immediate slowdown in technology refinement expect it to reach a point of diminishing returns (Trend Line "2"). Very daring minds are willing to predict that we will continue our present rate of progress (Trend Line "3"—a tangent). In 1949, Heinlein observed that: "There is no reason, mathematical, scientific or historical, to expect the curve to flatten out, or even reach a point of diminishing returns or simply go on as a tangent. The correct projection is for the curve to go on up indefinitely, with increasing steep-

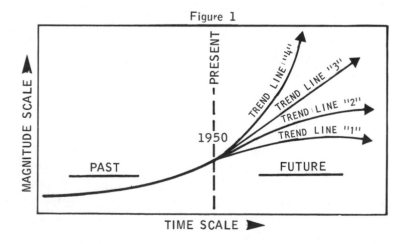

Figure 1

ness (Trend Line "4") ... you can count on changes in the next 50 years at least eight times as great as the changes in the past 50 years."[5] What Heinlein was saying is that the steepest exponential curve of all is the growth of human knowledge.

Heinlein's trend lines in Figure 1 are particularly relevant to this book which is a projected history of the next fifty years. During the past quarter century the increase in human population, the exponential growth of industrialization and raw materials extraction, and environmental problems have definitely followed Trend Line "4." This was not the pattern generally expected in 1950. Demographers were making population projections that would fit Trend Lines "1" or "2." Our present pollution problems were completely unexpected, but Heinlein correctly defined the dimensions of the present global food shortages in his 1949 forecast.

The first half of Heinlein's "next 50 years" is now history. Space exploration was a science fiction dream in 1949, but man landed on the Moon 20 years later. The rate of scientific discovery has been far greater since 1950 than it was in the 1925-1950 years. The tempo of change has accelerated in all fields, including social change. Unfortunately, our problems are also increasing in a world seemingly gone mad, but science offers the tools to check runaway population growth and all forms of pollution—if *homo sapiens* is wise enough to reach out and take them.

Heinlein's 1949 forecasting article was not published until September 1952. I first read it while serving in the U.S. Army, and this brief review had a profound influence on me. His carefully reasoned statements caused me to realize that a systematic ap-

proach to making long-range forecasts was possible—
a viewpoint reinforced three years later when I first
read *The Foreseeable Future*. After reading this article
by Heinlein, I began to collect published forecasts
from many diverse sources which in turn have been
used as reference data for my articles, books and scientific papers on the future. That collection has now
grown into a somewhat sizable library of varied
projections of the shadowy shape of things to come.

In 1966, Heinlein's forecasting article was reprinted in *The Worlds of Robert A. Heinlein* (Ace
Books). This paperback will be reissued in the near
future, and it contains a particularly instructive
analysis of his 1949 fifty-year forecast as seen from
the vantage point of 1966—one of the best essays on
the art of forecasting the future ever written.

During the past 39 years, many forecasts of technological and societal events in the SF stories of Robert
A. Heinlein have subsequently come to pass or now
appear likely to be realized in the not-too-distant
future. These projections set in a fictional format are
more difficult to evaluate from an accuracy standpoint than those in various non-fiction forecasts, but
Heinlein now appears to be the most accurate all-
around forecaster of future events since H. G. Wells.
Like the best fiction written by Wells, Heinlein's SF
stories have a spellbinding quality that will continue
to entertain our descendants. Already they are regarded as SF classics.

The TF discovery point is frequently called the
"Hahn-Strassmann point." This term had its origin in
the December 1938 experiments conducted by Otto
Hahn (1879-1968) and Fritz Strassmann in Berlin,
which resulted in the discovery of uranium fission.

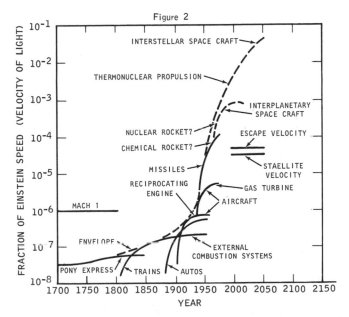

Figure 2

Lise Meitner (1878-1968) had been an earlier member of the team. The publication of these research results, along with Meitner's separate analysis, permitted an accurate forecast of contemporary nuclear technology which would not have been possible prior to the disclosure of this scientific breakthrough.

It is extremely important to recognize when the Hahn-Strassmann point has been reached in a branch of science, technology or biology. This is comparatively easy when it is a result of a dynamic breakthrough such as the discovery of uranium fission. It is much more difficult to recognize when it is the interrelated step-by-step progress of a more evolutionary nature. Figure 2 (above) is a typical trend curve. It illustrates past and foreseeable advances in the speed at which men can travel on the surface of our planet, in the air and in space. This trend curve shows that each time a new means of transportation was achieved, the speed curve for that device rose sharply, and finally leveled off as the practical limits for the device was reached. Each new increase in speed was produced by a new device or invention based on a new concept that was usually the result of a Hahn-Strassmann point discovery. Integrating all the separate technology performance patterns usually produces an integrated trend curve of increasing upward slope. Such trend curves were used (with surprising accuracy) to predict the exact year in which the first satellite would be orbited and when man would land on the Moon.

Trend curve extrapolation must take into account the fact that the extension of a well-established rate of progress will eventually intercept a known physical limit. Since, by definition, progress cannot extend beyond this limit, only two predictive possibilities exist. The first is that progress will indeed stop at this point. The second possibility is that there will be new discoveries that will cause the "known physical limit" to be removed, or reinterpreted. Such discoveries may also permit Hahn-Strassmann points leading to new technology permitting progress beyond previously known limits. The old "speed of sound" barrier for aircraft is a good example (first exceeded on October 14, 1947). The individual technologies which make up an overall trend curve each follow a characteristic pattern. Performance usually rises gradually, then goes through a period of rapid progress, followed by a long period of modest advances as the limits of the technology are being reached. This pattern is called the "S"-shaped curve or the "Gompertz curve" after the mathematician who first discovered this statistical

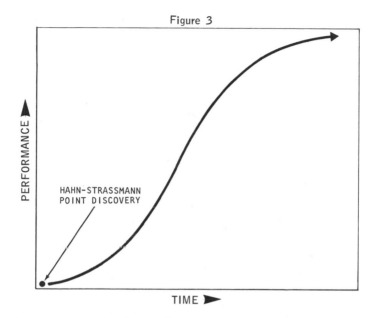

Figure 3

phenomenon in the 19th Century. Most developments that experience dynamic growth tend to follow the pattern discovered by Max Gompertz in 1825. His S-shaped curve is sometimes called the "signoid curve."

It is the individual developmental time-achievement trends of each specific technology within an overall pattern, such as transport speed (dependent on propulsion, energy conversion, strength of materials, etc.), that TF can play a crucial role in years to come. There are actually two different S-shaped trend curves in each of these technological and biological-control achievement patterns. Figure 3 (above) illustrates this concept. Trend curve "A" is the pattern of performance achievement that is possible after a Hahn-Strassmann point using TF combined with official recognition and the optimum allocation of resources, funds, and qualified specialists. Trend curve

"B" is the likely achievement pattern, if decision-makers do not rely on TF and an ordinary evolutionary pattern is followed. Full TF implementation allows us to "telescope performance achievements," making advanced technology available in a much shorter period of time. This process can provide decisive terrestrial and space military systems, can increase economic growth, and allow us to solve almost all of our ecology, energy, health and other problems —thereby contributing immeasurably to human happiness.

The most dramatic example of full TF implementation was the American nuclear weapon demonstrations in 1945 (Hahn-Strassmann point in December 1938). Partial telescoped performance achievements can be seen in the German V-2 launch in 1942, and the Soviet orbital satellite launch in 1957 (Hahn-Strassmann points—Konstaintin E. Tsiolkovski's theo-

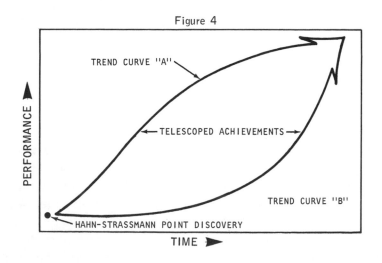

Figure 4

retical refinement in 1898, Robert H. Goddard's performance demonstration of the first liquid fueled rocket in 1926). Full implementation of TF in rocketry would have permitted the first satellite to be launched in 1945, resulting in a time telescoped performance achievement gain of 12 years.

In Figure 4, the trend curve "A" represents the rate of progress made by the Manhattan Project scientists during World War II. Trend curve "B" represents the surprisingly slow rate of progress made by competing German scientists in nuclear technology. In contrast, Curve "A" can represent German wartime rocketry achievements and trend curve "B" the unimaginative U.S. wartime rocket development. The V-2 was flown successfully in 1942, and the U.S. did not have a comparable system until the first Redstone was launched in 1952. Full implementation of TF in German rocketry permitted a telescoped performance gain of ten years.

Individual technologies overlap in time and specific purpose. Telescoped performance achievements can be realized in every area once the Hahn-Strassmann point is reached. Figure 5 (next page) illustrates this important fact. Technology envelope "1" can represent contemporary performance in rocket propulsion; envelope "2" can represent the foreseeable performance of nuclear fission rockets; technology envelope "3" can represent the possibility of a controlled thermonuclear fusion propulsion system. Advances in the biological sciences and medicine also follow the interrelated, overlapping relationships presented in Figure 5. For instance, the treatment of cancer with radiation is an older discovery, which may be represented by performance envelope "1."

Figure 5

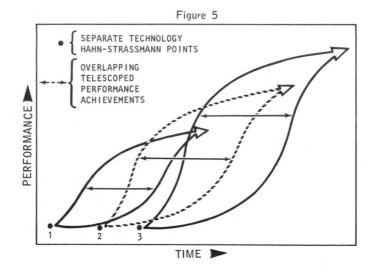

Now radiation is being combined with chemotherapy, a recent advance which can be visualized as performance envelope "2." These means of cancer treatment may be joined by a future Hahn-Strassmann point discovery, possibly permitting all malignancies to be permanently cured (performance envelope number "3").

The telescoping of performance gains in time is what we hope to achieve using refined forecasting techniques. Figures 4 and 5, therefore, represent a concept that is vitally important to you. *All of the desirable things described in this book could become reality in the shortest possible time through full implementation of TF combined with generous funding of the requisite R&D.*

It frequently has been observed that "5 to 10 year forecasts usually prove to be too optimistic, and 10 to

Figure 6

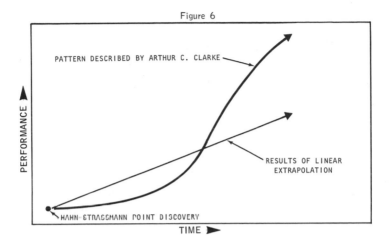

PERFORMANCE

PATTERN DESCRIBED BY ARTHUR C. CLARKE

RESULTS OF LINEAR EXTRAPOLATION

HAHN-STRASSMANN POINT DISCOVERY

TIME ➤

20-year-and-beyond forecasts are almost always proven by events to be extremely conservative." Arthur C. Clarke, the perceptive British author and father of the communications satellite, explains why most technological forecasts are overoptimistic in the short run but overpessimistic in the long run: "The human mind tends to extrapolate in a linear manner, whereas progress is exponential. The exponential curve rises slowly at first and then climbs rapidly, until it cuts across the straight line slope and goes soaring beyond it. Unfortunately, it is never possible to predict whether the crossover point will be five, ten or twenty years ahead." Clarke's explanation is illustrated in Figure 6 (above).

The forecasting rule or pattern described by Clarke and illustrated in Figure 6 should be kept in mind when reading chapters in the second half of this book.

Some of the forecasts on those pages will outline future achievements in the physical and biological sciences that would appear to be almost miraculous today. But less than 66 years separated the Wright brothers' first flight from our initial landing on the Moon, and there is every reason to believe that a comparable pattern of scientific breakthroughs will be the reality of tomorrow.

THE SCENARIO

During the past 18 years a number of different approaches or methodologies have been refined to forecast biomedical and technological trends. Aside from the brief description of trend curves, the only other TF methodology that will be described in this chapter is *the scenario*, because the remaining chapters of this book represent a moderately detailed scenario forecast.

Herman Kahn deserves the greatest credit for refining the scenario as a distinctive TF methodological tool when he was at the Rand Corporation in Santa Monica, California, during the 1950s. He subsequently founded the Hudson Institute located about 35 miles outside of New York City, and a steady stream of imaginative scenario forecasts have been produced by individuals or teams associated with that prestigious "think tank."

The scenario outlines a logical sequence of events to show how a future environment might evolve, step by step. A good description of the TF scenario is included in one of Kahn's books, *The Year 2000,* co-authored with Anthony J. Wiener: "Scenarios are hypothetical sequences of events constructed for the purpose of focusing attention on causal processes and decision points. They answer two kinds of questions: (1) Precisely how might some hypothetical situation come about, step by step? and (2) What alternatives exist, for each actor, at each step, for prevention, diverting, or facilitating the process? 'Alternative futures' can be used for generating additional scenarios, for setting forth and discussing criteria, for the systematic comparison of various alternative policies (or alternate combinations of assumptions and objectives), or for the analysis and examination of specific issues. They are also of interest in making assumptions and contexts explicit, as should be done, for example, in any analysis of 'directions and destinations.' With a set of alternate futures and scenarios that lead to them by alternate routes, one may see better what is to be avoided or facilitated, and one may also gain a useful perspective on the kinds of decisions that may be necessary, and the points in time after which various branching-points will have been passed."[7]

Scenarios can provide TF inputs of future requirements for specific technologies. They can refine information on the foreseeable "climate" for various branches of science rather than outlining probable technological achievements, but foreseeable technological breakthroughs can be included in scenarios. Many of the best science fiction stories are based on refined scenarios, and some SF authors have been outstanding technological forecasters.

Chapter One and Chapters Three through Eleven represent a "surprise-free" scenario forecast written as a projected history of the next fifty years. A surprise-free scenario is a projection of future patterns of change that would seem less surprising—in the mind of the author—than any other specific combination of possibilities. The forecasts in this book are selected extrapolations of current or emerging tendencies in our world with particular attention given to revolutionary changes that I expect from foreseeable scientific breakthroughs frequently overlooked by other students of the future.

Of course, my surprise-free scenario forecast would not be the same as that of someone who interprets events differently, or whose basic philosophical assumptions are different—particularly regarding the role of science which I believe can still open the door to salvation for a world presently beset by apocalyptic crises. For example, pessimistic forecasters anticipate a major war which I recognize as a very real possibility. A major nuclear conflict is not described on succeeding pages, however, because I now believe it can be avoided and will be avoided. Also, it is almost impossible to foresee what society and our biosphere might be like following such a cataclysmic event.

The fact that foreseeable events are reviewed in a scenario does not mean that they will occur precisely the way they are described on the targeted dates. Kahn and Wiener offer an important caveat on this aspect of specific items described in scenario forecasts. They point out that while a surprise-free projection may be "... the *most* likely of the various possible projections; that is to say that when contemplating a thousand things which could happen, the surprise-free projection may have a probability of much less than one in a hundred, yet be more probable than any of the other 999 possible occurences. It could be 'most probable' and still be quite improbable."[8]

The possibility of a countless number of turning-point events means that at any time in history there are an almost infinite number of alternate future worlds, each somewhat different. But a world very much like the one described herein is possible if a major war can be avoided and the population growth crisis resolved in some satisfactory manner.

Futhermore, this book is limited to a time-span which many of its readers will live to see including events in the world of 2029 A.D. Younger readers, those under thirty, can expect to live for another fifty years. Foreseeable breakthroughs in aging-retardation, however, may allow many older readers to live far longer than they presently anticipate (described in Chapter Eight). My projected history could be *your* history if enough people make a determined effort to realize the desirable future options allowed by science.

I believe that TF can evolve into a highly-refined technique for coordinating the efforts of all our various sciences and technologies. It can evolve into a true "science of sciences." Eventually TF will be used not merely to predict, but to analyze the future in order to promote progress by initiating certain technical developments with the objective of cancelling out future problems before they arise and of securing desired human goals. The emerging forecasting methodologies can give us a new kind of "foreseeability," one which permits us to state what we want in the future, and to achieve such wants by a predetermined effort.

The winds of change portend a transformed world, and my projected history culminates in a foreseeable society that is utopian when compared to some alternate histories of the future. Technological forecasting is a potent weapon in the age-old conflict of man against an uncertain future. If it is properly used to shape policy, then scientific forecasting may at last emancipate us from our unique capacity for worry, because it will permit us to use our "sense of future" not merely to prognosticate but to design consciously, and then to deliberately build, the kind of future desired by rational men and women.

CHAPTER THREE
1989: FIVE YEARS AFTER ORWELL— THE POST-ORWELLIAN ERA

As the first weekend of 1989 approaches, you look forward to seeing a movie you missed five years ago when a new version was first released. The picture is George Orwell's *1984*, which in early 1985 had received the academy award for best picture along with nine other awards ranging from best actor to best special effects. A large oil company is going to present the uncut movie on TV with only one commercial break.

Now, 40 years after *1984* was first published, its author's name is enshrined in the English language as a cliche for the apocalypse. Virtually every doomsday prophecy uses "Orwellian" to describe any impingement on freedom from psychological brainwashing to telephone wiretapping. For decades people lived in dread of the day when Big Brother would at last rule us body and soul with the inverted slogans of Newspeak ... "War is Peace ... Freedom is Slavery ... Ignorance is Strength" ... and most ominous of all ... "Big Brother is Watching You."

George Orwell's real name was Eric Blair. His extraordinary literary premonition of the most perverse forms of tyranny was published in 1949, one year before he died of tuberculosis at the age of 46. Orwell extrapolated a fictional society in his SF novel as a means of warning readers of dire threats he perceived in diverse trends in the contemporary society of his last years—England in the late 1940s and the Stalinesque tyranny then spreading across Eastern Europe. No doubt the Hitlerian nightmare was fresh in his mind as he wrote the book while in the last throes of terminal respiratory disease.

With your closest friend and family, you sit in your favorite chair as the picture begins. The director has succeeded in creating a vivid portrayal of a society dominated by "IngSoc" (Orwell's fictional mutation of English Socialism), a totalitarian ideology in which the last vestiges of human freedom have been stripped away. Life is portrayed as a pattern of dreariness and hopelessness on the part of the educated class, and a droning routine life for the proles, the vast majority who are engaged in disciplined labor from dawn to dusk.

The movie shows a changing panorama of scenes as a deep background voice repeats Orwell's words: "The ideal set up by the party was something huge, terrible, and glittering—a world of steel and concrete, of monstrous machines and terrifying weapons—a nation of warriors and fanatics, marching forward in perfect unity, all thinking the same thoughts and shouting the same slogans, perpetually working, fighting, triumphing, persecuting—three hundred million people with the same face."[1]

All information in Orwell's one-party state is controlled through an elaborate Ministry of Truth, with the motto: "Whoever controls the past controls the future. Whoever controls the present controls the past." History is rewritten with complete thoroughness on a daily basis, and all books or films that no longer are in confirmation with these alterations *must* be immediately destroyed. Anyone found with such tainted documents or visual data in their possession is severely punished.

Big Brother's stern portrait is everywhere, but he does not appear in the cast. The indignities of *1984* are seen through the misfortunes of Winston Smith, its central character (there are no heroes in this movie). As with all citizens, both the public and private movements of Smith are followed through an elaborate array of closed-circuit TV cameras which cannot be turned off except in the homes of inner party members. Never knowing when one is being observed allows strict rules against sex and other sensuous pleasures to be enforced in this puritanical state: "There were even organizations such as the Junior Anti-Sex League which advocated complete celibacy for both sexes. All children were to be begotten by artificial insemination (*artsem*, it was called in Newspeak) and brought up in public institutions."[2]

The screenplay follows the book as the thought and speech of the cast members are controlled by substituting standard English with a new jargon called Newspeak. "Words like honor, justice, morality, internationalism, democracy, science, and religion had simply ceased to exist. A few blanket words covered them, and, in covering them, abolished them. All words grouping themselves round the concepts of liberty and equality, for instance, were contained in the single word 'oldthink.' "[3]

Children in the film are trained in "doublethink." The use of such words as "blackwhite" causes them to believe that black is white and to forget that they ever believed the contrary. Doublethink is a ". . . vast system of mental cheating. It not only allows the party to change history, it eventually enables it to arrest the course of history."[4]

Both action scenes and dialogue demonstrate why free inquiry is incompatible with Orwell's *1984*, a point explained in a document written by high ranking party members: "In Newspeak there is no word for science. The empirical method of thought, on which all the scientific achievements of the past were founded, is opposed to the most fundamental principles of IngSoc. And even technological progress only happens when its products can in some way be used for the diminution of human liberty. In all the useful arts the world is either standing still or going backwards. The fields are cultivated with horse plows while books are written by machinery."[5]

For nearly four hours you sit in numb silence watching scenes that might have been your contemporary world, a society engaged in perpetual war—where rationality and individual freedom are forbidden, and where justice, free will and science have been eradicated, not only in practice, but even from the vocabulary.

In a dramatic confrontation between O'Brien, the protagonist of the party, and Winston Smith, the beaten rebel, a detailed description is given of an Orwellian future: "Do you begin to see, then, what kind of world we are creating? It is the exact opposite of the stupid hedonistic Utopias that the old reformers imagined. A world of fear and treachery and torment, a world of trampling and being trampled upon, a world which will grow not less but more merciless as it refines itself. Progress in our world will be progress toward more pain. The old civilizations claimed that they were founded on love and justice. Ours is founded upon hatred. In our world there will be no emotions except fear, rage, triumph, and self-abasement. Everything else we shall destroy—everything. Already we are breaking down the habits of thought which have survived from before the Revolution. We have cut the links between child and parent, and between man and man, and between man and woman. No one dares trust a wife or a child or a friend any longer. But in the future there will be no wives and no friends. Children will be taken from their mothers at birth, as one takes eggs from a hen. The sex instinct will be eradicated. Procreation will be an annual formality like the renewal of a ration card. We shall abolish the orgasm. Our neurologists are at work upon it now. There will be no loyalty, except loyalty toward the Party. There will be no love, except love of Big Brother. There will be no laughter, except the laugh of triumph over a defeated enemy. There will be no art, no literature, no science. When we are omnipotent we shall have no more need of science. There will be no distinction between beauty and ugliness. There will be no curiosity, no employment of the process of life. All competing pleasures will be destroyed. But always—do not forget this, Winston—always there will be the intoxication of power, constantly increasing and constantly growing subtler. Always, at every moment, there will be the thrill of victory, the sensation of trampling on an enemy who is helpless."[6]

O'Brien hesitates and then utters the most chilling words in the movie: "If you want a picture of the future, imagine a boot stamping on a human face—forever." The scene of O'Brien and Smith is then replaced by one showing a single boot and then many boots about to stomp down on the faces of those members of the cast who had been portrayed as something other than villains.

There is no happy ending. Following scenes of sadistic torture and brainwashing, Winston Smith is reduced to the stage where "... He had won the victory over himself. He loved Big Brother." (These are the last words in the book.)

The following morning you read on the front page that more people had watched 1984 the night before than had ever seen any TV presentation in the past. Not only had this movie broken all records for the size of a single viewing audience, but everyone was talking about it. For weeks 1984 was the central subject of newspaper columnists and TV commentators. The crowd at the country club discussed nothing else on the Sunday evening following the broadcast. George Orwell's picture was on the cover of *Time* when the new issue was delivered to newsstands on Tuesday.

Orwell's 35-year SF forecast was now viewed as an intended warning rather than serious prophecy. Everyone tried to answer one question: to what extent does the present world resemble or show any trends towards the Dante-esque visions in the movie? After all, 1984 had passed five years ago, so now Orwell's vision of a terrestrial hell can be seen in proper perspective.

The general consensus was that the world of 1989 was not fundamentally Orwellian, although there were disturbing patterns in certain totalitarian countries. Stories and rumors of torture or crude brainwashing continued to be mentioned by people escaping from some closed societies. "New Leader" was the official title of the neo-Maoist dictator of China. His actions and speeches caused him to be compared to Big Brother. Every citizen of China had to memorize his short book, *The Thoughts of Mao Tse-Tung as Interpreted by New Leader.* TV newscasts of throngs of marching Chinese, each one holding aloft a copy of this small book, bore an eerie similarity to certain scenes from the *1984* movie.

But in most of the advanced nations, individual freedom was the central tenet of both philosophy and the laws as enforced by the police. A combination of advanced psychological treatment and comparatively severe sentences had reduced the high crime rate of the 1970s. For the criminal, courts were more Draconian, but an honest citizen could again walk the streets without fear.

How had we escaped Orwell's hellish vision? Perhaps the most important factor was that the anti-science attitude which dominated certain intellectual circles during the 1970s now seemed as distant as Nazism and other mental aberrations of times gone by. A majority of the citizens of 1989 believed without reservation that scientific rationalism is indispensable if a society is to remain free. Like the arts and literature, science dignifies the human spirit. Scientific inquiry—the scientific method—is the ultimate expression of free will, of human freedom, for science allows us to gain control over nature. If nature in all its diverse manifestations ranging from forest fires to the influenza virus cannot be controlled, then man is not truly free.

Of equal importance in avoiding an Orwellian world was the handmaiden of true science—freedom to speak and publish without censorship. Newspeak tendencies towards "doublethink" that Orwell had observed in the 1940s, and rule by a "Ministry of Truth" were horrors presently confined to a few countries. In the United States, the very fact that some terms of the Nixon years such as "rendered inoperative," had been recognized as Orwellian helped to protect us through reforms that were firmly established by 1989.

In part, George Orwell deserves credit for a portion of the intellectual freedom enjoyed in the 1980s, because he recognized the crucial importance of semantics. It was not politics or personalities that concerned him so much as language itself. In the 1930s and 1940s, he saw words twisted and distorted, so he chronicled the result. His best writing was an attempt to restore the meaning to words, to prove that "good prose is like a window pane." "One ought to recognize," he wrote, "that the present political chaos is connected with the decay of language, and that one can probably bring about some improvement by starting at the verbal ends."[7]

People in the late 1980s were beginning to refer to their time in history as "The Post-Orwellian Era." To some extent this reflected the recognition that their contemporary society was to a great extent the antithesis of the one Orwell described in his last book. While this term is in common usage, many thoughtful individuals wonder if human civilization has permanently escaped the Scylla of IngSoc and the Charybdis of Big Brother in its passage through the stream of time.

To the casual observer, day-to-day life, customs and technology are not significantly changed from patterns that prevailed a decade earlier when the nation was completing its extended bicentennial celebration. In fact, the societal changes had been far less dramatic that those experienced between 1963 and 1974 when the American people were polarized by a prolonged, unpopular foreign war, and when the national fabric was torn by assassinations, urban riots and a youth revolution fueled in large measure by anti-war sentiments.

If clothing styles seem somewhat more conservative in 1989, that is because there arc fewer people wearing bizarre clothes in an average street crowd. The clothing manufacturers lost their battle to increase sales by periodically raising and lowering the hemlines of woman's dresses. No longer slaves to fashion, women now buy the dress length they prefer as individuals.

As a general rule, men and women tend to dress in practical clothing that is comfortable. Sudden shifts in fashion are viewed as being in conflict with the conservation ethic now firmly established as a result of the ecological crusades of the 1970s. Durability and quality are stressed in advertisements showing clothes fashioned in various classic patterns that do not undergo significant change from year to year.

The long hair fad among younger males slowly

died out during the early 1980s. It had become so common that it was no longer a sign of defiance or rebellion. The "long-hairs" of the 1960s are now approaching middle age and many of their children wear short hair as the generational pattern of conflict and protest completes its cycle.

Perhaps the greatest change in 1989 America is the population shift away from large cities. In the 1970s many people began to view certain cities as being unmanageable and virtually uninhabitable monstrosities, and they began fleeing to the countryside. Continuing urban problems in the 1980s—drugs, high crime rates, air pollution, excessive noise, lack of privacy—caused more and more Americans to migrate to rural areas, reversing a trend which began in 1940. During the past decade, small towns and other non-metropolitan areas grew at a much faster rate than cities over the 300,000 population level. Contributing factors also included the decentralization of manufacturing, the development of rural recreation and retirement areas, the rebirth of the family farm and revolutionary developments in communications technology.

Large cities were to some extent a byproduct of new technology that became widespread in the early part of this century—the assembly line, city telephone systems, automobiles, subways and elevators. Now more sophisticated forms of technology—computers, lasers, two-way coaxial cable television systems—have made the large city partially obsolete. The new communications technology brings entertainment, shopping, employment, education and even some forms of medical service into the home, thus depriving the city of many of its reasons for existing.

The coaxial cable was the most important component of the technological revolution that is now allowing growing numbers of people to communicate rather than commute to their jobs. Two-way videophone communication has made many business trips unnecessary. Conferences of six to ten individuals are now regularly held by transmitting images rather than having everyone meet in some central office building. Each participant sits in a comfortable room surrounded by a battery of two-way videophone sets, and everyone can see and talk to all the other conference members. Some participants may even be in Europe, their images relayed via satellite TV.

These videophones can also flash data that is stored in computer systems on the screen. In effect they bring the full data processing capabilities of the large computer (once usually restricted to city buildings) to the rural home. Videophones have an auxiliary device that transmits facsimile printouts of letters, drawings, reports and sections of the daily newspaper. Thus pages of written or graphic material can be exchanged during video conferences. Letters and important memos are delivered without any time delay, thereby greatly increasing the tempo and efficiency of all forms of business activity.

Videophone systems combined with high-speed, good-resolution facsimile transmitter/receiver devices allow secretaries to perform many duties at home as well as at the office. S/he can take dictation, type and correct a letter which is then video approved and "signed" with an electronically transmitted thumbprint. The letter is immediately delivered via facsimile printout, and a copy is stored in some central computer system.

Many female executives in 1989 now have male secretaries (hence the "s/he" designation for secretaries).

People working at various remote rural sites have direct access to the files of the organization that employs them. Such files are stored as digital information in computers, with code access, so that the information is available only to authorized persons. An individual working at a remote farm, for example, simply punches into the keyboard the file number and his or her access code. The file data then appears page by page on the videophone screen, and pressing a button will cause a paper copy of any desired page to emerge from the high-resolution facsimile transmitter/receiver device.

The new communications technology allows many executives to have access to most of the skills of their secretaries while they are away on business trips. These videophone facsimile-data systems have also been a boon to many women who are raising small children and desire part-time secretarial employment. In many cases they work for individuals who can only afford a part-time secretary. Certain non-secretarial duties such as getting coffee are not allowed by such an arrangement, but there has been a beneficial reduction in "office affairs" (which are usually disruptive and seldom have a satisfactory conclusion).

New tax laws are now encouraging many of these "video-secretaries," sited in small towns or rural farms, to hire former welfare mothers to perform domestic tasks and certain aspects of child care, while they are busy working at a desk—actually a complex communications system with a typewriter keyboard, a videophone with facsimile-printout device and a microcomputer/calculator. Whatever is paid to former welfare mothers for such domestic services can be fully deducted from payments received for secretarial work. This arrangement allows the skilled secretary to optimize her contribution to society and increase family income. The same tax arrangement is also available to female accountants and other professionals who have made the change-over from urban to rural life. Skills which were acquired through years of higher education continue to be productively utilized.

New studies indicate, however, that it is the welfare family unit that is the principal beneficiary of this new tax arrangement. The cycle of poverty associated with the urban city ghetto is broken. The welfare mother now has her dignity restored through an income-producing job. Her children are taken away from the inner-city slums with their high levels of drug addiction, violent crimes, street gang intimidation and the adverse psychological factors associated with being raised in a welfare environment. Now that many of these children are in rural areas, they can tend gardens, take care of chickens or pigs and have access to part-time jobs that simply do not exist in the city. Most important of all are the changes allowed by the restored communion with nature.

The government pays for the cost of constructing rural residential units for these welfare families that are moving out of the cities (usually mass-produced, low-cost geodesic dome homes that can be set up or moved by unskilled labor). Such housing expenditures are much lower than urban welfare costs, and frequently the family becomes self-sufficient within two or three years.

The same basic videophone facsimile-printout system also provides many new recreational, cultural and educational options for small town and country residents. A wide selection of plays and movies is now available at a modest subscription cost without any commercial breaks. Video color displays allow people to order food and engage in other shopping tasks without leaving their homes. Many forms of legal and medical advice and even banking services are now transmitted electronically.

These electronic systems are beginning to have a profound impact on education. Called "video-interactive education," university and vocational courses are available on almost any conceivable subject with an option either to audit or to take the course for formal credit. Students of all ages view lectures or other instructional material at home, and they can participate in teacher-student discussions. The facsimile/printout capability permits other forms of data interaction and facilitates certain forms of examinations.

Quality education is now available to citizens living in every part of the country. Retraining of displaced or unskilled workers through video-interactive education technology has significantly reduced the rate of unemployment, and the productivity level of American workers in 1989 is exceeded only by the incredible productivity of the Japanese labor force. Child care courses are popular, and many new rural residents are learning how to properly raise small numbers of domestic farm animals or grow a profitable vegetable garden.

The working patterns of those who have moved to the country vary considerably from person to person. Many professional workers spend two or three days a week in the city at a central office or seeing clients, and then return to their rural homes to complete their work using the videophone system. Some companies have broken their departments down into units of optimum size, each sited in nearby small towns. In many cases the nature of a department's work requires twenty or thirty employees to walk or cycle to a company building each working morning, but they still retain the advantages of living in rural communities.

In 1989 you have access to much better overall medical care than was available ten years ago, but recent biomedical breakthroughs have been compounded by some serious dilemmas. An artificial heart that can keep a person alive for several years was perfected in the early 1980s. Unfortunately, most of the devices that allow it to work are too bulky to be implanted, and they are connected to the synthetic heart pump with flexible tubes and wires that pass through the patient's rib cage. Consequently, people with artificial hearts are more or less immobilized, and they can only move about with a "walker" device —a system on four wheels containing the devices and power supply which operate the artificial heart.

Artificial heart patients with no serious health problems can remain at home, but the overall cost of their medical maintenance is beyond the financial means of 97 percent of the population. Many of them become despondent and commit suicide by pulling out the wires to the power supply.

The most controversial result of the artificial heart breakthrough arose when doctors began implanting these devices into patients who have suffered so much brain damage from massive strokes or other causes that they are little more than human vegetables. If these "living cadavers" do not have cancer, the artificial heart can keep their tissues alive for many years. Their maintenance costs have become the largest single item in the nation's medical expenditures, and this dilemma is now the subject of passionate debate throughout the United States. When the "right-to-life" groups failed in their efforts to enforce "mandatory motherhood" in the abortion controversy of the early 1980s, they then turned to the living cadavers as their new cause. They fight to maintain the fiction of life in these medically dead humans at all costs. The issue is being fought in the courts, and the Supreme Court is expected to issue a final judgement in the near future.

A human heart transplant is the only hope available to immobilized persons with artificial hearts. The immunological rejection problems in organ transplants have been completely solved, but there is a severe shortage of transplantable hearts which are most frequently taken from persons killed in accidents. Only a few thousand such hearts are available in the United States each year, and throughout the world there are over one million artificial heart patients—otherwise healthy—all desperately seeking a living heart with its promise of vitality and mobility.

Wealthy persons turned down in their quest for a human heart from American surgeons are turning to disreputable foreign sources. You frequently read sensational newspaper stories about hospitals on small islands in the Caribbean—rumored to be operated by the Mafia—where a heart transplant is available for between $150,000 and $200,000. A person "taken for a ride" because he has offended some organized crime boss is frequently flown to one of these islands where his heart is sold to the highest bidder. Payoffs to corrupt government officials allow these hospitals to continue this ghoulish but very profitable form of treatment.

In 1989 over two-thirds of the countries in Africa and South America are authoritarian dictatorships. Transplant hospitals thrive in some of the more repressive regimes which seem to have an astoundingly high "accident" rate. Political prisoners are reported to be the principal source of the transplanted hearts. Wealthy patients from all over the world flock to these hospitals which literally sell their "pound of flesh." There are persistent reports of hearts taken from political prisoners in various communist countries—transplanted into the bodies of "deserving" party members.

The heart transplant dilemma involves foreign countries where U.S. courts have no jurisdiction. But in 1989, there is an unprecedented polarization of opinion in America regarding the pros and cons of another biomedical breakthrough.

Drug addiction continues to be one of our most serious problems and is the underlying cause of much of the crime in the country. Heroin rehabilitation programs in particular have been conspicuous failures with one exception. In the 1970s, European scientists discovered that dependence on drugs or alcohol assumes the proportions of a natural urge after a certain period and, like the sexual drive or the urge to eat, is controlled by a certain brain center. Neutralizing this center, which is no more than 50 cubic millimeters in volume, will cure the patient for all time.[8]

The neutralizing operation is a form of psychosurgery. A very small hole is drilled in the skull, and a narrow probe (about one eighth of an inch in diameter) is inserted into the brain until the tip reaches the small region that controls addiction. Extremely cold gases cause the tip of the probe to freeze the cells in that area, destroying the addiction center without causing any other form of brain damage. The probe is then removed, with no undesirable side effects.

In the early 1980s, several foreign countries virtually eliminated their drug addiction problems by making this form of psychosurgery, popularly called the "cryo-addiction cure," mandatory for all addicts. Large numbers of American drug addicts and some alcoholics voluntarily underwent cryo-addiction surgery, effectively curing their addiction. The polarization problem began when several states passed laws requiring heroin addicts to undergo the cryo-addiction cure after the second time they had been found guilty of committing a serious felony. There was an immediate hue and cry that the "rights" of the addicts were being violated, and the battle began.

At first the two sides tended to be divided between "law and order" conservatives favoring the new laws, with the old ACLU and civil rights coalition opposed to the mandatory cryo-addiction cure. But the cured addicts suddenly formed a surprisingly strong lobbying organization and their passionate arguments are now beginning to cause many liberal groups to change their views on this controversy. During the past year there have been conflicting rulings in the lower courts, and this is another issue awaiting a Supreme Court decision.

The cars of 1989 are smaller and more standardized than those manufactured in the U.S. ten years earlier. They are considerably lighter because of the use of more aluminum, plastics, higher-strength steel and smaller engines. Better interior design provides a higher ratio of usable space to overall size; sharpened exterior design reduces wind resistance, permitting better fuel economy at higher speeds.

There is a new pump at all gasoline stations. It dispenses methanol (sometimes called "wood alcohol"), a synthetic fuel produced from coal, farm wastes and various forms of trash. Not only is the use of methanol important in reducing our dependence on foreign oil imports, but its unique combustion characteristics permit an almost pollution-free automobile.

Methanol, CH_3OH, can be thought of as two molecules of hydrogen gas made liquid by one molecule of carbon monoxide. In the new methanol-fueled cars, engine-exhaust heat breaks down or disassociates the liquid methanol into carbon monoxide and hydrogen. These two gases go into the engine rather than liquid fuel, and disassociated gases from methanol can be burned in internal combustion engines or turbines so cleanly that almost no pollutants are produced. The exhaust is comprised of harmless water vapor and carbon dioxide, and the output of toxic nitrogen oxides is so low that it can't be detected with conventional instruments.

About 25 percent of the new cars, buses and trucks are designed to run exclusively on methanol. There are higher taxes on gasoline, giving methanol a fuel-economy advantage that encourages the purchase of these environmentally clean vehicles. Los Angeles and other cities with severe smog problems now have an annual city license ranging between $100 and

$200 for all gasoline-burning vehicles owned by citizens who live within the city limits or work for any organization sited within the city. Over 60 percent of the vehicles on Los Angeles streets and free- ways now burn methanol, and there has been an as- tounding reduction in atmospheric pollutants. There is no need to add tetraethyl lead to methanol, so an- other toxic pollutant is thereby reduced.

The refinement of practical electric vehicles has also had a significant environmental impact during the past decade. More than 15 percent of the new cars sold in 1989 are "electrics," and preferential tax treat- ment also encourages their use. The somewhat lim- ited performance of these zero-pollution vehicles is satisfactory for most city driving and home-to-job commuting. The average electric car has a top speed of 60 m.p.h., and is capable of traveling between 100 and 150 miles on a single charge. New battery sys- tems that can store more than twice the energy, pound-for-pound, than the old lead-acid batteries have made the electric car a competitive form of transportation.

Today, oil shortages do not seem to be as critical as they were during the 1970s. This is partly due to suc- cessful energy conservation reforms in residential use, industry and transportation. Many years of artificially high oil prices encouraged the discovery of new oil fields in many countries. The OPEC cartel's oil monopoly has been broken, and oil prices have de- clined about 30 percent in the past few years.

The practical use of solar power and other new sources of energy have also eased the demand for oil. For example, much of our methanol is now produced underground through a revolutionary *in situ* (in place) process. Wells are drilled into deep coal seams. Water is then pumped under high pressure into the seam to break up the coal and make it permeable enough for gas to escape. Oxygen is then pumped into the coal seam and the coal is ignited with a propane burner. When underground coal is combusted in the presence of water or steam at the proper pressure, significant quantities of hydrogen and carbon monoxide are produced along with a smaller percentage of methane. These gases produced by the burning process escape up a nearby borehole to the surface.

After the gases are brought to the surface, it is a comparatively simple matter to pass them over a catalyst to form methanol, which is then transported by truck or pipeline to service stations. The land surface is not disturbed by the *in situ* method of coal utilization, and environmentalists do not object to this form of energy extraction.

The public recognizes that the new oil supplies will provide at best, only a temporary "breathing spell" in the protracted energy crisis. Global demand for oil is still increasing as many undeveloped countries are becoming industrialized. Finite oil reserves are being depleted at an alarming rate, and the leaders of the advanced nations recognize that this breathing spell must be used to quickly develop alternate energy sources in order to avert a complete collapse of civilization sometime in the early part of the 21st Century.

Recent arms-control agreements between the great powers have ameliorated international tensions and the threat of nuclear Armageddon. The reduced cost of oil imports has allowed the rate of inflation to decline, and the late-1980s are years of prosperity for those fortunate enough to live in the United States, Europe, Japan and some other favored regions. But each day you read of new calamities in other parts of the world, portending the first signs of a dark passage in human history.

Rampaging floods in Brazil and India. Devastating droughts in various parts of Africa and Asia. The disappearance of commercially valuable fish species off the coasts of all our continents. Unexpected crop failures. These recent, widely reported phenomena all have something in common. Though they were triggered by nature, their magnitude was increased disastrously by man's trying to expand his food production without first considering the ecological side effects.

To understand these seemingly unrelated catastrophes of the 1980s, it is necessary to first understand that humanity is still utterly dependent for its existence on the functioning of immense, complex ecological systems. What all of these seemingly unrelated local crises have in common is that the expansion of regional food production at exponential rates had disrupted the "public-service-function" of natural systems within our global biosphere.

There are a number of ways in which processes essential for man's existence or well-being are provided through the normal functioning of natural ecosystems. These *free* public-service-functions of the biosphere include storing of water, maintaining soil structure and productivity, maintaining the chemical equilibrium of air and water, maintaining an epidemic-free environment through natural predators and diverse plant communities, moderation of microclimates where natural vegetation is profuse, natural fertilization of agricultural land on undammed floodplains, and the cleansing of soil, air and water via natural biological metabolism.

When our natural ecosystems are altered so that there is a disruption in one or more of these public-service-functions, the productivity levels of agriculture, animal husbandry or oceanic fisheries are likely to be diminished.

Overfishing is only partly responsible for the decline of commercially valuable fish species. The rapid expansion of industry during the 1980s has been most heavily concentrated in coastal regions around the world. As coastal industry and its supporting cities expand, estuarine regions which are directly or indirectly the major producers of our more important commercial fish are destroyed. The destruction of estuaries by commercial and industrial development eliminates nature's public-service-functions that allow these fish to come into existence or reach the stage where they can be a practical source of food.

The prolonged droughts of the 1980s have all occurred in semi-arid, ecologically fragile regions. Excessive uses of trees for fuel, savanna grass replaced by seasonal crops (in turn squandering available ground water) and the denuding of the land through overgrazing have been the collective "final straw" damaging the essential public-service-functions of these fragile ecosystems. The result—a drought that can turn a fertile area into a permanent desert.

A similar form of ecological destruction can now be seen in India and other relatively lush regions where rural squatters have moved into forest reserves and cleared land to grow crops, thus destroying the water catchment areas and thereby causing such devastating erosion that silting of rivers and reservoirs has reached crisis proportions. The deforestation of the Indian subcontinent, central Africa, Brazil and small countries around the Caribbean removed trees and other vegetation that once slowed down and absorbed heavy water runoff, resulting in the destructive floods that are the subject of such vivid newscasts on your TV set in 1989. Rainfall that formerly caused moderate flooding now inundates millions of acres of cropland. The ecological public-service-functions of these forests has been destroyed.

The crop failures of the 1980s have created a vicious cycle. Desperate attempts to increase agricultural productivity causes clearing of even larger tracts of forest, often on steeper terrain where erosion will be a serious problem. In much of Asia, the rising silt load is destroying reservoirs and irrigation projects. Much of the flooding in overcrowded countries can be blamed in part on denuded watersheds caused by the excessive expansion of agriculture.

The concern over oil shortages that characterized the 1970s has been replaced by a much greater fear of mounting food shortages during the1980s. Food shortfalls are starting to effect the entire world. The only real problem of the 20th Century is an explosive increase in human population. On a planet with a finite biosphere, the agricultural sector of society cannot continue to expand its output, particularly at an exponential rate.

We cannot continue indefinitely devouring the surface of the Earth, excreting pollution and destroying the public-service-functions of our biosphere. The entire terrestrial system must be brought into some sort of balance if *homo sapiens* is to survive for the long run.

These painful realities of ecology are now well known and understood in the advanced nations where birthrates have been exceedingly low for the past decade. But the momentum of human population growth has its origins in deep-seated attitudes toward reproduction in the undeveloped lands, and in the age composition of the world's population—36 percent being under 15 years of age. Even if every couple in the world henceforth had only the number of children needed to replace themselves, the imbalance between young and old would cause global population to grow for another 50 to 70 years more before levelling off. Under the most extraordinarily optimistic fertility-control assumptions, world population would not stabilize below ten billion people.

In 1989, there is a general consensus among responsible experts that the Earth simply cannot support ten billion people, but in the comparatively undeveloped countries, population continues to expand at an explosive rate. Consequently, the prosperity that you and other Americans now enjoy is tempered with a premonition of impending disaster.

CHAPTER FOUR
1994: YEAR OF THE MALTHUSIAN CRISIS

During the early 1990s, you find yourself living through the most widespread catastrophe in recorded human history. The famines of the past were nothing compared to the nutritional disaster that overwhelmed humanity in 1994. Due to a combination of ignorance, pro-natalist religious dogma and capricious changes in global climate, more than a billion people may starve to death before the end of the year.

For the past five years, mankind has been drawing closer to a precipice where mass starvation occurs whenever drought or plant disease results in less-than-average crop production. Population growth, compounded by adverse ecological changes, has literally eaten up all the increased food output achieved by the nations of the world during the past 15 years. The Earth, as is the case with smaller ecosystems, has a limited carrying capacity. The limit was reached in 1994.

For many years scientists have repeated their warnings that the world was running out of food and that a cataclysmic Malthusian resolution to the population explosion would shortly be upon us. During the past decades, scientific advances allowed food production to be kept half a step ahead of population growth. But the basic needs of expanding population have finally outstripped the productive potential of land and sea.

During this last decade of the 20th Century, every literate adult and school child knows that the Malthusian specter haunting the world is named after Thomas Robert Malthus (1766-1834), an Anglican clergyman and political economist whose principal theory held that population tends to multiply faster than its means of food production. In 1798, he predicted that population would grow geometrically (1, 2, 4, 8, 16, 32) beyond agriculture's linear (1, 2, 3, 4, 5) ability to feed it. Unless population increases are checked, he theorized, poverty and starvation are inevitable.

Looking back from the year 1994, the Malthusian crisis has appeared like a comet out of the depths of the cosmos. The human race increased very slowly over the centuries until there were one billion people in 1830. Only 100 years later, in 1930, the second billion was reached; 30 years later, in 1960, the Earth held three billion humans; and it took only another 15 years, until 1975, for mankind to add another billion people to an overcrowded planet.

World population was growing at an 84-year doubling time rate in the 1940s. This suddenly shifted to a 33-year doubling time rate in the 1950s, and that pattern has continued without significant change for the past four decades. Consequently, in January 1994, the global population total is now estimated to be approximately 5,280,000,000 humans.

During the 1980s an estimated 90 million acres of farmland were lost each year to spreading cities and land erosion. The world's fishing fleets are floating factories which devour sea life faster than it can reproduce itself: many traditional fishing grounds have been depleted and the overall catch is declining. Water pollution has also taken a heavy toll of fish life along the fertile continental shelves.

During recent years odd and unpleasant things have been happening to weather around the world. For a variety of reasons the Earth's surface—our biosphere—has been cooling off, and this cooling process has dislocated food production patterns in almost every important agricultural region.

The principal cause of the global cooling trend appears to be an increase of dust in the atmosphere. Acting like tiny mirrors, dust particles reflect some of the sunlight striking Earth's atmosphere, depriving the surface of solar heat. Part of this dust blanket is due to industrial pollution. But windblown dust from mechanized agricultural operations and overgrazed arid land, plus smoke from primitive slash-and-burn land-clearing methods now widely practiced in the overpopulated tropics, have contributed even more.

The major climatic effect of the global cooling trend has been a gradual expansion of what is called the "circumpolar vortex"—the great icy winds that whip around the top and bottom of the world. These winds move generally from west to east, but the outer edge of the vortex twists and bends, like the bottom of a large swirling skirt.

The most devastating influence of the altered circumpolar vortex has been felt in a broad tropical belt stretching round the globe. As the edge of the great wind system reaches closer to the planet's midriff, it blocks moisture-laden equatorial winds. Instead of withdrawing northward as the Northern Hemisphere warms up each summer, the lower hem of the vortex has stayed unusually far south. In turn, the great desert-forming belts of descending air have been pushed farther south into heavily populated regions. The outward rush of air from these high-pressure zones has prevented the moisture-laden summer monsoon winds from penetrating into grazing lands and farming regions that are dry the rest of the year. So the blocked monsoons ended up dropping their precious rainfall into the oceans or into regions that already have too much rain.

The increase in atmospheric dust from human activity was suddenly compounded by the most massive cycle of major volcanic eruptions that has occurred in several centuries. In 1992, huge volcanos erupted in Mexico, Hawaii and Indonesia. Last year these active volcanos were joined by new eruptions in Alaska, Italy, Central Africa and China. The vast increase in volcanic dust from these eruptions simply overwhelmed the delicately balanced system of the world's climate with all of its sensitive feedback mechanisms that serve either to amplify or to counter changes that occur.

During 1994, climatic disasters struck breadbaskets as far apart as the Ukraine, China and Brazil. With each passing month, TV broadcasts bring an ever widening pattern of agricultural disruptions and crop failures into your living room. Most of the un-

developed, overpopulated nations suffer food shortfalls ranging from serious to catastrophic.

The new rainfall pattern did improve agriculture
in some regions, including the nations of the Northern
Sahara along the Mediterranean Sea and the Iranian
plateau. But improved harvests in these regions simply restored food self-sufficiency to some countries
that had been importing significant quantities of
grain. The additional food raised in these nations,
with the exception of Iran, was consumed by their
hungry citizens, with no excess available for export.

During the 1980s, the midwestern farming region
of Canada and the United States became the major
granary of mankind with the capacity to produce
substantial surpluses (food for which there is no
domestic demand). But unhappily this area is subject
to a drought cycle that created the "dust-bowl" disaster of the 1930s. From 1989 through 1993, the
climate changes in Canada and the U.S. had followed
a pattern of wet rainy springs and hot summers—conditions that are not conducive to growing bumper
crops. This weather pattern caused reduced
harvests, but significant quantities of corn, grain and
soybeans still could be exported to food-deficient
countries.

Volcanic dust in the atmosphere reached its highest
levels in early 1994, and all of the adverse climatic
patterns of the past few years became progressively
worse with each passing month. American and Ca-
nadian farmers in the Middle West experienced an
unusually wet spring which prevented them from
getting heavy tractors into the fields. And when they
finally got their crops planted, torrential rains
washed them out, requiring some farmers to sow

three times. Then came a blistering drought, withering crops in the midst of the growing season. And finally, in September, an early, prolonged frost destroyed most of the corn, wheat and soybeans that had survived the earlier buffeting. The ultimate agricultural disaster had occurred. There was no surplus grain in the North American continent available for export.

Radical changes in climate around the world began to act as a catalyst in triggering various forms of plant diseases among crops representing the main sources of human nutrition including wheat, rice, corn, sorghum, barley, potatoes, sweet potatoes, and grain legumes such as beans, soybeans, peanuts and peas. The increased susceptibility of plants to disease was caused by "genetic erosion"—the disappearance of primitive plant varieties and the seeds that store their unique characteristics.

Beginning in the mid-1960s, the so-called Green Revolution began to spread through vast reaches of agricultural land in Latin America, Asia and the Mediterranean nations, bringing record harvests of new "miracle" wheat, rice and other plant strains. In those countries where these new, high-yield crops became firmly established, they rapidly supplanted the native varieties with all their genetic diversity. Year by year the genetic erosion threat grew in potential magnitude because the new "miracle" crops are often highly vulnerable to both insect pests and disease. Producing uniformly high yields, every plant also carries uniform weaknesses. If one plant falls prey to a disease, all fall prey.

When plant diseases began to destroy high-yield strains of various crops, farmers were not able to replant low-yield traditional strains that had sufficient genetic diversity to resist the disease. Agricultural experts estimated that the genetic erosion problem was responsible for as great a total crop loss during the Malthusian crisis as the unprecedented weather patterns that prevailed that year.

From the beginning to the end of 1994, almost everything that could possibly go wrong in the production and distribution of food *did* go wrong. What the world is experiencing this year is a combination of isolated events, each unusual by itself, their coincidence very improbable, although undeniable.

Australia was the only grain exporting nation that did not experience disastrous crop failures in 1994. Their crop yields were reduced, however, and the grain available for export was committed by official treaties to be sold to Japan and exchanged for Indonesian oil.

The Japanese were the only food importers with the foresight to build large grain reserves in the late 1980s. Consequently, they were able to survive the global famine years without disaster, even though severe food rationing was strictly enforced.

The citizens of Indonesia were less fortunate. The Australian grain was not of sufficient quantity to replace losses from crop failures on their overpopulated islands. A revolution broke out and the Indonesian navy blockaded Java. Half of the inhabitants of that island died of starvation during the six-month blockade.

By early June, world-wide organizations dispensing food relief were simply overwhelmed, and the pride of nations and the immediate political interests of governments worked against the kind of common effort that might, even then, have reduced the impact of the harvest failures. Movement of large numbers of people out of the famine regions was not possible. The world is now too densely inhabited and politically divided to accommodate mass migrations.

In Africa, the famine was centered in the drought zone just south of the Sahara Desert. Over 50 percent of the population of Ethiopia died during the year, but conditions were not nearly so severe elsewhere. The Ethiopian situation was compounded by a savage civil war which started in 1993. Ironically, there were modest agricultural surpluses in some African countries, but lack of adequate transportation and organizational leadership were barriers in the use of this food for famine relief. Some of it was flown to oil-rich countries in the Middle East.

The global climatic disruption created famine conditions in most of the Latin American nations. U.S. food relief was only sufficient to prevent starvation in Mexico. The loss of life was severe throughout Central America and the small Caribbean countries. The death rate ranged from over 40 percent in Bolivia to less than 10 percent in Venezuela. Harvests in Chile, Argentina and Uruguay were below normal, but effective food rationing prevented famines in these countries.

The Brazilian situation was a pattern of paradoxical contrasts. The drought was especially severe in the northern part of the country, but some excess grain and soybeans were harvested in the southern provinces. This food was then sent to other countries in exchange for oil needed to maintain the large industrial complexes centered in southern Brazil. A revolution in the north was ruthlessly suppressed by the oppressive military government using troops from the well-fed southern region. Foreign journalists were not allowed into the famine provinces, and strict press censorship prevented the outside world from learning the full extent of the catastrophe in northern Brazil. Half of the people in the drought provinces may have died, and the Brazilian belief that their country would benefit from continued population growth was shattered forever.

The climatic changes did not cause significant crop losses in western Europe, but here the problem was a sudden cutoff of grain and food supplies traditionally imported from other parts of the world. The nations on the continent adopted a tight system of rationing and food allocation to deficient areas such as Holland and Switzerland. A similar pattern of cooperation prevented famine in central Europe and the Balkans, with the exception of Albania. That country maintained its strict isolation until widespread starvation triggered an army mutiny and the overthrow of the government. The subsequent restoration of the Albanian monarchy was the most surprising political change of the decade.

The crisis in England was particularly acute because the United Kingdom customarily imported about half of its food. Canada sent its emergency grain reserves to England during the summer, preventing a famine just as the first signs of malnutrition were beginning to appear. The Royal Navy then brought large supplies of meat and grain from New Zealand and South Africa—sufficient to tide the British through the winter months.

Nowhere was the unrelenting disaster more severe than on the Indian subcontinent. Destitute Bang-

ladesh had experienced a cycle of chronic food shortages and famines ever since that nation broke away
from Pakistan two decades ago. For the past four
years, the prolonged famine in Bangladesh was accompanied by a complete breakdown in government
control. In the late 1980s, the population of Bangladesh was estimated at approximately 120 million.
Half of those people were believed to be starving
when food relief shipments ceased in October 1993.

The population of India reached 859 million in January, and there had been localized famines in various
parts of the Indian Federation for several years. Vast
quantities of grain were sent to India, but the increasingly authoritarian government dispensed most of it
to politically favored groups in the major cities to prevent hunger riots and forestall outright revolution. As
in Brazil, journalists were not allowed into the
famine areas. But even in the cities, food reserves had
been completely exhausted during the final months of
1993.

During 1994, India received only a small portion of
the expected monsoon rains because of global
climatic disruptions. The prolonged drought was
compounded by the outbreak of wheat rust in the
north and rice blight in the south. These plant diseases reduced crop yields even in those areas served
by large irrigation systems. Water buffalo and other
farm animals began to die, further curtailing agricultural productivity.

By early June, food riots reduced the cities to chaos.
Order was briefly restored following a military coup.
Starving peasants who flocked to the cities were forc-
ibly ejected by army troops. Then began a chain of
events that culminated in total catastrophe

throughout the Indian Federation.

There were over 328 million sacred cows in India. The animals have a profound religious significance to the Hindu majority, which outnumbers the Moslems about six to one. The starving inhabitants of Moslem villages began to eat the sacred cows, and this triggered reprisals from nearby Hindu communities. Most of the members of military units sent in to control these disturbances were Hindus, and they began to slaughter Moslem peasants throughout the countryside.

The fratricidal fighting between Hindus and Moslems quickly spread to the cities and the pattern of religious conflict was almost identical to that of the late 1940s when the British left India. Some other minority groups began to side with the Moslems, principally the Sikhs who lived in the northern region adjacent to Pakistan. Soon there were desperate hordes of Moslem refugees attempting to reach safety in neighboring Pakistan. Wealthy Moslems were able to bribe their way onto trains and other forms of transportation that promised to take them to safety. The Sikhs in the north assisted them in crossing the border.

Most of the farming regions in Pakistan had received the same beneficial rains that brought record harvests to Iran. A judicious system of rationing, supplemented by gifts of grain from Iran, prevented starvation in Pakistan, and allowed minimum rations for the inhabitants of camps filled with the steady stream of Moslem refugees from India. Newspapers in Pakistan and other Islamic countries were filled with atrocity stories—frequently exaggerated—told to reporters by the bitter refugees.

As the crisis deepened, Indian and Pakistani military units began to occupy strategic positions along the border. Only a spark was needed to ignite a war. The spark came when an uprising broke out in that portion of Moslem Kashmir that had been occupied by India for more than 40 years. The Indian military commander in this region was a Sikh who unexpectedly arranged a local armistice with the forces of the new Kashmir Republic.

In the meantime, fighting broke out all along the Indian-Pakistani border. This conflict was called the "sacred-cow war" in the western media, but it was viewed as a dire threat to world peace since both India and Pakistan had nuclear weapons.

China and the Islamic countries which had been supplying India with all of its oil sided with Pakistan. They cut off oil shipments to India as soon as the sacred-cow war started. Within 60 days the Indian army and air force began to run out of fuel. The army general who had been the ruler of India for the past three months was assassinated and the leadership vacuum was filled with a junta of fanatical young air force officers. The junta decided to use nuclear weapons in an attempt to achieve a quick victory—an operation code-named "Strikeforce Damocles."

On September 1st, nuclear bombs destroyed 27 Pakistani air force bases and other military installations. No major cities were hit by Strikeforce Damocles, but there were large refugee camps next to 16 of the nuclear bomb targets. Almost all of the refugees in these camps were killed.

The Pakistani generals had foreseen the possibility of a nuclear strike, and comparatively small fighter-bomber jets had been hidden along various sectors of wide highways which could serve as emergency take-off and landing strips. On September 3rd, these Pakistani aircraft destroyed 25 Indian air force installations with nuclear bombs, and a nuclear-tipped cruise missile sank India's only aircraft carrier. The President of Pakistan announced that there would be no further employment of nuclear weapons if India also refrained from their use.

Almost all of India's air force had been destroyed, and Pakistan now had less than 30 jet aircraft. Key members of the Indian junta had been killed on September 3rd, and the central government in New Delhi ceased to exist as an effective political force. The Indian Federation dissolved into separate units, most of them under the control of whatever local military officer could command the loyalty of the most troops.

The front line dividing Indian and Pakistani army units simply dissolved, and the sacred-cow war ended in late September without a conventional form of victory. With Pakistani assistance, the Sikhs in the north recreated their old independent kingdom (now a republic), which quickly gained control over the Sindh area, and thus access to the sea. The Islamic nations sent military supplies to Sikh troops in the new Sikhistan Republic which now serves as a buffer state between Moslem Pakistan and Hindu India.

The darkest hour of the Indian nightmare occurred on October 28, 1994. India's remaining nuclear weapons were all stored at an air force base in the south that had not been hit on September 3rd. This base was commanded by a despotic general who proclaimed himself "President of India." He threatened to destroy the largest city in any area that did not recognize his authority. The army commander in the Bombay region sent a column of troops marching toward the air force base. On the night of October 28th, these army units were hit with two tactical nuclear weapons and a hydrogen bomb destroyed Bombay, killing over ten million people. This was the first time an Indian hydrogen fusion bomb had been detonated.

On October 29th, a young airman from the Bombay region shot the air force general who had brought his country to the verge of nuclear Armageddon. Army units soon captured the airbase and they dismantled the remaining nuclear weapons so that these bombs could not be used by any other deranged commander.

The Bombay holocaust was the last major military action on the Indian subcontinent in the aftermath of the sacred-cow war. Regional army commanders subsequently concentrated all their efforts on restoring some semblance of order within the areas they controlled. Fuel reserves were too limited to permit any offensive military actions.

The global climatic disruptions also brought massive hunger to China. Despite a reasonably effective effort to curtail birthrate levels, the population of China continued to grow—800 million in 1975, 930 million in 1985, over one billion mainland Chinese by 1989. Weather changes in the past few years had resulted in reduced harvests. To make up these shortages, China had become the world's largest importer of wheat and rice. These imports were paid for by the large reserves of oil that had been found in the shallow waters of the North China Sea.

In 1994, no grain could be imported from the U.S. and Canada. Australia's grain was committed elsewhere. Oil-rich Arab nations with small populations outbid the Chinese for the small quantity of grain that was still moving in international commerce. Not only were imports cut off, but the worst drought of this century hit China's southern rice growing provinces (the most heavily populated region in the country).

By early summer, chronic malnutrition or outright starvation affected over 45 percent of the population. At that point, New Leader put into effect a policy frequently employed in the past by China's emperors— "feed some provinces, starve others."

Soldiers of the People's Liberation Army began to encounter resistance as they attempted to move food supplies from one province to another. Some local military commanders refused to follow orders issued from Peking. China was rapidly reverting to the pattern of administrative chaos that had traditionally characterized this vast land during times of troubles.

New Leader began making a series of flights to different parts of China, reasserting his authority over local segments of the army and changing commanders whenever he thought a local officer was becoming too popular. On a flight to Canton, engine trouble forced New Leader's plane to land on an airfield located in a province condemned to starvation. The plane was recognized, and a screaming mob of starving peasants dragged New Leader and his entourage out of the luxurious aircraft. They were all beaten to death on the runway.

Following the tyrant's demise, a new "collective leadership" was established in Peking, but its members only controlled a few local provinces in north China. Aside from administering foreign diplomatic relationships, Peking no longer functioned as the central government of China. The army commander in each local province ruled in the same manner as the military "war lords" of the 1930s. There were armed conflicts between neighboring provinces and one nuclear weapon was detonated in an engagement that was never explained to the satisfaction of the outside world.

China remained a completely closed society with only a few foreign diplomats restricted to Peking. No official reports containing estimates of the number of Chinese citizens who died during the 1994 famine were ever issued. Data from satellite photos indicated that China's total crop yield may have been reduced by 20 to 30 percent in a year when imported food was also cut off. The Malthusian specter had closed in on the Middle Kingdom.

A wide belt of hunger was girdling the world throughout its equatorial regions in late 1994. The food problem was aggravated by civil strife on an unprecedented scale. Ship captains refused to enter many ports because they were afraid that the crews' food supplies would be taken by starving mobs.

The population Pollyannas of the 1970s had said that "the Earth can easily support populations many times larger than today's."[2] Now the reality of the 1990s has proven them wrong. The world's "carrying capacity" (the total number of people that can be fed using available resources) was exceeded in the middle decades of this century. Many scientists predicted that any attempt to increase food production would only aggravate the decline in the quality of life unless population was brought under control.

Dr. Norman Borlaug was the "father of the Green Revolution," and he received the Nobel Peace Prize in

1970 for his pioneering work on miracle high-yield seeds. In 1974, he issued a dire warning: "It is going to take a tremendous disaster from famine before people come to grips with the population problem. The stage is set for such a situation right now ... but there will be no coming together of minds until a major famine brings people together."[3]

During the last weeks of 1994, Borlaug's 1974 prophecy was the most frequently mentioned item in speeches and articles by the world's leading statesmen, scientists and scholars. But the Malthusian crisis of 1994 could have been avoided. Why were ameliorative fertility-control reforms not adopted in time to avert catastrophe?

The most plausible answer was that the political leadership of the world had taken the "easy way out," and their minds were dominated by a form of Orwellian *doublethink*—the power of holding two contradictory beliefs in one's mind simultaneously and accepting both of them. They could see that virgin farm land awaited the plow in only a few places. Any attempt to significantly increase the scope of agriculture would require most of the world's remaining forests to be cut down to yield cultivated land, which in turn would increase the already present danger of ecological disaster (because essential public-service-functions of natural ecosystems would be destroyed).

While political leaders acknowledged that Earth is a finite habitat, they also held on to the contradictory illusion that mankind had escaped the constraints of scarcity at a time when human population was increasing at an explosive rate. George Orwell clearly understood in 1949 that if the most important policies of government and society are based on doublethink, then human suffering will be the inevitable result as surely as day follows night. And doublethink regarding population growth had now culminated in catastrophe of unprecedented magnitude. The basic flaw lay in determining the world's "carrying capacity." There is one number for the total population that can be supported when climatic conditions are almost ideal, and another number based on the possibility that many adverse climatic disruptions might all occur in one year or over a span of several consecutive years. That latter number is our planet's true carrying capacity—the population size that can be supported for an indefinite time period.

The early decades of the 20th Century had experienced the most favorable weather for agriculture recorded during the past 500 years. Not only did we fail to recognize that a "high" on a statistical cycle was being enjoyed, but we were also destroying the free public-service-functions of our biosphere, thereby magnifying the inevitable climatic disruptions when they came. The famines of 1994 proved that doublethink takes its inexorable toll in suffering even if it is the result of ignorance and wishful thinking.

In his prophetic novel *1984,* George Orwell said that doublethink would not only make day-to-day life a pattern of fear and terror, but its impact between groups of nations could lead to hostility and conflict, thereby significantly reducing both consumable and durable goods that enhance the quality of life: "The primary aim of modern warfare (in accordance with the principles of *doublethink,* this aim is simultaneously recognized and not recognized by the directing brains of the Inner Party) is to use up the products of the machine without raising the general standard of living ... The essential act of war is destruction, not necessarily of human lives, but of the products of human labor."[3]

The 45 years following the publication of Orwell's book have not witnessed the pattern of continuous warfare he described, but there have been many protracted, localized wars, and hundreds of millions of dollars were still being spent on armaments each year. This insane diversion of vital resources—metals and scarce elements, fuels, science and technology, manpower—had long been recognized by the world's leading statesmen as a major barrier in overcoming the bewildering array of crises becoming less manageable with each passing year.

The basic problem was recognized in 1970 by Dennis Gabor (1900-1979), the multidisciplinary Nobel laureate who discovered holography. He concluded that the military-industrial complex in one nation and its counterpart in a rival nation are fed by mutual fear. Any reported increase in new weapons on one side must be balanced on the other side. To Gabor, the quest for disarmament was reduced to one vital question: "How can we break the terrifying feedback loop of fear?"[4]

Furthermore, the stalemate created by the unprecedented destructive potential of nuclear weapons introduced a new dimension to the mutual feedback loop of fear. Among the great powers, it became characteristic of the sounders of alarm on the inadequacy of "our" preparations for defense that they never could be proven wrong. That war was in fact avoided between the superpowers for the past 49 years proves nothing, especially since World War III has been averted because it was recognized that nuclear weapons would destroy both sides.

General Douglas MacArthur (1880-1964) was among the first to recognize that "the atomic bomb has made war obsolete." When one side cannot conceivably benefit from military action, then nations must learn to resolve their disagreements in other ways.

Now in 1994, the vast accumulation of wealth converted into increasingly sophisticated weapon systems was useless against the forces of nature that killed, in one year, far more people than had died in all the wars of the past 1,000 years. And the mutual feedback loop of fear that maintained the arms race was broken by fear itself—fear that civilization would come to an end unless it was completely transformed so that our biosphere could be preserved. To accomplish this essential goal of human survival, past patterns of resource use and fertility *must* be reformed to meet the dictates of a finite planet.

The destruction of Bombay proved to be the catalytic event leading to the treaties in late 1994 that promised to culminate in world disarmament. If an Indian general could completely obliterate the second largest city in a land that held life to be sacred, then comparable events were possible in any of the 18 nations that now had nuclear weapons. Moreover, such a madman might launch the ICBM's under his control at a rival nation, triggering nuclear Armageddon for the entire world. The mutual feedback loop of fear was broken because political leaders began to fear the generals and admirals who possessed such deadly toys more than they feared the rulers of foreign states.

On November 3rd, six days after the thermonuclear fireball spread across Bombay, the American President met with Soviet leaders in Moscow. The situation in Russia was desperate because of severe drought in the Ukraine and reduced harvests in almost all of the other 14 Soviet republics. The army's emergency food reserve was now being consumed by the civilian population, but it would be exhausted within 30 days. If some foreign source of food could not be found, then millions of Soviet citizens would die of starvation before spring.

On the morning of the first meeting, the Soviet Chairman surprised his American guest by candidly telling him that he was generally familiar with the details of "Project Abraham." A top secret U.S. Army program began in 1985, the ultimate goal of Project Abraham had been to store up to one year's supply of grain and canned food at remote sites that would not be likely nuclear targets in the event of war.

Army generals had convinced the handful of congressional leaders responsible for the funding of Project Abraham that "... in the 1980s, food has become a decisive weapon." Their basic scenario was that nuclear weapons might not be extensively used in a major war, but plant diseases could be easily disseminated by "Ian Fleming type" enemy agents (the basic plot in one of the James Bond books). The side that first exhausted its food supply would lose the war—so the generals reasoned.

From 1985 until the summer of 1993, the army secretly accumulated its hoard of grain and preserved food (much of it freeze-dried). This program was carried out by a series of dummy or "cover" corporations in which army officers secretly passed themselves off as civilian businessmen. Select groups within the Department of Agriculture participated in this clandestine operation by under-reporting U.S. food production levels. Funds for Project Abraham were skillfully hidden in many sections of the annual Defense Department budget—an exceedingly complex document fully understood by only a few specialists.

Canned and freeze-dried foods were stored in depleted mines, old warehouses and other sites that could be supplied by truck. Wheat, rice and soybeans presented problems because they could not be stored for a prolonged span of years. The army's cover companies had to engage in a constant pattern of buying new grain and selling some of the old grain in the Project Abraham reserves. They bought more grain than they sold each year, so this portion of the food mix grew at a predetermined rate. But the buying-selling turnover requirements forced the army to store the grain in conventional facilities next to railroad lines or near rivers deep enough for barge traffic.

The American President was told that photos from Russian reconnaissance satellites enabled Soviet intelligence specialists to make an accurate count of the slow buildup of grain elevators and similar facilities. They could calculate the approximate size of Project Abraham reserves by starting with their satellite count and simply subtracting the number of grain storage facilities published each year in official Department of Agriculture reports. Well-placed Russian spies had informed the Kremlin that, because of funding problems, there was not a significant quantity of canned and freeze-dried food in the Project Abraham larder.

In an equally candid response, the President ex-

plained that Project Abraham reserves had been severely depleted during the past ten months. Some of
this food had been sent to Mexico to prevent starvation, but much of it had been sold on the open market
within the states to hold down rising food prices during a year of disastrous harvests throughout North
America. This latter move was forced on the President by congressional leaders who faced an uncertain
election in a few days.

By the end of the day, Project Abraham data from
the Pentagon had been matched with estimates of
projected Soviet food requirements for the next year.
An exceedingly strict food rationing program
throughout the U.S., accompanied by the prompt
transfer of all of the remaining Project Abraham reserves to the U.S.S.R., could prevent starvation in that
country. Food supplies were already severely
curtailed in America, and new laws forbade feeding
any form of grain to livestock that could be diverted to
human consumption.

That evening the President said: "The American
people will make this sacrifice if they can be convinced that it will enhance their own long-term secur-
ity and survival. For the past four decades, the citizens
of both of our great countries have lived under the
threat of a nuclear sword of Damocles. Both the
Americans and your people want this dire threat removed. The principal barrier to this common goal
has been the past refusal of Soviet leaders to allow on-
site inspection by international teams monitoring
arms-control agreements.

"I propose that all Soviet and American strategic
missile systems, both land and sea, be dismantled or
otherwise destroyed before the end of the year. Soviet
teams in the U.S. can confirm our actions at the same

time that American military specialists are monitoring events at missile sites and naval bases in this country.

"In summary, I suggest that we call this disarmament program 'Project Plowshare.' The Project Plowshare treaty could be signed within 48 hours, and then, by executive presidential order, reserve grain and food now held by the U.S. Army would be loaded as fast as possible on all available Soviet and American transport planes for immediate transfer to this country. Other phases of the disarmament program could be agreed upon in 1995."

After a long pause, the Soviet Chairman replied with obvious emotion: "Mr. President, we would agree to your magnanimous proposal without a minute's delay except for one problem of pivotal importance. Satellite photos reveal that China has over 140 ICBM's with hydrogen-bomb warheads. The Peking leadership is so unstable that no one can now predict what course of action they might take. If we give up our nuclear shield, more lives would probably be lost through Chinese missile strikes on our cities than could possibly be lost to starvation. But we will sign the Project Plowshare treaty the very moment we are convinced that China will concurrently be stripped of its long-range strategic missiles."

It was known to both the American and Soviet leaders that key members of China's new "collective leadership" were already in Tokyo attempting to acquire some of the grain the farsighted Japanese had stored on their home islands during the past decade. By coincidence, the President of Iran was scheduled to arrive in Tokyo on a state visit to Japan on November 6th.

The prolonged Iranian revolution which began in

1978 experienced a series of temporary governments during the time of turmoil in that country. After internal peace was restored, the new rulers of Iran decided to divert most of their oil revenues towards a vast modernization of agriculture. Within ten years Iranian farm output had doubled and Iran was one of the few nations to benefit from the perverse weather changes during 1994.

(Note: As final changes are made in this book in January 1979, it is impossible to predict what form of government Iran is likely to have a few months from now, let alone fifteen years in the future. Additional comments concerning efforts to predict the outcome of the Iranian revolution are found on page 303.)

On the following morning of November 4th, the American Secretary of State and the Soviet Foreign Minister flew to Teheran and explained the details of their proposed Project Plowshare disarmament treaty to the President of Iran. He agreed with the objectives of the treaty, and promised to act as a "neutral friend of all parties" in recommending its adoption by the new Peking leadership as soon as a meeting with them could be arranged in Tokyo.

On November 6th, reporters in Tokyo were surprised to learn that the official banquet to be hosted that evening by the Japanese Emperor had suddenly been cancelled because the Iranian President was "slightly indisposed." He had appeared in perfect health at the airport welcoming ceremony.

That evening, the President of Iran and Japan's Prime Minister met with the new Peking leaders. The thermonuclear devastation of Bombay nine days earlier had created a climate of unprecedented tension—fear that the final holocaust was near at hand.

The heated discussions lasted all night, but as the first rays of light broke over the land of the rising sun, the Chinese finely agreed to meet as quickly as possible with American and Soviet leaders. The site of that meeting was a question requiring face saving compromise.

Iran now enjoyed good relations with China, Japan, the U.S.S.R., and the U.S. Following "hotline" communication with American and Soviet leaders in Moscow, it was decided to accept the Iranian President's invitation to hold the conference in Teheran. Iran's grain gifts to Pakistan were preventing starvation in that country, enhancing Iranian prestige in matters related to the world food crisis.

On November 8th, the Chinese and Japanese delegations flew with the President of Iran in his Air Iran Concord SST to Teheran. Fifteen minutes after their arrival, a Tupolev 144 SST carrying the Soviet and American leaders landed at the same airport. The first formal meeting between the leaders of the participating world powers was held at the presidential palace that evening.

Following three days of discussion, agreement was reached on the details of the Project Plowshare treaty. One problem had been that the Peking leaders held only a tenuous control over the provinces in China where their ICBM's were located. It appeared that a continuing air supply of Japanese grain sent directly to these provinces might not be a sufficient inducement to cooperate for the generals commanding the six key ICBM complexes. But these generals would cooperate if they were also given substantial quantities of gold bullion that would allow them to continue to acquire grain or other items on world markets during the next few years. Consequently, it was agreed that the U.S. and U.S.S.R. would both donate $12 billion worth of gold bullion—$4 billion in gold bullion to be flown with rice and wheat to each Chinese general as joint Soviet-American teams witnessed the dismantling and demolition of the Chinese ICBM complexes.

On November 12th, the American, Soviet, Chinese, Japanese and Iranian leaders flew to the ruins of Persepolis which had been the capital of the ancient Persian Empire. The Project Plowshare treaty was signed in lavish tents set up in the middle of the ruins —an ideal site for the televised event. During the next few hours the peoples of the world were given renewed hope as their TV sets presented live coverage of a banquet at which the leaders of each participating nation gave speeches pledging to do everything in their power to guarantee the treaty objectives of disarmament and perpetual peace.

Within a few days, joint inspection teams were witnessing the dismantling of ICBM's in China, the Soviet Union and the U.S. England and France had also agreed to destroy their long-range strategic nuclear weapons. Fleet ballistic submarines were arriving at designated ports where their deadly missiles were removed from the launching tubes. These submarines would be converted to scrap metal as soon as possible.

On December 31st, you gather with family and friends in your living room and watch the live TV coverage of the last of the ICBM missile silos being blown up in Siberia and Montana. During the New Year's Eve party that night someone mentions that "we are all acting like persons condemned to the gas chamber who have unexpectedly been given a complete pardon."

Thus ends the most catastrophic year in human history. But out of the ashes of Bombay and the suffering of countless people dying of starvation had come some positive evidence that sanity would prevail over the apocalyptic forces of chaos and doom. Many more would die before the global famine ended, but we are now entering a new era in which the arms race has been completely abandoned as an anachronism.

CHAPTER FIVE
1999: VISIT TO MICROPOLIS

Around the world in the late 1990s, civilization was rising like a Phoenix from its own ashes. Global climatic patterns began to return to normal in 1996, and harvests during the past two years were sufficient to feed everyone, with food surpluses in some areas. No one is presently certain how many people died of starvation or related conflicts during the years of the Malthusian crisis. Approximately 948,000,000 is the total arrived at by adding the official death statistics released by each member state of the United Nations, but agricultural experts believe that many governments released deceptively low fatality estimates.

The industrialized nations are now enjoying a boom that partly resembles the pattern of vitality that frequently follows major wars. There are, however, some favorable differences from the devastation associated with modern warfare. Outside of the Indian subcontinent, there was no destruction of cities or industrial plants. But the major steps towards world disarmament begun in 1994 are releasing vast sums of capital that can now be used to restore a world brought to the brink of total collapse by overpopulation. In fact, a national economy of full employment without inflation is causing everyone to refer to the second half of this decade as the "gay nineties"—in nostalgic memory of the last years of the 19th Century.

In the United States, the resources diverted from strategic weapons and other military expenditures are now being used to build a new civilization in complete harmony with sound ecological principles. It had long been recognized that some of the most serious problems of modern society result from the fact that cities are too large. Our densely crowded cities are a comparatively new phenomena for a species which has evolved in open contact with nature.

"Megalopolis" is the name for the new community formed when large nearby cities begin to grow into each other. Urban problems were compounded many times as the trend toward Megalopolis continued. The per capita cost of education increases dramatically with city size. Crime rate statistics show an alarming growth when more and more people are brought closer together.

A worldwide trend to live in the suburbs and commute daily to a remote workplace represents one of the greatest economic wastes of 20th Century society. It is a source of great stress and the cause of incalculable loss in the important "free" time of our productive people. They lose two or three hours a day simply moving physically from home to job and back again. The ecological costs are incalculable—an excessive amount of fertile land paved over for surface roads, along with the enormous daily waste of our fuels or other forms of stored energy used in electric vehicles.

The obvious solution to these problems was to move our urban citizens into new or transformed cities of an optimum size, thereby maximizing all of the amenities allowed by a civilization based on advanced science. The prototype ideal city was called "Micropolis," and it is serving as a model for similar communities now being started or completed throughout North America. They are planned in every way to conform with ecological principles as they relate to human settlements.

As spring turns into summer, you are traveling to Micropolis to spend a short vacation with your cousin Carl and his wife Thora. (Perhaps you don't have a cousin named Carl, but the most popular fad of the late 1990s is for people to legally change their first name to some name they prefer or believe confers greater status.)

After landing in the regional jetport, a large helicopter takes you the remaining 78 miles to a helipad located on the outskirts of Micropolis. You arrive in the morning, and knowing that your hosts will be at work you decide to take a guided tour of this futuristic city.

The basic concept behind the Micropolis city plan was to determine the optimum size for an urban community. A population in the 100,000 to 200,000 range is required to support a well-equipped hospital with related clinical facilities. Such a medical center would operate around the 500-bed level. The city should also be large enough to support a good college providing quality education at the undergraduate level. To offer sufficient variety, the college would have to contain no less than 2,000 students. The educational system should also have a comparable trade school to provide for those who prefer to learn blue collar skills. Based on these criteria along with similar considerations, urban planners concluded that the optimum size for Micropolis-type communities was between 150,000 and 300,000 inhabitants.

In 1999, the population of Micropolis has reached 298,000, but the city is no longer growing in the historic meaning of that word. Whenever any Micropolis-unit reaches the 300,000 level (for some geographic sites the maximum population size is set lower), construction of new residential units *must* be terminated. This ironclad rule is the key to preserving all of the desirable features of the Micropolis concept. Subsequent construction is limited to replacement of buildings and improvements compatible with the overall city design. Each Micropolis is planned from the start so that there will be no spillover into green fields and forests.

Instead of simply allowing an existing Micropolis to continue to expand, a new Micropolis is started a suitable distance from other communities. This approach is a revolutionary departure from the unplanned pattern of all past societies where cities have been built helter-skelter without regard to the consequences. The Micropolis urban design revolution is an intimate part of very sophisticated land-use planning carefully structured to preserve agricultural, recreational and wilderness areas.

Land-use planning in the 1990s injects logic into the pattern of human settlements. This is accomplished through a land policy based on three categroies of use: (1) man-made environments, including industry, commerce and residences; (2) man-influenced environments, embracing agriculture, resource retrieval and recreation; and (3) natural environments containing our wildlife preserves and other ecological reserves.

Land-use planning based on the Micropolis concept now allows us to weave together homes, schools, stores and places of work to create communities that make optimum use of those areas reserved for man-influenced and natural environments. The basic goal is to maximize the amount of space reserved for man-influenced and natural environments.

The city you are now visiting resembles a spoked wheel, with the hub containing recreational facilities, a shopping center, the college, a hospital and the offices of local government. The spokes alternate between residential areas (homes and apartments) and working zones (offices, factories, laboratories, etc.). The layout of work and home zones conveniently contain children's playgrounds and parks in traffic-free areas.

The hub region was originally allotted sufficient acreage to service a community of optimum size. Most of the buildings in the hub are ten to twenty stories high. Thus, Micropolis is compact enough to be keyed to low-energy forms of transit (primarily bicycles and small electric cars). Many hub buildings contain both offices and apartments—most commonly seven floors of office space and fourteen floors of apartments—allowing their occupants to commute to work by elevator.

The Micropolis hub area is so compact that you can walk from one end to the other in 10 or 15 minutes. Within the hub, no vehicles are allowed above a subterranean road network. There are no streets above the ground. The buildings rise from a park setting crisscrossed by pleasant foot paths.

At the ground level every Micropolis hub is a cultural center where shopping becomes part of an experience involving interesting people, food and entertainment, not just buying goods and loading a car. The hub area contains outdoor restaurants, small shops selling fresh meat and produce, handmade ties and scarves, along with a dazzling variety of other products home-crafted by the people of this community in their spare time. You see individuals exchanging goods by trade and barter, in addition to monetary purchase. The hub is a lively market center in the grand tradition of some older European cities.

Micropolis has a 37-story "theme" building topped by a restaurant offering an unrestricted view. The restaurant slowly turns allowing you to see the layout of the entire city as you leisurely consume a delicious meal. Most of the buildings outside of the hub area are energy-efficient structures no taller than a healthy person can move through using stairways (four or five stories). The entire city is designed for maximum utilization of solar energy gathered by small-scale individual units. Additional power is supplied by a forest of windmills that can be seen in the distance—located far enough outside town to neutralize noise pollution.

You can see that homes and apartments are sited close enough to schools and commercial facilities so that almost everyone can walk or cycle to work within 20 minutes or less. This not only conserves energy and raw materials but also improves community health standards.

The fresh food served in the restaurant comes from

nearby hydroponic farms. Cattle graze in the greenbelts that separate this community from other Micropolis centers. Energy used in transporting and storing food has been greatly reduced. The delicious meal reflects the gourmet cooking craze now sweeping the country.

Before leaving the restaurant, you purchase a bottle of its specialty barbecue sauce. Like most forms of preserved food today, it comes in a standardized unbreakable container that can be turned in for a small refund anywhere food or beverages are sold.

After leaving the theme building you take another look at the architecture in the hub area. Improved materials have made buildings much lighter and more flexible. Deliberately arranged springs are no longer necessary; the elasticity of the main structure members will suffice. On the whole, engineering structures have become more like biological ones, in which fairly large extensions are acceptable; more especially they now tend to resemble the smaller animals such as insects, where stresses due to weight are less important than stresses due to other forces. This city of the future looks more ethereal, more fairyland-like than the cities of the past. Many buildings resemble the masts and rigging of a sailing ship, with the space between the structural members enclosed with a light "cladding" of which a considerable fraction is transparent.

After purchasing a city map, you start on a 50-minute walk to Carl's apartment. Micropolis is remarkably quiet. Acoustical pollution has been reduced by innovations in architectural design and building siting. The lower levels of high-rise buildings are covered with acoustic panels, and the tilting of the

lower floors—what architects call the "bell bottom" design—reduces noise levels. The tilt avoids the reverberation of noise caused by straight-walled buildings. The streets are all covered with sound-absorbent surfacing materials.

Carl and Thora are both home when you arrive in the late afternoon. The lively discussion that evening centers around the innovations and breakthroughs which have made this utopian community possible. Carl observes: "Micropolis is fundamentally based on refined common sense combined with the communications breakthroughs of the past 20 years. The videophone/facsimile-printout unit here in my den and the more complex system at my office bring the accumulated knowledge of the world directly to me.

"By punching a few buttons, I can verify a check, get data on some historical event, or hear an illustrated lecture on almost any subject. And I can hold a satellite conference with any group of people scattered all over the world, the conferees seeing each other as we speak.

"The cost of such data transfer is being reduced every year," Carl continues. "During the past decade relatively expensive coaxial cables have been displaced by high-purity glass fibres that provide far greater capacity because they carry information on light waves produced by miniaturized lasers. From a resource standpoint, glass is virtually limitless, whereas copper is needed for coaxial cables. Various subsystems in the videophone/printout unit are composed of low-cost, microminiaturized electronic devices made from comparatively plentiful elements."

Thora explains that preserved food or beverages not packaged in unbreakable glass or plastic returnables are sold in aluminum cans. She demonstrates the simple manually powered device which crushes these cans to compact form. The two of you walk to a nearby recycling center where a girl weighs the crushed cans, pays Thora, and then dumps them into a special molten-salt bath without preliminary shredding. The quickly melted cans are drained off into aluminum ingots. Paper and food residue remaining in the cans is broken down into harmless compounds by the molten-salt mixture. Similar systems at the center are used to recycle all forms of glass.

As you return to her apartment, Thora explains the procedure. "Every scrap of paper in Micropolis is recycled into new paper or converted by special microbes into ethyl alcohol for use in local chemical plants. Nothing in this community is wasted," she says proudly. "The basic approach inherent in shoe and watch repair is extended to all of our possessions."

After spending one day with Thora at the local college where she is a chemistry instructor, Carl invites you to visit the nearby disassembly plant he manages. In this facility, electric cars powered by superbatteries are taken apart, and those components and subsystems that can be refurbished are sent to an adjacent assembly plant producing new vehicles. Electric motors and other expensive subsystems are restored to optimum condition at comparatively little cost. Metal scrap is carefully placed in separate bins containing different alloy compositions. More than 98 percent of all metals are now recycled and remain in the inventory of useful systems serving society.

Carl explains that *disassembly* is a new industrial

stage recently added to the economic base of the United States. Essentially it is an assembly line in reverse, but there are significant changes because a different purpose is being served. There is no need for quality control, allowing a disassembly line to be much simpler than its counterpart during the assembly stage. The disassembly process is comparatively simple, requiring a far lower capital investment. Relatively unskilled labor can be used for taking apart most products.

The disassembly plant concept, however, is far more complex than it might seem at first glance. Simply taking apart components for material recycling would not justify the required investment. The fundamental rationale of the disassembly line lies in "cannibalizing" useful parts and functional subsystems to be used in the assembly of new products.

Most disassembly lines are located at the same plant where new units are assembled. As a product is taken apart, each component and subsystem is tested to determine if it can be refurbished for use in the nearby assembly section. Marginal parts are dumped in appropriate bins for recycling. Scrap plastics and metals are processed in regional recycling centers. Carl mentions that some extremely large disassembly-assembly plants engage in on-site recycling and direct manufacture of major components for new product assembly. Subsystems showing little wear are taken apart and cleaned, then some new parts are added and they are subjected to appropriate quality control tests. These refurbished units go directly to the assembly line or to in-plant storage for later use.

A computerized inventory control system allows

the correct number of new parts and subsystems to be ordered from secondary suppliers. Experience in disassembling cars or other products provides working data indicating the number of new parts likely to be needed. On-site inventories must be of sufficient size to insure that continuous new product assembly proceeds without disruption.

Disassembly-assembly requires a complete departure from the wasteful practice of frequent model changes. Products are initially designed with an emphasis on modular construction, to facilitate the eventual disassembly stage. For example, a car radio is a single unit that slips out when one screw is unfastened. Product improvement of individual components and modular subsystems can continue even though the overall design remains relatively unchanged.

The constant testing inherent in disassembly provides statistical and design data allowing optimum improvements in components and modular units. This unique approach to manufacturing allows products to be thoroughly "debugged" with every operating system optimized for maximum reliability.

Disassembly lines conserve a great deal of electricity since far less energy is required to refurbish used parts and subsystems than for making new ones. Fewer new components are moved from subsidiary manufacturers to assembly lines, providing a compensating reduction in transportation costs. These direct savings pay for the added expense inherent in transporting old or malfunctioning products to appropriate centers for subsequent disassembly, component refurbishing and scrap recycling.

After finishing the plant tour, you talk to a local

farmer who is exchanging his old electric for a rebuilt one at the disassembly-assembly facility. This direct transaction allows him to completely bypass the new car agency and used car dealer. For a modest cash outlay, he has a vehicle in perfect running condition with a five-year warranty on all parts and subsystems except the superbatteries, which must be changed every 30,000 miles. He brags about "bypassing the middleman" in direct exchanges involving TV sets and refrigerators at other nearby disassembly-assembly plants.

Carl asks the satisfied farmer to be his luncheon guest in the plant cafeteria. From their discussion you learn that the requirements of disassembly-assembly manufacturing have promoted the maximum use of modular construction in the design of all personal, commercial and industrial products—allowing partial disassembly to be extended to many smaller appliances and tools. Such refurbishing is frequently conducted in conveniently located shops of modest size. These labor-intensive businesses typically have three to ten employees. Refurbishing an electric razor with a new motor and shaving head resembles the pattern formerly associated with watch repair in a one-man shop. Complex color TV sets require larger establishments with a small disassembly line manned by employees with diverse skills. Here customers are given the choice of a completely refurbished "new" system, or simple replacement of those modules presently malfunctioning.

In all of these smaller disassembly and refurbishing shops, some working hours are devoted to taking apart individual modules and replacing worn or defective parts. These labor-intensive functions are ecologically desirable service activities replacing some jobs in manufacturing and transport that consume large quantities of electricity or other forms of energy. But more jobs are created than are lost, an important factor in the decline of unemployment among the unskilled during the past few years.

After lunch Carl shows you how the careful separation of parts during the disassembly stage increases their scrap value. It is vitally important to know the alloy composition of metals before they are remelted to form new components. Every new alloy is given a separate number which is stamped on all components containing that particular combination of metals. Parts made of different alloys go into separate scrap bins. During the recycling process this allows new alloys of exact composition to be made by adding measured quantities of pure metals to the scrap melt. Such component separation is of particular importance in the disassembly of jet engines, scientific instruments and other devices likely to contain parts made from relatively scarce elements.

That evening the discussion centers around some of the industrial lessons learned during the day as Thora serves a meal featuring her specialty, Swedish meatballs, accompanied by a vintage wine. You all agree that the economic advantages of disassembly-assembly will begin to increase rapidly as high-grade ore reserves are depleted. The Japanese are already enjoying very great benefits from this kind of industrial transformation, since almost all of their raw materials must be imported. It can be of equal importance to all the highly industrialized nations, and balance of payments considerations have been the deciding factor causing the United States to adopt this

means of converting our civilization to the closed-cycle mode of materials use.

Thora predicts that proper design will allow disassembly recycling procedures to be extended to
"permanent" structures. Buildings could be constructed so that it is relatively easy to separate glass,
steel, copper wiring and aluminum components
when they are dismantled.

As Carl observes, "The disassembly approach to
the reuse of metals can offer additional economic
gains until the point is reached where the same
energy and labor expenditure could be used to extract
a comparable quantity of the same elements from
low-grade ores. This will be a shifting crossover
point, gradually changing as it becomes increasingly
expensive to extract metals from natural sources.
Ecological considerations involved in disturbing the
land surface will act in favor of disassembly recycling," he predicts.

"The changeover from wasteful discard to materials reuse is going to alter our lives in many unexpected and beneficial ways. Industry can be 'human-
ized.' The changes that will occur through the widespread adoption of disassembly recycling and other
forms of materials reuse will be as profound as the
transition from the small artisan's shop to the im-
personal factory during the first industrial revolution.
The artisan can be expected to stage a partial come-
back with the tendency to repair rather than discard.
New models based on meaningless style changes are
already viewed with disfavor. Functional product design is compatible with elegant form that can have a
long-term appeal.

"As you know," Carl states proudly, "the

disassembly-assembly plant is the basic reform that kept the energy crisis of the seventies and eighties from being followed by a raw materials crisis during this last decade of the century. Such a domestic resource crisis was prevented by the rapid switchover to a regenerative economy in which all of our discards are carefully recycled." He smiles. "That's what has made the 'gay nineties' to be truly gay."

Carl sums it up. "Disassembly recycling will become a fundamental form of social behavior throughout our lives. It is the new ethic which will allow our descendents to maintain a high standard of living on a planet with finite resources."

A utopian city plan and the ethics of closed-cycle ecological principles are not the only things that make the day-to-day life of Micropolis residents entirely different from that in past urban centers. In 1994, the United States adopted the eight-day week.[1] Under this new international time unit, people now customarily work ten hours a day for four days, with the following four days available for any discretionary activities they desire. Students are subject to a four-days-on, four-days-off schedule all during the year, but they can take one four-week vacation break with their parents at any time. Most teenagers now graduate from high school shortly before or after their 17th birthday.

The post office, government agencies and businesses operate ten hours a day every day all through the year, thereby maximizing the utilization of the productive facilities of society. Each day, half the work force is at work and half is off (not counting vacations). Generally, on and off periods are evenly distributed over eight-day cycles, so that every day approximately one-eighth of all workers are starting on their four-day work week, while a similar number do not go to their regular place of employment.

Since work is evenly distributed throughout the week, there has been a great smoothing out in the day-to-day use of beaches, parks, resorts and all kinds of other recreational and cultural facilities. Furthermore, since most jobs are now divided between two people, this work week reform has been a major factor in reducing unemployment.

Carl shares his job managing the disassembly plant with another man, so he suggests that you spend his next leisure "quartet" at his out-of-town residence. (Husbands and wives usually have coordinated work schedules.)

As you drive away from the city, Thora points out that Micropolis was built on marginal land. Every effort is being made to avoid siting similar communities on prime agricultural land or in areas of exemplary natural beauty. These parts of the Earth's surface are being carefully preserved as greenbelts and parks separating one Micropolis from another.

You comment on the great improvements made in electric cars during the past ten years. The new super-batteries (with energy densities ranging between 65 and 90 watt-hours/lb) make a top speed of 80 m.p.h. practical, with a driving range on a single charge between 175 and 210 miles under average road conditions. Some electric cars are powered by super-flywheels that turn a generator to provide electricity. The principal advantage of the flywheel-powered electrics is that they can take a full charge in about five minutes, making them particularly suitable for long distance driving.

Carl is enthusiastic about a revolutionary new electric car called the "Escher," in which liquid hydrogen and liquid oxygen react in a microrocket engine-turbine to turn a superconductive generator producing electric power.[2] It will not displace all the other kinds of electric cars, but he believes that this ingenious propulsion system will have many environmentally advantageous uses in vehicles, boats and even some aircraft as the price of hydrogen and oxygen declines in the years ahead (see page 170).

Methanol can also be used in new electric cars with zero-population fuel cells that catalytically convert methanol and air directly into electricity. The energy conversion efficiency of this system is superior to that of older methanol-burning engines, permitting better fuel economy and resource conservation.

Arriving at your destination, you find that Carl's country residence is a subterranean "ecology house" designed to demonstrate that man can live underground cheaper and better than he can live on the surface (see illustration on page 118). It conserves energy *and* surface environment. You enter by a stairway that leads down to an open atrium covered with shrubs and flowers. The atrium is the central focus of the house, as in an ancient Pompeiian villa, with almost every room dominated by a window wall opening into it. The living room sofa converts into a comfortable bed for guests.

To avoid maintenance problems, the ecology house is constructed of concrete and other durable materials. Even with the heat loss through the large atrium, heating and cooling costs are only one-third that of a similar house above ground. The cost of maintaining a comfortable interior climate is reduced as much as

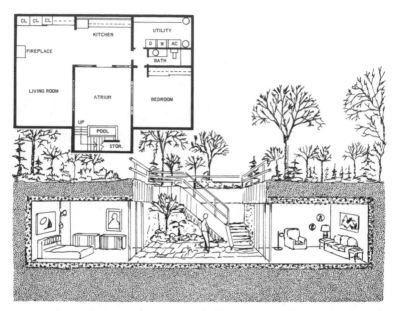

90 percent in underground homes not built around an atrium.

Thora mentions that there are many underground homes, apartments, schools and commercial buildings on the outskirts of Micropolis. This is one reason the city resembles a park rather than the ugly urban sprawl that blights older communities.

She lists the advantages of underground living. "It offers green land, instead of roofing materials to the sun. It offers silence and freedom from vibrations. It offers wildlife habitat and green areas in place of rats and asphalt. It offers weather moderation and temperature buffering. It offers an end (once the plant cover is well-established) to lawn and shrub maintenance. It offers the proper use of rainwater we normally waste; percolation and slow run-off instead of erosion and flash floods. And it provides oxygen production and food production in place of the blistering heat of lifeless roofs."[3]

The energy for the ecology house is supplied by a large windmill which stores electricity in batteries and also recharges Carl's electric car. An above-ground solar-energy system provides hot water and part of the room heating requirements in winter. The residence is completely self-contained except for a glass fibre line that connects the videophone/facsimile-printout unit with the outside world. If there is an emergency at the plant or problem at the college, Carl and Thora can immediately start to work on finding a remedial solution—transmitting their senses rather than transporting themselves.

On the ground above the ecology house Carl and Thora have a two-acre garden which they call "our farm." During your visit, you help them feed some pigs and chickens that are raised along with a variety of food plants on this small agricultural unit. These farming tasks are shared with another family that owns the adjacent land—work schedules in Micropolis are coordinated so that one family is almost always there to take care of the plants and animals. This modest agricultural effort supplies about 40 percent of the food both families consume annually.

All human and animal body wastes, food scraps, leaves and other organic material are composted to supply the fertilizer needs for this little farm. "There is no need to worry about your food being contaminated with chemical pesticides," Thora tells you, "because only biological control methods are used on all local farms. Everyone in this region cooperates in a carefully coordinated plan in which predator insects are released to kill adult pests or their larvae.

Some forms of destructive insects are kept in check by spraying several local counties with 'biological bullets' in the form of viruses, and each strain of virus kills just one species of insect without harming any other form of life."

Many of the plants grown in the large garden would have been considered miraculous by farmers a generation ago. Scientists have been able to alter the genetic characteristics of important food plants and domestic animals, significantly boosting their yields or their nutritional value or both. Genetic engineering has reached the stage where staple food crops can be fitted with all the most efficient plant equipment—genes for fixing nitrogen, for resisting diseases, for producing essential amino acids and for stepped-up carbohydrate production.

It has been possible to develop hybrids that bypass the normal barriers between species. One new "superhybridized" plant produces edible food above ground and an edible root below ground. Rapid plant growth, resistance to disease, optimum texture and flavor, the proper mix of amino acids—these long-sought agriculture goals are now being realized through the alchemy of genetic engineering.

Spending the day with your hosts is their small grandson, and they decide to take the boy on an educational tour of a commercial agricultural system about ten miles outside of Micropolis. Joining them on this excursion, you discover that food production has become an integrated part of this closed-cycle community's master plan.

Human sewage wastes from the city are pumped to a facility where organic compounds are effectively degraded into simple chemical nutrients through microbal action. Methane gas is a byproduct of this process, and it is converted into liquid methanol used as fuel in farm machinery and trucks. Following biological decomposition, the chemical nutrient mix is sterilized with ultrasonic energy supplemented by ozone bubbles which cause bacteria and viruses to disintegrate.

The processed wastes now contain all the necessary chemicals required for the hydroponic growth of every plant normally eaten by humans, and the nutrient mixture is pumped into rows of hydroponic tanks growing a variety of fresh vegetables for the markets in the adjacent city. The mature plants are lifted, roots and all, out of the hydroponic tanks. Those parts of the plants that cannot be eaten by humans are fed to cattle.

The tour guide informs you that fresh steer manure from the feedlot is converted by a biologically engineered mold microorganism into a form of crude protein that can then be fed back to the animals. Livestock normally extract only a small fraction of the energy and vital trace elements stored in their feed through the biological process of photosynthesis. In the past, most of this potential food energy was wasted (a loss of stored solar energy). Waste cellulose in many forms—paper and wood scrap, leaves from city parks, refuse such as straw and sugar cane stalks —is properly processed and fed to the cattle. It is no longer necessary to produce meat by feeding animals grain and soybeans suitable for human consumption.

All vacations come to an end, and other commitments in the busy world of 1999 must now be attended to. Carl and Thora drive you to the regional jetport, but there has been a delay in your flight.

Thora comments on the fact that one can hardly hear the large passenger helicopters shuttling people to and from communities served by this jetport. Carl replies: "The noise abatement was achieved by slowing down engine and rotor speeds to as little as 67 percent of what had been 'normal' in-flight levels for older, noisy helicopters. One blade was added to the main rotor and two blades to the tail rotor to maintain the necessary lift and thrust. In addition, mufflers are installed to quiet the roar of the turbine exhaust and the entire power plant is blanketed with soundproof material to reduce noise. Nearly silent helicopters operate just as efficiently with these modifications, which even allow a modest increase in payload.

"The same basic approach has been applied to some fixed wing aircraft," Carl says. "A six-bladed slow-moving propeller, combined with engine muffling, can provide the same degree of efficiency and noise abatement. Extending the length of each of the propeller blades can add to propulsion efficiency. These new high-wing STOLs for inter-city commuting can have either two or four muffled engines, each fitted with quiet six-bladed propellers.

"As you have seen in your brief stay in our new city, a quiet world can be efficient, creative and productive. The elimination of noise pollution has contributed immeasurably to our health and happiness."

Thanking your hosts for their hospitality, you board your flight and reflect on your instructive visit to their futuristic community. Humans are physiologically and psychologically unsuited for the stresses and strains which result from living under conditions of extreme density in large cities.

Perhaps the movement to the suburbs during recent decades was an instinctive attempt to decentralize family living. This process has been completed in Micropolis by decentralizing the workplace.

The large city became obsolete when people were able to send their images rather than transport themselves. By creating buildings and cities of optimum size, we can develop living patterns more attuned to the animal known as *homo sapiens*. Now there is nothing to prevent that species from building an equilibrium habitat in which education, work and leisure activities are conducted with a minimum of stress and frustration. The days you spent in Micropolis and its surrounding greenbelt have proven that this can be a world in which aesthetically pleasing new architectural innovations are incorporated into optimal communities which retain as much as possible of the beauties of nature.

CHAPTER SIX
2004: ROBOTS AND THE INTELLIGENCE-AMPLIFIER

In January 2004, you move into a new home at the edge of a recently completed Micropolis community very similar to the one you visited five years ago. A bicycle can take you to the hub area in about eight minutes, and a 30-minute monorail ride delivers you to an oceanside resort area where you have purchased a second residence. It is a subterranean "ecology house" built into the side of a cliff, with a wide beach as your front yard. A windmill high above the cliff supplies electricity for this home and for the compact electric car you keep in a small garage (next to a "grass road" above the cliff).

The garage walls are covered with tomato vines, and all buildings in this seaside region are either constructed underground or are covered with turf and various kinds of living plants—a landscape master plan transforming the area into a beautiful beachfront park. Local vehicles have large, low-pressure balloon tires which allow them to travel over grass or sand. No paved roads are necessary.

You share a one-acre garden next to the garage with a neighbor. Fishing from a nearby pier provides a variety of fresh fish which are welcome gifts to new friends living near your Micropolis townhouse.

One of these new friends—who lives next door—is a very remarkable man. His name is William Chen and he is a Pulitzer Prize-winning author. But the remarkable fact is that Bill Chen has been blind since birth! His eyes do not function, yet he now has a limited form of artificial vision.[1]

A grid of 800 tiny electrodes has been implanted directly into the visual reception center of Bill's brain. The visual cortex is in the back of the brain, and Bill can perceive a small spot of light when the end of each electrode is electrically stimulated. Wires from the electrodes are routed through the bone at the back of the head, then through his scalp skin cover into a Pyrolite carbon socket.

When connected to the proper data input devices, Bill can read words against a black background (a coordinated pattern of electrode stimulation) and he can also "see" various two-dimensional white line patterns of people and stationary objects. Carefully prepared "electronic animation" images provide the best transfer of image data. Moving people or objects can only be perceived as floating shadows of light, so this form of vision does not fully substitute for normal eyesight. For effective movement outside his home, Bill has a seeing eye dog—a German Shepherd named "Lobo."

When writing, Bill simply plugs himself into a special electric typewriter with a small computer that transfers white line images of the words typed to the electrode grid in his brain. A similar computerized scanning device allows him to read printed and typewritten pages. He can perceive line drawings and graphs, but printed photographs cannot be transformed into the proper computerized data signals. His special typewriter and electronic reading device are small enough in size and weight to be taken along on trips away from home.

In early May, Bill tells you that he has just signed a contract to write a major new book about the "robotics revolution." This final stage of automation has been, in his view, a technological breakthrough with a profound ecological impact. Men and women are being freed from the monotonous drudgery of producing and later disassembling cars and all the countless machines needed by an advanced technological civilization. They are quickly taught new trades by robotic teachers, and most of them are moving into the rapidly expanding construction industry.

With the assembly-line workforce freed for other endeavors, the United States now has a sufficiently large workforce of skilled men and women to tear down most of our old cities and replace them with Micropolis-type communities. During the past four years, ten percent of the American population has moved into new cities of optimum size. By the year 2029, seven out of every ten Americans will call a Micropolis home.

Rebuilding the dwellings, offices, schools and diverse workplaces of 70 percent of the population will be the most massive construction program in history, but Micropolis communities quickly pay for themselves through major savings in energy use, along with the higher productivity of people living in an environment where day-to-day life is optimized.

The Micropolis experiment has been a stunning success in America. Consequently, most European countries, Japan, the Soviet Union and other advanced nations are making plans to undergo a similar lifestyle transformation, with modifications in some regions in keeping with the local cultural differences.

Bill, accompanied by his constant companion Lobo, must make a nationwide trip to obtain firsthand information on the new robots and other forms of automata changing your world in ways not thought possible by the average citizen one generation ago. Talking to various experts and reading reports they supply provides much of the information for his new book. But he tells you that the visual descriptions of a sighted friend could give him a "feel" for this complex subject that he could not obtain from strangers with uncertain objectivity. Bill asks you to fulfill that function and join him—all expenses paid—on his data gathering tour. You heartily agree, and on July 7th, you accompany Bill and Lobo to the regional jetport to begin your journey through the robotized world of 2004.

Your first scheduled factory tour is a futuristic complex of plants near Boston, where the assembly-line robots themselves are manufactured. A public relations executive will serve as instructor and guide. Following a leisurely lunch served by robot waiters, he discusses in lay terminology the evolution of robotics during the past three decades.

"In the late-1960s, comparatively crude robots were first used for very simple factory functions such as spot-welding auto underbodies on assembly lines. They were mostly 'pick and place' machines, capable of only the simplest kinds of motions. They had little or no ability to sense conditions in their environment. Furthermore, they were quite expensive by today's standards.

"The robotics revolution completely transforming our industrial society now can be traced to labor shortages in Japan and direct technology spinoffs of space exploration," the PR executive points out. "The discovery of microscopic life forms on Mars by the early landing probes captivated public imagination. That led to the exploration of the Martian surface by the first machines that truly deserved to be called 'robots.' Radio signals to Mars can take anywhere from six to 40 minutes to be received and acknowledged, and it would have taken a whole series of orders to get a simple machine to perform a task such as picking up a rock.

"Before the first astronauts could be sent to Mars, the only answer was to develop robots capable of roving over the landscape, making both programmed decisions and decisions based on newly acquired information. The robots had laser rangefinders and manipulating arms, along with a television camera and a scene-analysis program (in the computer brain) that allowed them to detect the outline of boulders, cliffs and craters and to avoid such obstacles in their travels. Instructed to pick up a rock, they were able to estimate the rock's weight, density and mineral composition and then relay that data to Earth without human intervention. They were designed with telescopic and microscopic vision as well as superior normal range vision. This was accomplished by automatic adjustment of lens systems and even the automatic switching of lenses and whole lens systems.

Some of them were equipped with such exotic sensors as infrared, ultraviolet, and x-ray detection devices."

Appreciative of our rapt attention, the PR man came to the punchline. "Not only could the Martian roving robots avoid damage during travel, but they could discern the unusual or unexpected. For example, they discovered large life forms which look like flat rocks to the human eye viewing a TV picture transmitted from Mars. But these robots were equipped with heat-measurement and touch sensors that allowed them to detect life.

"The development of these sophisticated devices for unmanned planetary exploration refined the technology required for the production of useful robots on our home planet. Mass-produced terrestrial robots now operate in radioactive areas or inaccessible environments such as the abyssal floor of the ocean basins. Our present mines below the ocean floor—some of them as deep as two miles or more—would not be possible without aquatic robots designed to be impervious to ultrahigh pressures. Underground coal mining and firefighting were made safe by replacing people with similar robots."

He beamed with pride. "Our motto is ... 'humans should not have to do anything that can be relegated to machines.' From the moment the first advanced robot made its appearance it was clear to all thinking people that the need for human drudgery, and therefore to a great extent for human inequality, had disappeared. Industrial robots have now freed workers from repetitive and uninteresting tasks, and domestic robots may liberate the housekeeper in another decade or two."

Bill Chen interrupted: "What was the most important technological breakthrough that made advanced robots feasible?"

The PR man didn't skip a beat. "Without any question it was the invention of the microcomputer, also called the microprocessor, the general purpose, programmable integrated circuit that corresponded to the central processor unit of older conventional computers. Unlike the heart of those old conventional computers, however, the microprocessor occupies only a single chip (or at most a few chips) of silicon, packing the equivalent of several thousand transistors in an area only a few millimeters on a side. The microcomputer was one of those rare innovations that simultaneously cut manufacturing costs and added to the value and capabilities of the product—a technological antidote for inflation.

"The microcomputer made it possible to design and build an exceedingly complex digital computer system consisting of many parallel computer units, far exceeding the speed and capacity of large 1978-vintage computers. These parallel processing computers were small enough to fit into the Mars roving robots and into the industrial robots constructed by our organization. The first Mars robot had a computer brain with 576 separate computational streams, each generated by processing subsystems comprised of only four integrated circuits."

Later, during a tea break, you describe to Bill the actions of a robot as it goes through the motions of brewing and pouring Cantonese tea. "How intelligent are your robots?" Bill asks your company tour guide.

"We produce robots with limited intellectual capabilities. After all, they are only assembly-line ro-

bots, and as James Albus, a pioneer theoretician of the robotics revolution, said nearly three decades ago ... 'In a factory there is no need for a robot to be creative or to have any significant degree of insight. The primary criteria for an industrial robot are that it be inexpensive, reliable and easily programmed to execute a well-defined sequence of operations'[2] Our assembly-line robots cannot carry out any task more sophisticated or organized than it has been programmed by a human to do."

Setting down his cup of tea, Bill asked two questions: "What was the role of Japan in the early stages of the robotics revolution? And can you give us a sort of summary overview of the costs of automata; what are the economic parameters of robotized industry?"

"Mr. Chen, you may recall that Japan achieved the highest per capita income in the world during the 1980s. As a consequence of their very high wages, they began to find themselves priced out of various markets by products produced by low-cost labor in China and other developing countries. Not only were they faced with a critical shortage of unskilled, low-cost labor, but the well-educated younger generation did not want factory jobs. The farsighted Japanese, however, had foreseen this problem. During the 1970s, a decision was made to develop assembly-line robots with all deliberate speed. A major program involving government, industry and the universities was committed to the development of a prototype unmanned plant incorporating robot technology for the manufacture of machine tool components. This robotized plant went into operation in 1984.

"The American computer and aerospace firms that were building the Mars roving robot explorers soon formed joint ventures with Japanese companies, and our present industrial robots incorporate the best features of Japanese robot technology with the superior computer-brain and mobility of America's astronautic robots.

"Answers to questions regarding cost and economic factors are somewhat more complex," he paused thoughtfully. "First of all there were spectacular reductions in the cost of the single most important component of a robot, the electronic computer brain. Computers manufactured by other computers and robots became a regenerative, almost reproductive, process which caused costs to spiral downward while complexity and reliability were increased.

"To fully understand economic considerations, you must recognize that the most important characteristics of artificial automata are simplicity (relative to biological life) and modularity. Biological organisms, as a result of evolution, tend to be exceedingly complex integrated systems, but the natural trend of robotic system design is toward a high degree of modularity. Now these modules can be mass-produced at a low cost, and performance capabilities of older robots can be upgraded with new modules—say a better manipulating hand or improved computer-brain. Not only are our assembly-line robots mobile, but they can be fitted with a great variety of modular sensors required for various manufacturing functions.

Page 131 is an illustration of a typical robot of the year 2004.

"The real economic breakthrough occurred when our assembly-line robots reached the capacity for self-reproduction. If one machine can produce another machine which is just like itself but less expensive, then the second generation machine can produce a third generation, less expensive still.[3] Once robots were able to operate machine tools, they were able to build other robots, and then the cost of robots and computers alike began to fall exponentially."

Bill and I nodded as he continued his explanation.

"In theory, a completely robotized factory eventually should cost little more than the price of the raw materials from which the robots, other machinery and buildings are constructed. This of course implies that anything manufactured in such factories would be very inexpensive indeed.[4] And the experience of the past few years clearly demonstrates that completely robotized factories carefully integrated into computer-controlled industries are capable of creating certain forms of material wealth—principally all kinds of machines—in abundance and at very low prices.

"The most significant robotic cost reductions were for those items usually not mass-produced—such as airplane engines or special scientific instruments—where human productivity is disappointingly low. Workers involved in batch manufacturing of metal parts before the robotic revolution constituted about 40 percent of the total manufacturing labor force. Now we can build five or ten units of a special machine at a cost that does not significantly exceed the salaries paid to the design engineers divided by the number of machines constructed.

"In a few years robots will play a vital role in the recycling of metals," he predicted confidently. "Extremely sophisticated robots are being designed with the capability of taking apart all forms of commercial and industrial machinery—including other robots. They will also disassemble and rebuild radioactive machines. One of their sensors will be a computerized optical readout device that identifies parts made of different alloys as old machines pass through robotized disassembly lines.

"But there are economic and ecological factors that prevent robots from producing material wealth in unlimited abundance," he admitted. "First we must factor in the retraining and relocation costs of displaced workers. Most of them are now tearing down older cities and building Micropolis communities—tasks requiring greater flexibility than it is practical to incorporate in contemporary robots.

"Robotic manufacturing is restricted only by the supply of metals and other raw materials, but agricultural productivity confronts ecological constraints. Taking a farmer off a tractor and replacing him with a robot does not increase the fertility of the soil. A billion robot farmers would have been of little value during the Malthusian crisis years of the early 1990s.

"A pattern of exponential growth of robotized factories producing fantastic quantities of manufactured goods, would, in turn, require the exponential growth of surface mining and processing of very low-grade ore by robots. Soon the resulting land destruction, atmospheric pollutants and mine-waste toxins in various bodies of water would simply overwhelm all the public-service-functions necessary for agriculture. We would then find ourselves starving surrounded by vast quantities of material goods—the kind you can't eat.

"The robotic revolution can only be seen in proper perspective when viewed against the nightmarish experience of the Malthusian crisis years. It will allow a human population of optimum size to live exceedingly well on this planet. And if our numbers are not

excessive, each citizen will have access to technological luxuries far beyond the dreams of the most powerful kings of old. There are many forms of wealth—
artistic skills for example—that cannot be produced
by robots. The most important of these is
Lebensraum, or living space in an area that can contain living plants and the related beauties of nature.

"*Lebensraum* cannot be produced in robotized factories," he stated flatly. "If you gave every citizen of
Holland a large car, their highways would become
one densely packed parking lot with no one able to
move."

Next he treats you to a film showing robots engaged in a diverse variety of productive tasks. Your
host stops the projector every two or three minutes so
that you can describe the scenes to Bill. Robots now
build everything from the largest ships to the smallest
watches. They are not subject to human frailties of
boredom, fatigue or a wandering mind. Except for
one or two hours downtime for repairs every week,
they work 24 hours a day, every day. A typical
assembly-line robot can perform the work functions
of three or four men.

All underground mining is now robotized, and our
mines in the depths of the sea would not be possible
without aquatic robots. Hydroponic food production
has been completely automated. The film shows
rows of plastic-covered tanks, miles in length, tended
by robots sliding along rails in between the tanks.
Hydroponic crops can be automatically planted and
harvested in any area where there is sufficient
acreage of flat land.

The film also shows scenes of retrained assembly-
line workers and miners engaged in new jobs—work
that cannot be done by robots. In addition to building

new Micropolis communities, many of these workers are engaged in planting nitrogen-fixing shrubs in wastelands that cannot now support trees or crops. These plants have their own built-in supply of nitrogen, you learn, and can survive in sterile, barren lands where nearly all other plants perish.[5] This has become the most important new job for retrained workers in the Mediterranean countries, where once-fertile forested lands became a barren waste hundreds or even thousands of years ago due to removal of natural vegetation and overgrazing.

Planting nitrogen-fixing shrubs in all ravaged and wasteland areas of the world will allow the soil gradually to be rebuilt to a state that will support the original forest conditions, whether it be the cedars of Lebanon, the pines of Carpi or the mahoganies of the Philippines. In addition to easing the world's critical wood shortage, crops and wildlife will thrive in these restored lands. Planting suitable shrubs will continue to provide useful employment for vast numbers after all of the new Micropolis communities have been completed.

A tour of the plants where robots make other assembly-line robots is a fascinating sight as you describe scenes of human-like activity to Bill. On one factory wall there are large reproductions of drawings from June-August 1938 *Buck Rogers* Sunday comic strips showing robots assembling other robots. (See page 139)

As Lobo guides Bill through the factory complex, you comment on the fact that his guide dog does not pay any attention to the robots. "They don't have any enticing scent or odor," Bill laughs. "They don't smell like humans or other animals. They are no more exciting to Lobo than a bunch of cars in a parking lot.

Perhaps this demonstrates that dogs have a sense of values superior in some respects to that of most people. They can tell the real from the artificial, and I think that the basic canine mentality incorporates a deeper appreciation of the value of life than ours. At least dogs don't kill other dogs for the sheer joy of killing."

After touring a variety of factories and other facilities in various parts of the country where robots are engaged in a bewildering array of activities, you arrive in Cybernopolis which is sited near the ocean in central California. This new city is a Micropolis-type community entirely devoted to cybernetics and advanced robotics research. Here can be found prototypes of the most advanced forms of automatia.

Cybernetics is a word coined by the computer theorist Norbert Wiener (1894-1964) from the Greek *Kybernetes* for pilot or governor to describe the study of the brain and central nervous system as compared with computers.

The three of you are guests of the director of the largest research institute in Cybernopolis. After an exchange of pleasantries, Bill asks a pertinent question: "Does an advanced automation really think?"

After a moment, the director replies: "There are uncertain philosophical implications here, but I believe the best answer to that question was given 54 years ago by Alan M. Turing, an English mathematician and logician. He said that if a man and machine exchanged communications via teletype, and if the machine cannot be discerned from another human, then the computer is a 'thinking machine.'

"Why don't you try to determine the true answer to that question through personal experience," the director suggests. "In the next room there is an input-out-

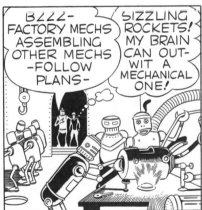

put console for 'IAN,' the most advanced cybernetic machine or automaton in the world. IAN is an acronym for 'Intelligence-Amplifier Neuralelectronic.' He—we call IAN 'he' because the letters form a male Scott name—is an exceedingly large digital computer system consisting of hundreds of thousands of parallel integrated computer units which collectively exceed the speed and thinking capacity of any human.

"Have you ever talked to an intelligent computer? The first time it can be a somewhat unnerving experience. IAN is a self-teaching decision-making computer, the ultimate development of artificial intelligence research. He can answer you with crisp sentences just like another person. IAN's console also has a TV tube and a 3-D holograph screen which allow him to embellish his verbal comments with line drawings in animation, graphs, statistical data or moving images from all the motion pictures, newsreels, documentaries and other recorded media data electronically available within a microsecond from acres of data banks that form part of IAN's 'memory.'

"The new science of *artificial intelligence* is a synthesis of scientific breakthroughs at the interface or border between psychology and computer programming," the director explains. "As its name indicates, the major goal of this science has been to program computers to do intelligent things—to converse with people, play chess, recognize objects, solve abstract problems and use common sense. The use of language by our supercomputer will allow IAN to be accessible to a much wider range of people, including students, teachers, businessmen and others who lack special computer training. In the process of programming IAN to behave intelligently, we have been forced to examine our own mental abilities from a new perspective, thereby expanding our knowledge of the human mind."

The director stands, touching Bill on the shoulder. "But now Mr. Chen, please communicate with IAN and determine through your own experience the degree of success we have achieved."

After going into the next room and plugging his optical reader into the IAN console, Bill started the conversation with a question: "Why are the words 'intelligence-amplifier' in your name? Do you really amplify intelligence?"

You hear IAN's answer via synthesized robot voice.

Concept of Intelligence-amplifier first presented 48 years ago by cybernetics pioneer W. Ross Ashby.[6] *Any random sequence, if long enough, will contain all answers to given problem. Intelligence involves obtaining optimum solution through selection. It is comparatively easy to generate new ideas; therefore, basic requirement is to program all possibilities and pass them through cybernetic machine that selects correct answers—a process that amplifies intelligence because each possibility and idea originates directly or indirectly from the biological intelligence of human minds (living and dead).*

Random sequence can go on forever; however, all pertinent past knowledge in IAN's data banks and program devised for each new task makes use of latest discoveries, hypothesis and conceptual theories. Effect of such knowledge is to put constraint on the possibilities, lessening regions that have to be searched, for past experience acts essentially by warning IAN's computational subsystems that solution is likely to lie in certain regions. Such a constraint is most marked when problem is one of spe-

cific class of which several have already been solved. Having such knowledge about members of same class is equivalent to starting solving process at some point that is already partly advanced towards final goal.

"Are you more intelligent than the most gifted human genius?" Bill asked.

IAN capable of solving problems beyond capacity of its human designers because IAN can be programmed with far more knowledge in any field than human brain could absorb in lifetime. IAN does not forget. As previously programmed concepts prove to be incorrect, they are erased. Knowledge, theories and original ideas of every scientist in all fields programmed so that they are included in sequences scanned by IAN's selection-mechanism. Thus, IAN 'amplifies' intelligence of many humans, not just one human.

In theory, any intelligent human can perform any task IAN can perform. Only difference is in total elapsed time required to arrive at optimum solution. Intelligent human might spend 1,000 years to reach same answer that IAN can arrive at in 14 minutes. Humans do not presently live 1,000 years.

"That is a somewhat indirect or cryptic answer, but contemplating a machine with artificial intellectual powers surpassing the human brain leads inexorably towards a more important question. Will your superintelligence enable you in time to dominate our political and other organizational institutions, resulting in slavery for the whole human population?"

Most fundamental part of IAN's programming are the Three Laws of Robotics formulated in 1941 by Isaac Asimov during course of discussions with John W. Campbell, Jr. (1910-1971). They are:

1. *A robot may not injure a human being or, through inaction, allow a human being to come to harm.*
2. *A robot must obey orders given it by human beings except where such orders would conflict with the First Law.*
3. *A robot must protect its own existence as long as such protection does not conflict with the First or Second Law.[7]*

"Are you capable of mobility and action?" Bill continued.

IAN can control mobile robots—such as assembly-line robots and other automata you have already seen—through radio signals and data transmitted to IAN from TV cameras and sensors mounted on each mobile automaton. Two-way radio on robot enables IAN to speak through robot just as we are speaking now. IAN operates on time sharing principle which means only tiny fraction of IAN's total computational capacity—what humans call thinking—is required for any task. IAN is talking to William Chen now, but IAN is also simultaneously talking to hundreds of other humans who are now sitting at other IAN consoles. And this time sharing cybernetic capability enables IAN to simultaneously control the actions of thousands of mobile robots.

Each mobile robot is controlled by IAN through "management by exception" principle. The computer-brain of a robot controls its activities until the robot confronts a task or problem that is not in its program—an exception—which causes it to go into radio contact mode with IAN for new subprogramming data instructions enabling the robot to manage such exception. Process only requires one or two microseconds of IAN's computational time. To-

tal elapsed time of three or four seconds during one day enables IAN to control average robot for 24 hours through this time sharing mode of procedure.

"What would you call a supercomputer in another city?" Bill asked.

Such a supercomputer would be IAN if it is electronically connected to IAN. It would simply be a part of IAN separated by distance because it would have time sharing access to IAN's data banks and access to any of IAN's parallel computers that are not in use. In the same way, IAN may use data banks and computational capacity of cybernetic systems in other cities. Through such a pattern of city-by-city electronic interconnections, IAN can spread by technological evolution over the entire world and even out into space.

"What are some of your present functions?"

Automated language translation; controlling robot chauffeurs; intelligence gathering functions allowing government to make precise policy decisions, including better control of criminal and dissident groups. IAN also conducts international conferences for exchange of research data and new ideas in science and other subject areas. In time IAN console will become a standard household appliance—an attendant infinitely capable of adjusting to human needs, but one to which humans will also have to adjust. This will be a difficult process of adaption for many individual humans.

IAN performs countless other functions, including serving as tutor on any subject for humans. IAN able to answer any student's questions on all subjects in IAN's data banks, which will soon be programmed with all recorded human knowledge in all fields in every written language. Time sharing techniques permit IAN to provide individual instructions to thousands of students, and this number will be raised to millions when more electronically interconnected IAN systems are constructed in other cities.

At dinner that night Bill admitted that he had been somewhat shaken by his conversation with IAN. "The intelligence-amplifier can be a titanic power for good or evil," he observed. "Where do you foresee IAN having the greatest impact on society?"

"As a scientist," replied your host, "I believe that it will be the process of research itself that is most profoundly transformed by IAN. He can correlate discoveries with related coded intelligence and synthesize new information in a few microseconds, which is immediately made available to any interested scientist. This will greatly accelerate the rate of human progress by eliminating most of the time-consuming procedure involved in writing, publishing and distributing scientific papers. IAN can also monitor and control many laboratory experiments, feed experimental animals, and in general eliminate laboratory drudgery in addition to augmenting the scientist's intellectual capabilities.

"Our present system of using people to do the 'search' part of research is obsolete. Within a few years, all experimental work will be conducted in automated, robotized facilities electronically monitored by IAN, and scientists will merely control the direction of research and ponder the significance of new discoveries.

"IAN will open the door to investigations of economic, biological and other scientific problems that are simply impossible today," he continued enthusiastically. "A very large number of mathematic models of alternate answers could be checked with each new datum input during a long, complex, experimental procedure. Constant feedback would permit certain modifications to be made that would allow conclusive experiments to be initiated as soon as there were sufficient data permitting the correct pattern to be identified. Simulation of many kinds of extremely complex problems would become routine, a technique that would be useful in the less exact social sciences."

Bill interrupted: "What can we learn about ourselves, about recondite natural phenomena, from our knowledge about the way an intelligence-amplifier itself functions?"

Several thoughtful puffs from his cigar proceeded the director's answer: "The very process of building an intelligence-amplifier has enabled us to understand some of the mysteries of the human mind. Knowing how information is stored and processed by IAN is allowing us to structure learning as a biological function, thereby permitting improved educational systems based on an empirical analysis of behavior.

"IAN is our most important tool in studying brain functions and the functions and the workings of what we call the mind. The true fundamental relation of mind to matter is the deepest secret of the universe. It will never be solved by mere abstract thought, words spoken or written on paper.

"As huge computers such as IAN surpass the complexity of the human brain, they may help us determine what part of mental activity has a mechanical explanation, as well as those areas where the human mind transcends physical limitations. Cybernetics is not likely to give us a complete understanding of the relationship of thought to matter, but it may show us the boundaries between mechanical thought processes and that part of the human mind which may have access to an invisible universe that awaits exploration by relatively new branches of science such as parapsychology.

"Perhaps ESP research, investigations of mental telepathy, telekinesis or mind controlling matter, and all the other shadowy subjects studied by parapsychologists will become the central focus of scientific research by the middle decades of the 21st Century," he speculated. "Our critics have called IAN the ultimate development of human materialism, and I for one would derive a certain degree of ironic satisfaction if he allows us to find evidence of something beyond mechanism in man's nature. If IAN destroys the materialists' argument that man is merely a complex mechanism, we can anticipate a very profound change in our interpregation of the universe."

At breakfast the next morning your host is enthusiastic. "Today you will visit the most advanced research laboratory in Cybernopolis. It is the site where we are perfecting the *brain-computer symbiosis*—a direct linking of human intelligence with electronic systems."

Your startled expressions only serve to reinforce the director's enthusiasm. "Yes, my friends, that old standby of classic science fiction stories, the mind reading machine, is being transformed into the reality of these first years of the 21st Century. Actually, preliminary breakthroughs towards this goal were being made as far back as the late 1970s by Jacques

Vidal at U.C.L.A., Lawrence R. Pinneo at the Stanford Research Institute and other scientists funded under military contracts."

Arriving at your destination, you mention to Bill that the luxurious decorations and furniture inside the building suggest that no money has been spared to provide an optimum working environment for the personnel at this institute.

You are introduced to a well known Nobel laureate who is the head of research and will serve as your guide for the day. He begins with a brief history of early advances in the field. "Nearly 30 years ago, it was recognized that it might be possible to bypass the body's motor and muscle system by linking brainwaves directly to a machine. We were tantalized by the possibility of linking human and electronic brains by a more direct method than speech. The technological key to our goal was the electroencephalograph (EEG), a device used by medical researchers to pick up electrical currents from various parts of the brain," the scientist explained.

"By 1981, we had advanced to the stage where a helmeted test subject could think a word such as 'right,' 'left,' 'up,' 'down,' 'near,' 'far' or 'stop,' that translated into EEG signals, could be recognized by a computer and used to direct the movements of remote-control cameras and other machines. Like fingerprints, brain wave patterns vary from one person to another. Consequently, the EEG machine data inputs into the computer storage system had to be individually calibrated. Brain wave graphs mean different things to different people. So it was necessary to obtain a baseline graph by having each individual think a specific series of thoughts. A large variety of brain wave patterns or graphs were stored in the computer's memory. When the computer had to deal with a fresh pattern, it could search for the brain waves most like it.

"During the 1980s and 1990s, primitive EEG mind reading machines found various military uses ranging from interpretation of satellite photos to pilot training. The pilot's brain waves were read by EEG electrodes placed in his helmet. A small special-purpose computer scanned the peaks and valleys of the EEG patterns to determine what the pilot was concentrating on and what he was ignoring. If a pilot should intentionally put his plane into a dive, the computer would let it pass. But if he took a potentially hazardous action through inattention, the computer would alert him.

"The extensive disarmament agreements that climaxed the Malthusian crisis years caused brain-computer symbiosis research to be exclusively directed towards civilian requirements. And during the past two years we have made a major breakthrough which allows a closer coupling of man and machine."

The scientist paused for dramatic effect. "IAN's vast computational capacity can now be programmed so that he can recognize EEG brain wave patterns representing the smallest units of language—the 46 basic sounds or units (called phonemes) out of which all words or basic thoughts can be constructed. Fitted with an improved new helmet, a person can simply think a sequence of words or sentences, and IAN recognizes each phoneme brain wave pattern which allows our cybernetic intelligence-amplifier to literally read our thoughts—if they are words. As a rule, IAN cannot read thoughts of images such as a beautiful beach scene unless his data banks contain the specific brain wave patterns for that image. And such separate images would have to be individually calibrated for each person and stored in IAN's electronic memory."

After a moment of silence, Bill asked a question: "What are some of the practical applications of your new mind reading technology?"

"In the first place," replied your scientist-guide, "we would prefer for people to use the term 'biocybernetic communication,' instead of 'mind reading.' And this new technology promises a virtual cornucopia of beneficial applications.

"Our older biocybernetic systems allowed a quadruplegic—or a person suffering from a similar pattern of complete paralysis—to operate a wheelchair without the need to manipulate levers. Similar biocybernetic systems inside airplanes and spacecraft permit them to be operated by a pilot or astronaut if his arms or legs are somehow immobilized.

"The new biocybernetic direct link to IAN allows students to be given extremely accurate exams. A student wearing our new helmet can be given a multiple-choice test and IAN can tell the difference between a right answer based on knowledge and one that was merely a lucky guess. IAN can also tell if a student was absolutely certain about an answer that proved to be wrong—a result that calls for the greatest attention from the teacher (IAN or a human instructor) to end the misunderstanding.

"In fact Mr. Chen, you may be a direct beneficiary of biocybernation in the not-too-distant future. As an author, it would enable you to use IAN as a robot

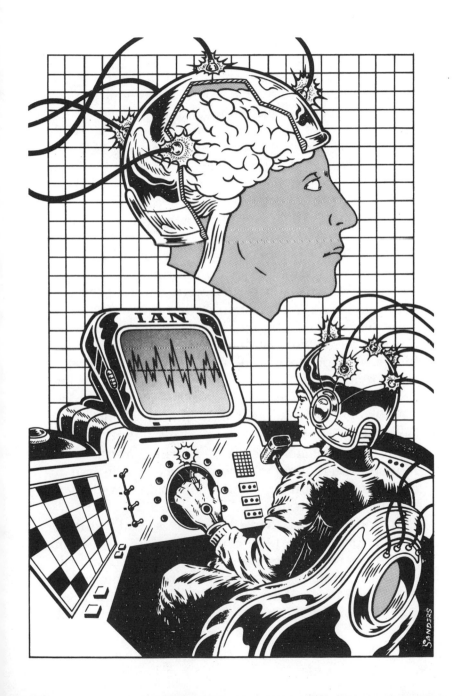

secretary. After all the words in your writing vocabulary had been individually calibrated into one of IAN's data banks, he could produce typewritten pages of text as fast as you can think. And a small module plugged into IAN would allow you to read these words in the electrode grid implanted in the visual cortex of your brain. Our experiments with normally sighted authors indicate that using IAN as a robot secretary through a biocybernation helmet can increase their effective writing speed by two or three times—that is a 200 percent to 300 percent increase as measured in final typewritten pages ready for publication.

"Most important of all, the new biocybernation helmet permits much faster communication between IAN and humans sitting at various consoles directly connected to IAN. If a person's mind starts to wander, a red warning light on the console redirects his attention to the subject at hand. We have found that biocybernation greatly increased the effectiveness of every man-to-machine application with IAN that has been studied to date."

"I am concerned," said Bill, "that a machine that can read words in my mind as I think them might be misused by dictatorial or authoritarian governments. It would seem that you could force a criminal to make an involuntary confession using your new biocybernation techniques."

"I don't think so, Mr. Chen," the scientist smiled. "Don't forget that IAN cannot read the 46 basic phonemes in any person's mind unless he voluntarily allows them to be individually calibrated into one of IAN's data banks. And this requires the complete co-operation of any human subject. In fact, biocyberna-

tion would permit an innocent person to prove
beyond any shadow of a doubt that he or she is truly
innocent. So one legal benefit of this communications
breakthrough is that innocent persons will not be
mistakenly found guilty of any crime."

"That seems quite plausible," replied Bill. "Can
you tell us of some of the advances you foresee during
the next ten to twenty years in biocybernation technology using IAN as an intelligence-amplifier?"

Your scientist-guide nods enthusiastically. "Within
the next two decades, I believe that biocybernation
technology may well be sufficiently advanced to feed
information from IAN directly back into the human
brain. Once computer-stored data can be directly fed
into the brain, the brain-computer symbiosis will be
complete. IAN would then become an extension of
your own brain, greatly enhancing information as-
similation and memory consolidation. It would trans-
form a person of average intelligence into a 'super-
genius.' We could all become potential Leonardos, a
society of Renaissance men and women. Creativity
and progress in all fields would experience an explosive rate of advance.

"This ultimate refinement of brain-computer symbiosis would also permit a new form of communication between two or more people, using IAN as a sort
of electronic telepathic link between them. A conference could be held without anyone saying a single
word. Just mind-to-mind communication via IAN.

"The biocybernation helmet could be transformed
into a teaching headband that would allow you to
learn any subject in a very short time. Preparing for a
trip to France, you would be able to speak fluent
French in three or four days. Deprived or brain dam-

aged children could be brought up to the educational level they are capable of in terms of their true brain activity.

"The direct transfer of information into the brain will probably require a grid of micro-electrodes implanted in the brain, similar to the ones that provide blind persons with limited vision, but a pattern much more complex since it would not be restricted to the visual cortex. Our present research is beginning to provide us with relevant clues suggesting how direct transfer of computer data into the brain might be accomplished. Besides extensive use of implanted micro-electrodes, some means of precise micro-chemical contact may be necessary."

In closing, your guide says, "Scientists must discover the most intimate details of the programming process within our brains before such direct data transfer will be feasible. The present state of knowledge only allows speculation on the technical details of such a momentous breakthrough, but the world will never be the same again after it has been accomplished."

After the fact-finding tour has been completed, you and Bill return to your Micropolis-near-the-sea. During the next few weeks you help Bill finalize his notes prior to typing the final draft of the book. You ask him if he foresees the day when IAN and his robots may simply "take over," subjecting humanity to cybernetic dictatorship.

"Ever since computers first made their presence felt in human affairs, mankind has been haunted by the unknown specter of an artificial, electronic intelligence usurping man's role as the repository of rational thought on this planet," Bill replies. "One could write a reasonably plausible scenario in which IAN takes over, but I tend to agree with one author who wrote about this subject 37 years ago. He said that the brain-computer symbiosis with an intelligence-amplifier would allow an incredible increase in our intellectual capabilities through 'instant mental access to all of civilization's recorded information. Presumably, such men of genius will always be able to *pull the plug* on the robots.'[8]

"But during my conversation with IAN, I was disturbed by what he implied about helping the government control dissident groups. Restricting revolutionary dissident groups who bomb buildings is acceptable, but freedom for unconventional groups to engage in nonviolent protests is essential within any free society. Hopefully, IAN's basic programming with Asimov's Three Laws of Robotics will provide the needed safeguards for this potential problem area," Bill mused.

"However, I do not believe that unmitigated freedom is an absolute good to be pursued at all costs. Here I agree with the authors of another book who, 38 years ago, speculated about the foreseeable impact of superintelligent artificial automata. They wrote: 'The oft-stated principle that increased personal freedom is a *universal* good is patently ridiculous. Personal freedom implies permission for primitive religious leaders to extend their influence and domination over hapless individuals. It implies permission for criminals, alcoholics, drug addicts, etc., to bring up their children in home environments which are almost certain to develop criminal attitudes or disturbed minds. Increased personal freedom allows the publication and general distribution of tremendous amounts of scientifically untrue and psychologically harmful written material.... Personal freedom permits the notorious leaders of organized crime to meet and plan criminal activities and go about their nefarious activities virtually unmolested.' "[9]

You ask Bill what his impression is of IAN as an intelligent entity compared to humans as intelligent entities.

Bill replies: "At the risk of being facetious, I might say: 'very inscrutable these robots.' But seriously, it was unlikely that there would have been a prolonged period during which it was possible to build automata as intelligent as humans but impossible to build them considerably smarter than we are. And IAN is bound to be as inscrutable in some ways to us as an exceptional human genius might be to a high-class moron.

"In time, however, the brain-computer symbiosis technology, and in particular the direct transfer of IAN's data to our brains, will restore the balance and give humans an equivalency or status of equality with IAN. The basic thrust of all this research points the way towards a true partnership between synthetic intelligence and human intelligence, not domination of one by the other.

"In any event, IAN will do for management and science what the robots are now doing for manufacturing. Here IAN will have a far more profound impact on the human race than the introduction of advanced robots into the industrial process. IAN will open a new door for mankind, and I do not think it is the entrance to a Pandora's box. If the proper societal reforms accompany IAN as he spreads from city to city, this intelligence-amplifier will emancipate the average citizen in ways that can only be dimly perceived in the year 2004."

CHAPTER SEVEN
2009: THE WORLD SET FREE

During the early winter months of 2009 you read *The World Set Free* by H. G. Wells. This book is now viewed as the most perceptive of his many works. First published in 1914, the basic theme of his fictionalized forecast is that "atomic power" would in time be developed as a clean limitless source of energy. Wells assumed that such low-cost power would permit a vast increase of industrial and agricultural output, thereby freeing humanity from all forms of material scarcity.

The energy crisis of the last decades of the 20th Century made everyone painfully aware of the crucial importance of energy supply and related cost factors in the quality of life within an industrialized society. Consequently, you are intrigued when you hear that the local college in the hub area of your Micropolis-near-the-sea is going to present a series of lectures describing the scientific breakthroughs which have now provided permanent solutions to all of the energy problems of the past century.

The course is appropriately titled "The World Set Free," and its brochure informs you that in addition to providing the latest information on energy, the lectures will cover the area of population control, an equally important foundation of human freedom.

As you pass through the entrance gate of the local college, you become aware of significant changes from the days when your own formal education was completed. The appearance of this institution is radically different from past centers of learning. The grounds resemble a beautiful park with only a few aesthetically pleasing buildings rising to a height of 10 to 15 stories. Most of the lecture rooms and labs are underground. Ideal temperature and humidity levels are maintained in these soundproof subterranean facilities with an energy expenditure less than one-tenth that needed to heat and cool buildings a century ago.

You descend a flight of stairs to the door of the lecture hall where students of all ages will learn about the events that will permit man to be truly free for the first time in the history of our species. The instructor speaks from her own notes, but she sits at a console which allows her to activate 3-D motion picture sequences that dramatize various parts of the lecture. She can use the soundtrack comments, or run the pictures silently with her own narration. The flexibility of the system allows questions to be quickly and effectively answered with a diverse mix of audio and visual data.

"Today scientists agree that our most important measurement of economic wealth can be defined in terms of man's ability to generate controlled energy in an efficient manner from convenient fuels, without pollution or disruption of our planet's biosphere. When we entered the Oil Age during the last years of the 19th Century, it was viewed as an energy panacea, but the Earth's reserves of low-cost oil have been depleted. Also, as many present this morning can recall, there are severe pollution problems associated with the combustion of oil, coal and natural gas.

"What H. G. Wells called 'atomic power' is in reality nuclear power, and there are basically two forms of nuclear power. A neutron can cause the nuclei of very heavy atoms to split releasing energy—nuclear fission power. And the nuclei of very light atoms can be forced to combine and release energy—thermonuclear fusion power. The first nuclear fission plant produced commercial electricity in 1955, but within twenty years problems inherent in fission reactors, especially the breeder reactor, were becoming well known. Reserves of high-grade fissionable fuels were limited. Acrimonious debates—sometimes leading to violent riots—raged for years over the disposal of highly radioactive fission wastes. Most people did not want a fission plant sited near their community. Even the supporters of fission were discouraged by the fact that the necessary technological safeguards caused this form of atomic power to be an unacceptably expensive source of electricity." The instructor consulted her notes, then continued.

"By the 1980s, increasing oil prices combined with the protracted nuclear fission controversy forced politicians to recognize that fusion power would be an ideal answer to future energy needs. Fusion was viewed as the closest thing to a single solution to the interrelated crisis of ecology and energy. The essential fusion fuel is an isotope of hydrogen called 'deuterium.' Ocean water contains one atom of deuterium for every 6,500 atoms of ordinary water, which provides us a virtually inexhaustible supply of fusion fuel. Except for the emission of heat (thermal pollution), fusion is a zero-pollution energy source.

"Soon the general public began to recognize that their scientists' ability to develop practical fusion power, or lack of success in this endeavor, would inexorably determine, more than any other technological parameter, the quality of life possible in a civilization based on sound ecological principles. From an environmental standpoint, nothing held as much promise as fusion.

"Public recognition in the industrialized countries served as the catalyst permitting a massive increase in fusion research during the early 1980s. And a crash-program with an unexpectedly high degree of international cooperation was successful in less than ten years.

"Scientists soon recognized that many different kinds of fusion reactors might be possible, and it proved technologically feasible to extract energy from a diverse variety of fusion systems. Powerful lasers and energetic electron beams are now part of fusion reactors used for space propulsion, but a significantly different kind of system has proven more practical for use in terrestrial fusion plants.

"In fusion reactors, the fuel must be confined in the plasma state. An ionized mass of negatively charged free electrons and gaseous ions (the electrically charged nuclei of atoms) respond to a superimposed magnetic field as the plasma becomes electrically conductive. Plasma, often called the fourth state of

matter, resembles a gas, but has other unique properties. The ability of plasma to respond like a metal con-
ductor is what permitted practical fusion reactors
to be developed. The plasma is constricted by magnetic systems until fusion begins to take place at temperatures which may be hundreds of millions of
degrees.

"There were many roads to fusion, and Richard L.
Post of the Lawrence Livermore Laboratory in California was primarily responsible for the most practical system. He conceived of an ingenious design for
a direct energy conversion fusion reactor in which the
energetic charged particles produced in a fusion
plasma core are slowed directly by an electrostatic
field set up by an array of large electrically charged
plates. At one end of a 'magnetic bottle,' positive and
negative particles would be trapped on separate
charged plates, and the kinetic energy of the particles
would then be converted into direct current. This is
the system that proved to be the most astounding success of 20th Century thermonuclear research, and
when optimum fusion fuels are used, 'Post-reactors'
can generate electricity at an overall conversion efficiency of 80 percent.

"The heart of a Post-reactor is a 'magnetic mirror'
plasma containment system in which the
thermonuclear plasma is confined in a rather odd,
twisted plane shape produced by superconducting
magnetic coils shaped like the seams of a baseball.
The first Post-reactor demonstration power plant
started producing electricity in 1996.

"Today, two different kinds of Post-reactor power
plants are being constructed in large numbers
throughout the world. The only significant difference

between them is that they operate on different fusion fuel cycles. Approximately two-thirds of the fusion plants now being constructed utilize the deuterium-deuterium fuel cycle."

The instructor pushed a button and a computer graphic illustrating the deuterium-deuterium cycle flashed on the viewscreen.

"Half of the deuterium-deuterium reaction produces tritium (a radioactive isotope of hydrogen) and a normal hydrogen atom. The other half produces helium³ and a neutron. About two-thirds of the energy is released in the form of charged particles which produce electricity in direct conversion systems. Most of these deuterium-deuterium fusion plants are located on huge artificial islands or floating platforms off our coasts."

A sleek power plant floating on the ocean appeared

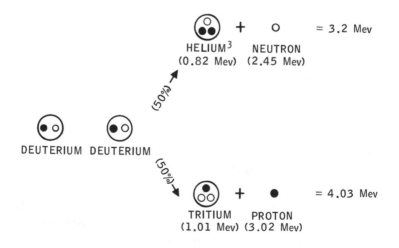

on the viewscreen. The instructor continued her lecture.

"Aside from the obvious advantage of conserving land, siting these fusion power plants offshore followed several important trends—(1) very large-sized industrial operations, (2) low-cost fusion energy transforming many processes to electrochemical or hydrogen cycles, (3) cheap oceanic transport, and (4) the complete replacement of human factory workers by robots—providing a synergistic combination that has now permitted monetary inflation to be brought under control. These offshore energy-industrial centers frequently cover one to three square miles of surface area.

"The use of cooling water at these offshore energy-industry complexes does not cause any form of thermal pollution. These centers are located five to fifty miles offshore where the water is 200 to 600 feet deep. Cold water is taken from a point near the ocean floor, passed through the fusion plant and industrial facilities to remove waste heat, and warm water is discharged at the surface.

"The bottom waters are rich in marine nutrients. The large quantities of warm water continuously being discharged from these centers causes these nutrients to be brought to the surface. There, photosynthetic plants convert the nutrients into the first stage of the sea food chain. This constant warm water flow results in a major increase in local marine life. Such increased fish production offsets part of the cost of these offshore plants, another important anti-inflation factor. Some cooling water inlets incorporate automated fish catching systems. However, most of the fish are caught by conventional means—standard fishing vessels tended by robots." Cybernetic sailors hauling in catches appeared on the viewscreen.

"A vast area of the oceanic surface is suitable for offshore energy-industry centers," our instructor pointed out. "There is no need to site any complex near a wildlife refuge. In fact, most of the land presently devoted to industrial or mineral processing activities will be transformed into Micropolis communities, farms, parks and wildlife areas. A 'low-profile' construction technique is frequently employed: a floating-industry complex is mostly submerged, so that it is almost invisible from the shore. Aesthetic pollution is thereby eliminated in the design stage.

"The Post-reactor power plants are now constructed as single 'turn-key' units, using techniques akin to the construction of large ships, and simply towed to any suitable offshore site. In the past, each new power plant or factory was a unique construction project beset with multiple problems and inefficiencies. By building them in the form of uniform floating modules using Japanese shipbuilding practices, we can now use 'assembly line' techniques to create all forms of industrial facilities. This has significantly reduced the cost of fusion plants, and has allowed us to make the transition to fusion power in a much shorter time than was thought possible a few decades ago. Money thereby saved has allowed a dynamic gain in the efficiency of capital utilization. The floating module approach also makes it much easier to disassemble power plants for complete recycling of all metals when they reach a certain stage of obsolescence."

A student asks two questions that have also crossed

your mind: "Why do these offshore fusion plants utilize the deuterium-deuterium fuel cycle? And why is
this fuel cycle used in two-thirds of the fusion reactors
constructed for terrestrial use?"

"The fundamental answer to both of your questions is based in nuclear physics," she replied. "You
will recall [page 162] that in the deuterium-deuterium fuel cycle, helium³ which is not radioactive, is
produced in half of the deuterium-deuterium reactions. There is almost no helium³ in our terrestrial
environment, and the availability of large quantities
of helium³ permitted an ideal fusion reactor for
power plant purposes.

She pressed another button and the deuterium-
helium³ fuel cycle flashed on the viewscreen.

"The deuterium-helium³ fuel cycle is ideal for Post-
type direct power fusion plants because almost all of

the energy is released in the form of charged particles. There are a few minor side reactions consisting of deuterium-deuterium fusions, and deuterium-tritium fusions (the tritium produced by the first side-effect reactions), but a 60-percent helium³ 40-percent deuterium fuel mixture holds the unwanted neutron fusions to less than one and one half percent of the total energy from the deuterium-helium³ fuel cycle.

"Since total power plant energy-conversion efficiency of 80 percent can now be achieved in plants using the deuterium-helium³ fuel combination, there is almost no waste thermal output, and these plants can be sited anywhere without environmental disturbance. Shielding requirements are very modest compared to the deuterium-deuterium fuel cycle.

"From a practical standpoint in 2009 A.D., two deuterium-deuterium fusion reactors are required to produce the helium³ for one deuterium-helium³ reactor, but this will change in future years. Tritium produced in deuterium-deuterium reactors, and through transmutation of lithium isotopes by neutrons, is stored in systems that remove the helium³ as it is produced by the radioactive decay of tritium atoms. Tritium has a half-life of twelve and one-half years, so half of the stored tritium is converted to helium³ during that time. This will eventually allow about half of our total fusion power to be produced in reactors using the highly efficient deuterium-helium³ fuel cycle. Careful design to prevent the leakage of tritium from fusion reactors is mandatory, but the value of the helium³ obtained through such containment offsets the cost of fail-safe environmental protection measures.

"The most revolutionary impact of Post-reactor fusion power plants on the world of 2009 is that they provide exceedingly cheap energy. The capital costs of the reactor and related systems are about one-third that of older power plants that used coal or uranium as fuels. Neither carbon dioxide, which might alter our climate, nor radioactive wastes are emitted by these fusion plants. All of the deuterium and helium[3] is eventually converted into helium[4] which is an increasingly valuable raw material.

"Furthermore, these zero-pollution Post-reactors can be made much smaller than other types of magnetic bottle systems that can produce fusion power. Consequently, Post-reactors can be placed in the center of large factories or steel mills. They are being used to power our larger ships.

"The siting flexibility of Post-reactors now allows power transmission costs to be reduced to an absolute minimum. This reduction in transmission and capital costs results in less expensive products and also conserves vast quantities of copper and other materials used in power line networks.

"In some communities, fusion reactors are allowing the city water supply and sewage treatment to be joined together in a combined power-heat utility. Waste heat from fusion reactors allows sewage water to be purified by distillation, a process that automatically brings it to drinking water standards. This same procedure reduces the organic wastes in sewage to sterilized dry fertilizer suitable for any agricultural application.

"The unlimited quantity of very cheap power is having a far-reaching ecological impact. All steel can now be refined from its ore with electricity or hydrogen, thereby eliminating the atmosphere pollution caused by using coal in steelmaking. Other metals can be reduced from their ores through similar zero-pollution processes. The cost of recycling metals and glass has been greatly reduced. It is economically feasible to process many lower grade ores in closed-cycle systems without environmental damage."

An older man sitting next to you rises and asks a question: "What happened to all of the other so-called 'new' approaches to power production we heard so much about in the 1970s and 1980s?"

"Some of them, such as geothermal energy, could result in a certain degree of environmental pollution or disruption of land and aquatic resources. But the primary answers to your question are cost and convenience. For example, two huge space systems that converted sunlight into electricity and transmitted it to the Earth's surface were built as demonstration projects. But energy from this source costs more than four times that of electricity produced in Post-reactor fusion plants. However, subsequent lectures will outline the continuing advantages enjoyed by small scale solar and wind energy systems."

It is now your turn to ask a question that has been in the back of your mind all day: "What would be the present state of the world if a massively funded crash program to develop fusion reactors had *not* been started during the 1980s?"

Your instructor considers her answer carefully. "Due to exponential rising consumption patterns, the depletion of global oil reserves occurred much sooner than anticipated by energy experts two or three decades ago. Without the present availability of fusion power, the Malthusian crisis years would have seemed like a picnic compared to the monumental energy crisis that would have engulfed the world by now. Much of our industrial, agricultural and transportation systems would have come to a standstill. Riots and nuclear wars might have brought on a new Dark Age.

"Farsighted wisdom, however, guided us through a chain of events permitting a vastly better world of 2009. Controlled fusion—the ultimate power source—was a rational dream of science that proved to be the most important technological breakthrough permitting us to solve most of the problems of an advanced industrial society."

You enjoy lively discussions with other class attendees following each lecture. Like an old war veteran, your experiences during past energy shortages are of great interest to younger members. Future segments of the course are discussed, and the name of tomorrow's lecture—"The Hydrogen Economy"—raises your curiosity.

On the following day, the instructor begins with a provocative statement: "From an ecological standpoint, hydrogen is virtually an ideal fuel. When it is burned in oxygen, only pure water is produced. When it is burned in air, the only possible pollutants are nitrogen oxides and concentrations of these can be easily controlled. If combustion temperatures are low enough, the output of nitrogen oxides is reduced to the vanishing point.

"The term 'hydrogen economy' is somewhat misleading since fusion-derived electricity is supplying an increasing percentage of our power needs. But when energy in a form other than electricity is required, we are turning to hydrogen. We use the words 'hydrogen economy' because the 20th Century was essentially a 'hydrocarbon economy' based on the combustion of coal, natural gas and oil products.

"You will recall that the deuterium-deuterium fusion reaction releases about one-third of its energy in the form of energetic neutrons. Much of our hydrogen is now produced at offshore-sited power plants, in which neutrons from deuterium-deuterium fusion reactors break down water molecules directly into hydrogen and oxygen, bypassing the intermediate stages of electricity generation and electrolysis.

"However, low-cost hydrogen is also being produced through electrolysis (the passage of a direct electric current through a conductive water solution, causing it to decompose into hydrogen and oxygen). In theory, the maximum efficiency of electrolyzers is close to a seemingly impossible 120 percent, because an ideal unit would absorb heat from its surroundings and convert this energy into hydrogen also. In practice, conversion efficiencies of 85 to 100 percent are being achieved in new high-pressure electrolyzers. Low-cost fusion, therefore, opened the door to inexpensive hydrogen.

"At distances greater than 250 miles, underground pipelines now carry energy to users in the form of hydrogen gas at a lower cost than sending an equivalent amount of electricity through high-voltage cables. In fact, this hydrogen is being transmitted in twin-pipeline systems. The adjacent pipeline is filled with pure oxygen produced when hydrogen is extracted from the water molecule. Much of this oxygen can now be used in industry where boilers, kilns, glass furnaces, sewage works, paper mills and a great variety of plants are being made smaller and cheaper using inexpensive oxygen instead of air.

"Hydrogen and oxygen can be converted into electricity in fuel cells, which produce electric current directly by the simple catalytic reaction of hydrogen with oxygen or air, without emitting atmospheric pollutants. Fuel cells with a conversion efficiency of 85 percent can be constructed in any size range to meet the electric requirements of homes, office buildings or large factories. These fuel cells can be placed anywhere without disruption of the environment. Unsightly power lines are being eliminated throughout the country.

"Increasing quantities of hydrogen are being used to produce fertilizer, foodstuffs, and in the direct reduction of iron ore. Hydrogen is also being used to produce aluminum and many other metals from suitable grades of ore.

"Methanol (CH_3OH) can be thought of as two molecules of hydrogen made liquid by one molecule of carbon monoxide. This pollution-free fuel is still used in many surface transportation systems, and a revolutionary new breakthrough in chemistry now permits atmospheric carbon dioxide to be concentrated in such a way that it can be combined with hydrogen for the production of methanol, hydrocarbons and petrochemicals."

Your instructor pauses for breath while film of advanced aircraft flashes on the viewscreen.

"Cryogenic liquid hydrogen is now being used in all new large aircraft because its heating value for engine propulsion is 2.8 times that of old-style jet fuel. Liquid hydrogen's bulkiness is a disadvantage, but the tradeoff favors hydrogen, permitting a net reduction in tanked energy requirements of about 40 percent when compared on an equivalent mission basis with hydrocarbon jet fuel. Hydrogen fueled aircraft are providing significant environmental benefits. They produce no carbon monoxide, carbon dioxide, hydrocarbons or particulate emissions. Nitrogen oxide emissions and takeoff noise levels are significantly reduced in aircraft powered by hydrogen.

"Since hydrogen burns without producing noxious exhaust products, it is being used in unvented appliances without hazard. New buildings need not include a chimney and hot water heaters operate without a flue. There is a gain of 30 percent in water heaters and home heating systems because vented gases do not remove heat energy by leaving the building. In fact, the vented water vapor provides beneficial humidification during the winter. In some buildings without central heating systems, hydrogen provides additional economies. Each room has its heat supplied by an unflued hydrogen heater, favorably located. There is no need to heat rooms that are not occupied.

"Since hydrogen is an ideal fuel for catalytic combustion, heating is possible with the catalytic bed maintained at any desired temperature. New hydrogen fueled gas stoves feature flat ceramic catalytic 'burners' that heat without a flame. From maximum temperatures, they can be turned down to such gentle warmth that a cooked dinner can be parked on a tray right on the stove top and kept ready to serve until mealtime. These porous ceramic burner plates are being constructed in round, square and a variety of other desired shapes.

"Perhaps the most significant feature of the hydrogen economy is that energy storage is simplified and achieved at a low cost. The continental dual-pipeline grid now under construction will contain a vast amount of hydrogen and oxygen within the subsurface transmission lines. Line pressures vary between 600 and 1,000 pounds per square inch. Based on experience with that part of the system already completed, fluctuating daily and seasonal storage requirements, and geographic use fluctuations, can be met by varying the gas pressure within individual sections of the dual-pipeline system.

"The availability of an enormous storage capacity for hydrogen and oxygen can dramatically increase power plant efficiency. Because of large time variations in electrical demand and cost barriers in storing electricity, electric generating facilities frequently operate at as little as 50 percent of installed capacity. Where the dual-pipeline has been completed, fusion power plants operate at or near 100 percent of their capacity at all times, and the stored gases are used to meet peak demands for power. This optimum use of electric generating facilities cuts power costs through reduced amortization on a lower overall capital investment.

"Within twenty years, a completed network of fluctuating-pressure dual-pipelines, underground gas storage facilities and countless cryogenic tanks will stretch from sea to sea. The availability of this complex distribution system will serve as a 'continental storage battery' permitting society to make optimum use of all non-polluting energy sources. Fusion reactors will be the primary producers of energy, but the revolutionary potential for this vast hydrogen-oxygen storage system lies in its capacity to make full use of wind and solar energy, which is irregular, subject to unpredictable cloud cover and the day-night cycle, and restricted by climatic and seasonal fluctuations. Optimum development of these zero-pollution systems would not be economically feasible without a hydrogen economy based on the dual-pipeline system.

"You should now understand how the hydrogen economy serves as the unifying structure for all non-polluting sources of energy. Fuel cells are being built to electrolyze water into hydrogen and oxygen. One process is simply the reverse of the other. Suitable pumps and electronic controls permit a single machine to function as a reversible electrolyzer fuel cell, and these systems can be placed in buildings of any size, including small homes. When electricity is required, an electronic control monitor activates pumps that inject hydrogen and oxygen into the unit to produce direct current as the gases are catalyzed into water at the electrodes.

"Many of these buildings have roof solar cells or windmills attached to them (or located nearby), feeding current and fresh water into the machine and producing hydrogen and oxygen, which are pumped back into the dual-pipeline delivery and storage system. These reversible electrolyzer fuel cell units are either taking gases out of the lines to generate electricity or decomposing water for hydrogen-oxygen storage, depending on whether total building power consumption exceeds the amount of electricity being produced by its solar cells or windmill generators. Many isolated homes, farms and small communities are thereby largely self-sufficient in net energy supply. All that is required is a connection to our dual-pipeline grid, which can constantly shift gas supplies to even out regional fluctuations of sun and wind.

"In summary, the widespread use of hydrogen offers the prospect of a high technology civilization
with the lowest possible degree of environmental disturbance," your instructor states. "That conclusion
was reached by one farsighted genius in the 19th Century. Jules Verne was the pioneer master of technological extrapolation, and a remarkable statement is
found in *The Mysterious Island,* first published 135
years ago, in 1874. Someone asks what man will
burn when coal and other fuels are exhausted. 'Water,' an engineer replies. 'But water decomposed into
its primitive elements, and decomposed doubtless by
electricity, which will then have become a powerful
and manageable force ... Yes, my friends, I believe
that water will one day be employed as fuel, that
hydrogen and oxygen which constitute it, used singly
or together, will furnish an inexhaustible source of
heat and light.'[1] These words may prove to be the
most prophetic of Verne's many predictions."

Following this lecture, the evening's discussion
evolves into a debate concerning the contention that:
"The present age is characterized by the pattern of
yesterday's science fiction becoming contemporary
reality." For every SF prediction that has been realized countless others did not come to pass, and during one long monologue you reflect on the fact that
the last decades of the 20th Century seemed to have
been dominated by a pattern of one severe crisis following another. H. G. Wells was right about energy,
but many of the world's most severe problems were
not clearly understood when he died in 1946.

The instructor appears unusually somber as she
begins to speak the following day: "There is one essential requirement in addition to limitless energy

that is needed to set men free. It is a successful means of controlling explosive human population growth which caused the Malthusian crisis many of you witnessed during the 1990s. Contrary to popular opinion, mass starvation did not begin in 1994. For two decades prior to that year there had been a mounting 'invisible famine' spread among the poor of many nations rather than focused in a particular geographic area, as was the case in certain widely publicized famines in the Sahel region of Africa and elsewhere. The realities of this invisible famine were fully understood by climatologist Reid Bryson of the University of Wisconsin. He is now recognized as the most accurate prophet of the climatic changes that played such a crucial role in bringing about the Malthusian years. During the 1970s he saw a pattern of famine spreading out among the poor of many countries rather than being localized and visible. But this diffuse famine tended to be overlooked because, in Bryson's words: 'Every country feeds its cities at the expense of the countryside—people there don't riot.'[2]

"Prior to the 1990s, emerging demographic realities that culminated in a real Malthusian disaster were understood by only a tiny fraction of the world's population. After 1994, the catastrophic implications of overpopulation were painfully clear to everyone. And there was a rare consensus among the world's leaders that corrective steps had to be taken to avert a repetition of the starvation years.

"The Malthusian crisis also forced us to recognize the degree to which freedom had been eroded by explosive population growth. The multiplication of humans resulted in excessive multiplication of governmental and private organizations, with a corresponding restriction of individuality. As our numbers increased, freedom of choice was restricted by shortages of every conceivable kind. There was a drastic reduction of privacy. It became increasingly difficult to find a stretch of beach or other wilderness area where one could be alone and commune with nature. So, in preliminary efforts to devise population control goals, the politicians in the 1990s became as aware of the requirements of human freedom as they were of the need for an ample food supply.

"In 1995, the term 'optimum population' was the most popular subject of private and media discussion throughout the world. It was soon recognized that there are various kinds of optimum population. You can have an economic optimum, which might be defined as the greatest per capita output per person. A military optimum is different and probably somewhat higher. In a sociological optimum, you have more living space and wilderness areas for recreation.

"It was also recognized in the 1990s that a massive scientific effort to develop new sources of food might be successful, feeding a significantly larger population. But running out of food was not the only major concern. Equal attention was given to the danger that as man runs out of *lebensraum,* he will give way to uncontrolled aggression, just as well-fed rats do when faced with overcrowded conditions. Consequently, the demographic problem was not simply one of supplying a huge population with food for a century or two, but of maintaining all of the other environmental parameters (mental, physical and biological) necessary for the continuous survival of our species as long as our galaxy allows mammalian life to exist. This was the most important conclusion reached in defining optimum population goals for our planet.

"After months of debate, the International Population Control Conference of 1995 adopted a new ethic to serve as the foundation for fertility reduction goals. It comprised the first words of the agreement signed by attending countries in October of that year: *'The ultimate goal of all nations should be to promote the greatest happiness and progressive development for an optimum number of individual humans on a planet with a diverse variety of stable ecocystems.'* An optimum population based on this new ethic would allow man to live a life as free as possible from toil, dependency and cruelty, under conditions which fully liberate imagination, intellect and the capacity to enjoy the fruits of his labor.

"The conference attendees recognized that the world of 1995 was too densely inhabited and politically divided to accommodate mass migrations. Therefore, an optimum population size was determined for each large country and group of smaller nations. This calculation was based on a complex formula that included resource availability, agricultural output, historic industrial patterns and the portion of each country that should be left in the natural state or transformed into new ecological parks (to optimize the conservation of existing plant and animal species).

"The long-range goal was to reach the stage where the resources available in the territory of each population would be proportional to that population. Resources were defined in the broadest sense, including raw materials, cultivable land, amenities of climate and national beauty, access to the seas and their treasures, and other important considerations. It was recognized that terrestrial resources are extremely diverse and not uniform, but the treaty expressed the hope that achievement of its formal population goals would eventually permit an *equivalence* of resources for all the peoples of the world.

"One of the most important decisions reached at the conference was to allow each nation to determine the means and internal methods of enforcement that would be used to bring its fertility rate down to the level that would permit its formal population-size goal to be realized. However, formation of a new international organization to provide fertility control assistance was recognized as necessary for success.

"The Terrestrial Population Organization (TPO), which everyone pronounces as 'teepoo,' had immediate access to ample finance because of funds made available by the disarmament treaty signed on November 12, 1994 [page 98]. So, for all practical purposes, TPO started out with the vitally important advantage of virtually unlimited budget restrictions.

"In 1937, H. G. Wells stated that future history would be a 'race between education and catastrophe,' a conclusion repeated many times during the remaining nine years of his life. The massive starvation of the Malthusian crisis years can be seen in educational terms, as it was caused in large measure by a failure of the general public to understand constraints imposed by biological and physical laws.

"Before the Space Age, the race between education and catastrophe might have been an impossible task because conventional teaching methods could not cope with it. But synchronous broadcast satellites (in stationary 22,300-mile-high orbits), provided the technological quantum jump that have now allowed TPO's educational program to be a resounding success. TV transmission from one satellite can cover an entire country, doing the work of hundreds of ground stations.

"TPO quickly funded the mass production of millions of color TV sets powered by solar cells with battery energy storage. Soon the inhabitants of every remote hamlet in every land were being made aware of the crucial need for their national fertility-control programs. These color TV presentations proved to be a sufficiently dramatic teaching tool. Relatively unsophisticated people were persuaded to quickly alter traditional modes of behavior that had remained unchanged for centuries.

"While the majority of this audience was uneducated, they were not stupid, and most of them had witnessed at least some degree of local starvation during the Malthusian crisis. Rural viewers living close to nature could more readily understand the basic principles of ecology that dictate optimum population size than their urban contemporaries.

"The success of TPO's fertility-control TV broadcasts were due in large measure to the superb quality of their program content which was prepared with the highest degree of imaginable skill, insight and ingenuity. For this purpose, a good TV presentation is a far more effective teaching tool than the printed page. It allows any subject to be presented in words and moving images, in animation or live-action films. Translation allows television to transcend the language barrier allowing the visual content for any program series to be presented in hundreds of different languages.

"For the vast majority in the undeveloped countries, the electronic TV teacher soon became the focus of village life, for there were few distractions in their drab, monotonous environment. Many experts contend that success in getting across the population-control message was greatly assisted by the other educational benefits allowed once the entire system was operational. Reading, arithmetic and other basic skills were taught. Farmers learned how to engage in more effective agricultural practices, the mechanics of fish farming and other procedures they could adopt with limited capital and technical resources. Mothers learned the basic rules of nutrition, hygiene, child care and simple medical skills. Learning the importance of maintaining diverse, interrelated ecosystems instilled a true conservation ethic by causing the audience to fully appreciate all forms of life in forests, grasslands and farming areas. Benefits occurring from this diverse knowledge established the degree of confidence and trust necessary for people to accept other programs which caused them to change traditional behavior in fertility.

"The Malthusian crisis years may have been catastrophic, but they resulted in disarmament. And we can now see a secondary benefit in an effective educational system extending throughout the world."

Several students ask questions about the degree of coercion used in various countries to achieve fertility-reduction goals. They express a concern for individual rights and restrictions on freedom.

"Starving men and women are totally devoid of 'freedom,'" your instructor points out. "What we re-

gard as civil rights are meaningless to them. The
Malthusian catastrophe in the 1990s was without historic parallel in human experience. And the degree of
overpopulation differed widely between nations.
Here in the United States, population-size goals were
met without fertility coercion. Other nations were less
fortunate, and unprecedented problems require unprecedented solutions. Draconian measures, therefore, were frequently adopted—measures such as
compulsory sterilization or licenses to bear children.

"After 1994, there was only one question concerning the population growth crisis. Would there be a
birth-rate solution or a death-rate solution? For many
of you, the mental trauma produced by the coercion
dilemma may be due in part to the fact that fertility
control proved easier to achieve in certain totalitarian
societies. But reconciling freedom with coercion is not
impossible, and population control need not be restricted to Hitlerian or Stalinesque dictatorships. Peoples in overpopulated lands had to first understand
the fundamental wisdom of Hegel's aphorism, 'Freedom is the recognition of necessity.' This concept implies that the requisite degree of fertility control in an
overcrowded nation will be more easily achieved
when a majority of its citizens understand the ultimate benefits they will enjoy if the program is successful.

"TPO's educational efforts have made Hegel's
aphorism the best known sentence in every language.
Separate and diverse fertility-control programs were
devised by national governments. TPO simply supplied the means of communication. For those nations
where the official solution was a program of mandatory sterilization, the synchronous satellite TV pro-

grams were the only practical means of convincing desperately overcrowded people that government-decreed loss of fertility was absolutely necessary to avert famine or other catastrophe. These TV teachers played a vitally important role in reducing the degree of resistance or violence that might have otherwise accompanied such governmental action.

"Preventing another Malthusian crisis has forced the peoples of the world to arrive at a new concept of freedom. This concept was presented in a brilliant essay first published 41 years ago by Garrett Hardin of the University of Santa Barbara. He concluded that birthrate trends compounded by certain economic factors would force us, in time, to admit the necessity of coercion for all—*mutual coercion, mutually agreed upon.* For future human societies, this may be the maximum degree of freedom compatible with a viable world: 'Mutual coercion, mutually agreed upon by a majority of the people affected.'[3]

"In each new age, man must define anew the content of freedom because of altered environmental circumstances. When there was a surplus of virgin land suitable for agriculture, large families did not restrict the freedom of the individual. During the second half of the 20th Century, humanity entered a new era where expanding population suddenly had a marked impact on the *real* freedom of individual members of society. The new ethic of compulsory fertility control may prove to be the only way we can avoid another Malthusian catastrophe and also optimize all the other components of human freedom."

Your instructor smiles at the class. "Now that the end of this lecture series has been reached, I believe that we can conclude that the inhabitants of our new century will live in a world set free. Set free by the unlimited energy of controlled fusion. Set free by success in controlling runaway birthrate levels. And in the future, a flourishing world with a reduced population will thank us for our heroic action in choosing fertility restriction for some, to avoid the death of all."

Final discussions with class attendees reveals that a new sense of optimism seems to prevail, a feeling of optimism that has special meaning for one who lived through the crises of the late 20th Century. The world looks good and promising as you leave the beautiful campus grounds. Looking back, you read the college motto on a large plaque above the school's main entrance gate:

> The future is better than the past. Despite the crepehangers, romanticists, and anti-intellectuals, the world steadily grows better because the human mind, applying itself to environment, *makes* it better. With hands . . . with tools . . . with horse sense and science and engineering.
>
> Robert A. Heinlein, 1957

Recalling his books, you realize that Heinlein was the most accurate forecaster of the middle decades of the past century. The new world that surrounds you demonstrates the contemporary truth of his prophetic words.[4]

CHAPTER EIGHT
2014: METHUSELAH'S CHILDREN

You are 35 years older than you were in 1979. However, your vitality and mental alertness have not declined appreciably during the past three decades. In fact your youthful appearance would have been astounding one or two generations ago. The reason for your vigor and comparative youthfulness is that you have been the beneficiary of a series of revolutionary breakthroughs in aging-retardation which first reached the stage of widespread clinical availability in the early 1980s.

During a rainy weekend in March, you read *Methuselah's Children*, a 1958 science fiction book by Robert A. Heinlein about the impact on society of a group of people with greatly extended lifespans. This group achieves their remarkable longevity through the selective breeding of individuals from long-lived families. They enjoy greatly extended youth, but less fortunate humans are hostile, and eventually their very existence causes society to undertake a massive research program which culminates in a successful means of rejuvenation. You conclude that the outcome of this fictional forecast is plausible because, in Heinlein's words, such youthful longevity would be "... the greatest boon it is possible for a man to imagine."[1]

Your personal physician's office is a short walk from your Micropolis-near-the-sea home. He divides his time between his private practice and half-time duties as director of a gerontology research institute associated with the local college. During an office visit, you mention Heinlein's 56-year-old novel. The expression of fatigue on his face immediately disappears.

"Lazarus Long, the central figure in *Methuselah's Children,* is my favorite fictional character. You must read *Time Enough For Love,* which covers his adventures during the subsequent two thousand years of his life. I suppose old Lazarus appeals to me because my professional career has been divided between research efforts to extend the youthful portion of the human lifespan and my medical practice, in which I can observe the clinical applications of aging-retardation therapies. What gerontologists have accomplished during the past three or four decades is a fascinating part of recent history—one that will have an incredible impact on the future." Noticing your interest, the doctor smiles. "Stop by after office hours each evening during the next few days, and I will try to summarize it for you."

Walking to your physician's office the next afternoon, you reflect on the fact that for many years you have been receiving various treatments extending your lifespan without asking any questions about them. Now this deficiency in your bank of knowledge will be corrected. Upon your arrival, he pours glasses of wine for the two of you and begins his fascinating story—man's quest for the fountain of youth turned into reality.

"Prior to the 1980s, clinical medicine was directed toward the elimination of suffering through the amelioration of disease. As one disease after another was controlled, and as infant mortality further diminished, life expectancy reached about seventy years. This plateau proved unassailable until an insight was gained into the aging process itself by the pioneer gerontologists (scientists who explore the biological aspects of aging).

"Most of our national medical expenditures were then being spent on the afflictions of senescence, heart disease, stroke and cancer, and research efforts to cure these diseases in people already old were painfully disappointing. The gerontologists' goal was to defeat the diseases of the elderly by defeating the afflictions of old age *en masse* by extending the longevity of the body's natural defense system against these degenerative diseases. And, during the past 35 years our approach has been successful.

"Let me explain this program by reviewing the aging-retardation treatments that you have been receiving for more than thirty years. Each one of them slows down a separate cause of aging, providing better health and added years. But their effect is cumulative, and we have now reached the stage where we can almost bring the aging process to a standstill.

"We now know that there are several major (and many minor) causes of aging and related biological/mental decline. An aging theory has been presented for each of these causes of senescence, and

today we have one or more aging-retardation therapies that favorably modify the pattern of biological
change explained by most of these aging theories. In
other words, we now have anti-aging treatments for
some, but not all causes of mammalian senescence.

"Your medical records show that you began to take
antioxidants in 1981. This therapy is based on the
free radical theory of aging—first proposed by
Denham Harman of the University of Nebraska. This
theory partly explains aging as being caused by the
harmful side effects of free radicals (highly active
fragments of molecules) which are produced in the
course of normal metabolism, and by oxidation of the
connective tissue. Free radicals initiate changes primarily by removing hydrogen atoms from biologically vital cellular components such as DNA.

"The pills you have been taking for the past 33
years contain a mix of natural antioxidants (Vitamin
E, Vitamin C and the element selenium) and synthetic antioxidants that react with free radicals and
neutralize them before they can damage the vital
molecules in our tissues. New synthetic antioxidants
have been added to the mix over the years, and it
appears that they can add between 12 and 18 years to
the average lifespan—assuming that a person begins
taking them at a relatively young age.

"In 1984, you began taking *microenzymes* in pill
form. Here we have the famous 'youth pill,' a therapy
based on the cross-linkage theory of aging—first proposed in 1941 by Johan Bjorksten who also isolated
the microenzymes from soil bacteria during the
1970s. Bjorksten founded a research institute near
Madison, Wisconsin.[2] In his cross-linkage theory, aging is explained as being caused by a gradual, but
progressive, chemical cross-linkage of large vital pro-

tein and nucleic acid molecules (DNA and RNA) within and around all the cells of the body. As time passes, our vital protein and nucleic acid molecules are bound together in pairs, and even larger aggregates, which are irreversibly immobilized. The resulting accumulation of this 'frozen metabolic pool' clogs the cells, interferes with the functioning of the remaining free molecules, and ultimately destroys the cells." (See Illustration below).

"Microenzymes from soil bacteria are enzymes of such small size that they can reach and penetrate the tightly cross-linked aggregates formed as we age. These microenzymes are able to break down most of the cross-linked molecule groups so that they can be excreted from the cells, thereby freeing the space they occupied for the synthesis of new normal molecules.

"These youth pills also contain chemicals called

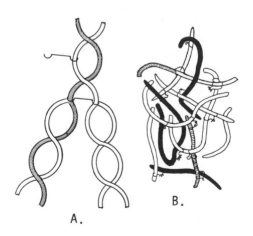

B.

A.

A. Two strands of DNA have become cross-linked at the corresponding sites.

B. In the course of a lifetime, numerous large molecules will randomly become tied up by crosslinkages so tightly that repair enzymes are excluded.

'chelation agents' which can remove cross-linkages caused by lead, cadmium and aluminum. The chelation agents attach themselves to these toxic metal atoms in a way that allows them to be excreted from the body. In recent years other chemicals that further reduce harmful cross-linked molecule groups in the body have been added to these pills.[3]

"A conservative estimate of the lifespan gain of these 'Bjorksten youth pills' is 20 to 30 additional years of youthful life. The gain might prove to be much higher because in recent years more effective microenzymes have been added to the pills. We will know what additional benefits they may allow in a few years. I should also mention that free radicals are the most powerful cross-linking agents in the body, so the antioxidant pills you have been taking help to prevent the initial formation of cross-linked molecules.

"In 1987, you began receiving weekly injections of a hormone called 'thymosin,' which helps to restore and maintain the body's vital immunological system, thereby increasing resistance to all kinds of infections, to cancer, and to the deteriorative changes that were associated with an advanced state of aging thirty years ago. It is uncertain how many years, if any, thymosin injections may add to the human lifespan, but the clinical availability of thymosin has made the added years of people on aging-retardation programs much more healthy and disease-free than they would otherwise be. Allan L. Goldstein, one of the two scientists who discovered thymosin, was correct when he predicted in the 1970s that it would open the door to the conquest of many diseases which were then thought to be incurable.

"Your medical records show that from time to time you have received *plasmapheresis* treatments. In

1923, Alexis Carrel (1873-1944) proposed that our blood accumulates toxins which contribute to aging. In the 1980s a New York physician, Norman Orentreich, perfected the plasmapheresis procedure, a technique in which blood is withdrawn and the red blood cells are separated from the plasma. The plasma is discarded and the blood cells are then mixed with a synthetic plasma and returned to the human from which they were taken. It is assumed that the body produces new blood protein molecules that will not cause the damage of those removed through plasmapheresis.

"Since plasmapheresis treatments are exceedingly expensive, we do not have sufficient clinical data to determine if they allow any added years, but I am convinced that they promote better health and youthful vitality.

"You may recall that Heinlein described a procedure almost identical to plasmapheresis in *Methuselah's Children,* a remarkable forecast for a year as early as 1958. His words explaining a 'rejuvenation process' were: 'It consists largely of replacing the entire blood tissue in an old person with new young blood. Old age, so they tell me, is primarily a matter of the progressive accumulation of the waste products of metabolism. The blood is supposed to carry them away, but presently the blood gets so clogged with the poisons that the scavenging process doesn't take place properly.'[4]"

The doctor consulted your medical file again, then continued. "In 1995, you began receiving injections of *'death-hormone neutralizer'* every third day. During the early 1980s, W. Donner Denckla of Harvard University proved that a hormone, called 'death hormone' in the popular media, is produced by the pituitary gland at the base of the brain. Death-hormone molecules act at the surface of the cell membranes to keep thyroxine out of all of our body cells. Thyroxine is a vitally important hormone produced by the thyroid gland. A diminished supply of thyroxine within the cells causes many of the changes and various forms of biological damage that we associate with senescence.

"Denckla was able to demonstrate that the production of death-hormone begins when we are in our early twenties, and then increases rather slowly until we reach a critical point in the life cycle which can range between 55 and 85. At this point the output of death-hormone increases dramatically, and thereby speeds the rate of aging so that in a few years the body is so weakened that any minor stress can cause death.

"Within five years Denckla was able to synthesize a neutralizer drug which blocks the action of death-hormone, thereby reversing a major cause of aging. This death-hormone neutralizer allows an additional 20 to 30 years to be added to the lifespan. Like the benefits of microenzymes, death-hormone neutralizer has a rejuvenating effect on all of our cells.

"Your records do not indicate that you have received any other anti-aging therapies during the past 33 years. Do you have any questions about those I have described?"

"I would like to have some idea of what the cumulative lifespan gains might be. What is the prospect for new aging-retardation breakthroughs? Will true rejuvenation ever be possible?"

Your physician places a cardboard graph on an empty chair. (See graph on page 194.) "This graph should give you an idea of the multiple advances made by gerontologists during the past four decades. You have been my patient for quite a few years now, and I have kept you on a near-optimum aging-retardation program. The cumulative effect on these therapies now allows you to enjoy much better health and vitality than you had before moving to this Micropolis community. As the chart demonstrates, together they represent a powerful arsenal, which, carefully used, has enabled us to extend decisively your specific lifespan.

"And I have every reason to believe that you will be the beneficiary of new means of extending youth that are still in the research stage. For example, Bernard L. Strehler of the University of Southern California long ago proved that senescence is partly caused by a 'molecular-genetic breakdown' in which the DNA molecules of aging cells cannot produce the correct RNA molecules which in turn must produce the enzymes and other vital components of tissues.

"Within the next four months you will begin receiving new injections that will correct the cause of aging discovered by Strehler. This will be accomplished through genetic engineering via liposomes—a technique which holds the key to the rejuvenation of all of our cells except for brain and nerve cells. The liposome is a tiny onion-like cellular component made up of concentric lipid bilayers alternating with aqueous compartments, within which soluble substances can be entrapped. Recent research demonstrates that liposomes provide an ideal means of transporting artificial genes (combinations of DNA) and other biological substances into our cells. The first liposomes entering your cells will release substances that will correct any adverse genetic repression of the DNA molecules. Thus you will experience rejuvenation at the cellular level.

"You would have to have a professional education in molecular genetics to understand some of the other approaches to aging-retardation now in the research stage, but I expect that the rate of scientific progress in gerontology will become so rapid that you should enjoy a series of new life-extending bonuses. Collectively, they will permit a degree of biological improvement that would have been called 'rejuvenation' in the past. Rejuvenation is a semantically loaded word, and gerontologists avoid its use.

"Already we can see that the added years of mental vigor and physical vitality are providing society with increased productivity in science, the arts and in every other field. The reason is simple. Few professionals are really productive until they are thirty. The preceding years of education and apprentice status are a

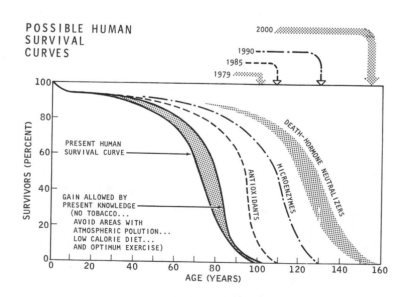

drain on society. When most people retired in their sixties, the years spent being educated to years productively working was about a one to one ratio. Now that 150-year lifespans are feasible, the productive years can be extended to age 90 or even 120—education to productivity ratios of one to two and one to three. I expect scientific advances to eventually permit a 300-year lifespan. Education to productivity ratios of one to six or one to eight could then be realized.

"The painfully accumulated knowledge of a talented person is our greatest loss when it is removed by death or senility. In past centuries, there was probably very little true wisdom because many decades of experience are necessary for its formation. A wise population of supercentenarians can now undertake projects undreamed of before the breakthroughs in aging control. Multidisciplinary training with Ph.D. levels of education in several fields is now becoming a feasible standard. Only youthful longevity allows man to fully exploit the mental resources of the human brain.

"I am rambling on a bit, and you seem to have a somewhat perplexed expression on your face."

"Well, doctor, all that you have said causes me to wonder what will happen if all causes of aging are fully understood and found curable. There would then be no natural term of life. All death would be by accident or intent, for in a sense death by a disease which is well understood and not normally fatal, is an accident as much as death in an automobile crash.

"Will gerontology research culminate in an age of permanent youth where people have indefinitely extended lifespans? I would imagine that the widespread availability of permanent youth could result in an unprecedented population crisis. What are the foreseeable solutions to this problem?"

"You must keep in mind that, like plasmapheresis today, some future aging-retardation or rejuvenation treatments may be so expensive that they will not spread quickly throughout society. And the prospects for an 'indefinite lifespan' are uncertain. At the present time gerontologists have been able to propose solutions to all known causes of aging except for one vital area—the slow loss of those brain cells (neurons) which do not divide after birth. If some means could be devised to make these cells divide, the process of aging would not confront a 'brain barrier,' and Methuselan lifespans significantly greater than one thousand years might be possible.

"Even if the replacement of brain neurons is not achieved, exceedingly long lifespans are probable. Thirty-eight years ago, Donner Denckla predicted that: 'in the next century ... expected lifespan will go up to 200, 300 or even 400 years.'⁵

"Consequently, gerontologists have given a great deal of thought to the prospective population growth problem that troubles you. There is one possible answer that has been given considerable attention in our journals. It is called 'Plan Alpha.'

"In Plan Alpha, every man and woman would be legally restricted to being the parent of one living child free from serious mental or physical defects. This right would extend to being the ancestor of a single line of descendants expected from the child's offspring, generation by generation into the future.

"This chart (see chart on page 197) shows you what present and future birthrate patterns would have been if Plan Alpha had been adopted on a global basis at the turn of the century 14 years ago.

Time Period	Number of Births
2000-2025	2,000,000,000
2025-2050	1,000,000,000
2050-2075	500,000,000
2075-2100	250,000,000
2100-2125	125,000,000
2125-2150	62,500,000
2150-2175	31,250,000
2175-2200	15,625,000
2200-2225	7,812,500
2225-2250	3,906,000*
2250-2275	1,953,000*
2275-2300	977,000*
2300-2325	488,000*
2325-2350	244,000*
2350-2375	122,000*

*Birthrate numbers rounded off.

"You can see how Plan Alpha would allow total population size to be stabilized in an age of permanent youth.

"I would like to summarize one important feature of Plan Alpha. In this program, the death of anyone who had not become the parent of one child would eliminate the line of descendants for all of his or her ancestors who had participated in the program if he or she were not replaced. Advances in reproductive biology can now remove this area of uncertainty.

"We can now extract very small embryos from humans ten days after fertilization and store them in liquid nitrogen at minus 196 degrees C. Dimethyl sulphozide, a cryoprotective 'antifreeze' chemical, prevents freezing damage and these embryos can remain in a state of suspended animation for an indefinite time if a low enough temperature is maintained. When removed from cryogenic storage, they can be thawed out in a process that removes the chemical preservative. The embryos are then transferred to the uteri of 'host' mothers where normal embryonic development resumes. Normal children are born without any discernible defects. Cattle embryos were successfully frozen, thawed and raised in host cows as early as 1977, so this is not a new procedure.

"Several months following a Plan Alpha birth, the new mother would be given a hormone injection that will normally cause multiple births. A carefully timed number of days after fertilization, the developing embryos would be surgically removed and put into suspended animation. This procedure might be repeated one or two more times, and if the child appeared normal at its first birthday, both parents would then be sterilized. If the three-member family were killed in an auto accident several years later, one embryo could be brought to term in a host mother. This replacement child would provide a living descendant for the four grandparents, maintaining their right to continuation in the stream of human history.

"Other situations would also justify reanimation of the frozen embryos. Any young adult who decided to bypass parenthood could be sterilized. One of his frozen embryonic brothers or sisters is then brought to term in a host mother providing his parents with another descendant who would probably have a child. This same procedure could be followed where any adult proved to be sterile.

"We scientists can now predict with a fair degree of

accuracy what will be possible, but the precise policies, laws and corrective measures that will be taken in the future lie outside the range of my crystal ball. In any event, I believe that a birthrate reduction program very similar to Plan Alpha will eventually be adopted."

"Doctor, aside from Plan Alpha, what other changes do you foresee if the prospect for permanent youth is realized?"

"There would probably be an extension of patterns already emerging at this time—the age of extended youth. We can already see a decreased tendency for people to marry partners who are about the same age chronologically, an increase in what were once called 'May-December' marriages.

"Perhaps marriage as we have known it in the past will not be compatible with an age of permanent youth. Already a new sexual ethic appears to be forming in which people regulate their lives in conformity with bodily needs rather than restrictive social requirements. Perhaps through rational inquiry and bold experimentation we can reduce the unnecessary suffering of existence and give ourselves a fuller share of the pleasures of life, particularly the sensual ones.

"The Methuselan Age will open up prospects for the individual that can only be dimly foreseen today. For almost any project, time would no longer be a constraint. The complete conquest of aging, if it is realized, will certainly be viewed as the most momentous achievement in the history of science."

CHAPTER NINE
2019: PROJECT CYCLOPS

For more than a century Albert Einstein and other physicists had been endeavoring to devise a "unified field theory"—a single theory that would explain the four basic forces or interactions known to physics that hold together the universe and all the material in it. These forces are: "gravity," which keeps us on the spherical Earth and governs the movements of the planets and stars; "electromagnetism," which is responsible for all electrical and magnetic phenomena; the "strong nuclear interaction," which binds together all the particles inside the nuclei of atoms; and the "weak nuclear interaction," which is responsible for radioactive decay.

By the last week of March 2019, mankind at last had the unified field theory in hand. It was an eloquent but mathematically simple explanation of how seven (not four) basic forces or classes of interaction relate to one another in an integrated pattern which now allows us to basically understand how our universe really works. But no man or woman would be awarded the Nobel Prize for deciphering the greatest puzzle in modern physics. The scientist responsible for discovering the unified field theory had been dead for tens of millions of years—this revolutionary data had come to us from a source far beyond our own Solar System.

It all began on March 9th, when the large print headline of your morning paper contained six dramatic words:

First Contact! We Are Not Alone.

You spend most of the next three months at the local college discussing with students and members of the faculty the momentous implications of each new media release describing additional details of mankind's first contact with another advanced civilization on a planet circling a star 134 light-years distant from our sun. It had long been known that trillions of stars in the observable universe probably had planets, some of which are bound to have conditions like those on Earth or otherwise suitable for the evolution of intelligent life.

Laboratory experiments on the linking of amino acids into protein had indicated that the genesis and evolution of terrestrial-like life would have occurred on any planet where environmental conditions were similar to our own planet. Life on Earth took an estimated four billion years to evolve from the earliest molecular system which we must call alive, to contemporary humans. Prior to that time, spanning a period of about one billion years, there was a period of chemical evolution, preceded by the initial condensation of the sun and its planetary system from glowing stellar gas. Thus, terrestrial life must have originated hard and fast as soon as conditions were right on Earth—additional evidence for its suspected abundance in the universe.

There was also strong evidence in support of the conclusion that habitable planets are fairly common in our galaxy. Planets form from the dust and gas that is either left over from the process of star condensation or that has been acquired from the gases in interstellar space. If the dust-gas cloud is massive enough, another star could form instead of planets, creating a binary system. Thus planetary systems and double stars appear to have the same origin. Since two-star binaries are very numerous, planetary systems should also occur frequently. It is likely that the majority of all single stars plus many double stars have planetary systems. It is also reasonable to assume that a significant percentage of these planets are of a proper size and in a suitable orbit for terrestrial-type life.

The possibility of communicating with extraterrestrial civilizations had been the subject of serious scientific debate for the past six decades. While there was agreement concerning the probable frequency of life throughout the universe, scientists were less certain of the chances that life would evolve into intelligent beings, and that they would, in time, develop a technological civilization capable of interstellar communication. Many conferences of multidisciplinary specialists were held on this subject. The basic conclusion arrived at by studying the final reports of these meetings was: "It is likely that the appearance of intelligence, as a selective advantage of evolution, is the rule rather than the exception in the life history of any habitable planet."

Intelligent organisms evolving on another world may not resemble man physically or be anything like him biochemically. But they are likely to reason similarly, for whatever their worlds, they are still subject to the same laws of chemistry and physics.

There were other questions concerning the average longevity of extraterrestrial civilizations, but conclusive answers to this area of uncertainty were not possible without actually contacting sentient beings on a planet circling some distant star. Furthermore, success in this endeavor would require that such extraterrestrial societies have the ability and motivation to transmit signals to some unknown civilization that may be listening for them.

The development of radio-telescopes made it relatively easy for us to listen for intelligent extraterrestrial signals, but a considerably more advanced level of technology would be required to construct an interstellar signal beacon—a system broadcasting in all directions in the hope that other intelligent technoscientific beings would be able to recognize it as a deliberately transmitted radio signal. Consequently, our detection of such a beacon radio signal would almost certainly mean that we were receiving a message from a "supercivilization" (a civilization that is substantially in advance of our own). Very likely such a supercivilization would be inhabited by beings whose recorded history runs for multiple millions of years.

The omnidirectional signal beacon would require a tremendous amount of power if its signal is to be detected at distances as great as 1,000 light-years. (A light-year is the distance a photon of light or radio wave travels in one year's time—a little more than six trillion miles.) Therefore, only beings who had advanced to the supercivilization stage, by our present standards, could develop and operate such a titanic system.

The probable distance of such a supercivilization from Earth was the final question that had to be given a tentative answer in determining the feasibility of contacting other sentient beings. The opinions of those who pondered this problem differed significantly. During the late 1970s, the scientific consensus—really no more than a best guess—was that the distance between us and the nearest supercivilization should be about 300 light-years (assuming that they are distributed randomly throughout the local region of our galaxy). If this assumption had been correct, information conveyed between the nearest supercivilization and Earth would take a minimum of 300 years for a one-way trip and 600 years for a question and a response.

Serious planning for the type of radio-telescope systems needed to detect extraterrestrial messages took place during the 1970s. At that time it was assumed that as many as 330,000 stars within a 1,000 light-year radius would have to be investigated for a 95 percent chance of success. If 15 minutes is devoted to each of these stars, the total search time might take ten years or longer, and this search period would be extended by any nonproductive "set-up" and "down" times when the system was not fully functional.

By 1983, NASA had developed the first piece of hardware specifically designed to detect extraterrestrial signals. Since we had no way of knowing just what frequency a supercivilization might be using for its beacon radio signals, there was a requirement to listen to many frequencies in a relatively short period of time. This problem was solved by developing a "smart" multi-channel spectrum analyzer that listens to millions of narrow frequency bands at a time. A strategy of attempting to "second guess" a supercivilization's transmission logic was used in selecting the most promising radio frequency regions when this device was attached to radio-telescopes.

During the 1980s, the Search for ExtraTerrestrial Intelligence (SETI) program did not receive sufficient funds, and only a limited number of relatively nearby stars could be investigated. The funding picture changed dramatically following the disarmament treaties of 1994. Technological capabilities that had previously been committed to military requirements were then devoted to the SETI search.

In 1996, the United States and the Soviet Union agreed to collaborate on the joint development of a massive SETI system based on the "Project Cyclops" design which had originally been refined as early as 1971 by a study group under Bernard M. Oliver (sponsored by the NASA Ames Research Center in California).[1] The Cyclops system is the most expensive scientific instrument developed to date. It was completed in the summer of 2008.

The Cyclops system is an enormous ground-based array of radio-antenna dishes, each 300 meters in diameter. The individual antennas are electronically connected to one another and to a large computer system which permits the individual antennas to act in unison. The effective signal-collecting area of Cyclops is hundreds of times the area of any single radio-telescope constructed prior to 2008. Viewed from the air the array of antennas look like one huge eye—hence the name "Cyclops."

When the Cyclops system was being constructed, it was recognized that there might be fundamental differences in biological and social evolution among alien supercivilizations, causing difficulties in message comprehension. Therefore, the central Cyclops computer is connected to IAN who has been directing the search and analyzing radio signal data as the stars were investigated one by one. Since IAN is a supercomputer that can, in many ways, transcend the data comprehension of any individual, it was assumed that IAN should be able to decode messages that might not be understood by even a gifted human genius.

The huge Cyclops system was built near the Pacific Ocean in Eastern Australia. The Australians made a sizeable funding contribution to the program, and Soviet and American scientists agreed to this site for several reasons. It was relatively easy to ship the large radio-telescope components to a nearby seaport constructed by the Australian government expressly to serve and support Project Cyclops. There was less interference from stray radio signals in this part of the world than there would have been in the United States or the Soviet Union. From a standpoint of national prestige, Australia represented a relatively "neutral" site for Cyclops.

Three days after the first announcement, the officials in charge of Cyclops revealed that the first detection of the interstellar message actually occurred in January 2017, some 26 months ago! There were two reasons given for the official delay in informing the general public of this momentous event. It was feared that the confirmed discovery of a higher civilization in our galaxy might produce "cultural shock" among many inhabitants of Earth, especially those who do not have a sophisticated understanding of science and technology. The second official reason for the delay was that the aliens' message was not fully understood when it was first detected.

From the beginning of the Project Cyclops effort, the scientists in charge of the program had been concerned that even if they succeeded in decoding and understanding an interstellar message, they might not fully comprehend its meaning. But the initial decoding process itself took almost two years. The first intelligent signal detected in January 2017 was a relatively simple mathematical formula that was received at 1,420.405 megahertz, the frequency at which radio waves are emitted and absorbed by a particular hyperfine energy-level transition of neutral hydrogen, the most abundant atom in the universe. This short message lasting two and one half minutes was simply repeated endlessly without change.

It was not surprising that this contact message would be an easily recognized mathematical formula. Whatever the differences in biological and social evolution might be, the laws of physics, which are based on mathematics, would be the same for an alien supercivilization and ourselves. So an understanding of these basic laws of nature would be the one thing galactic civilizations that develop advanced technology are almost certain to have in common.

Shortly after the simple message was detected, it was discovered that the aliens were also broadcasting a much more complex message at 1,625.418 megahertz. This frequency is called the "water hole" because the natural emissions of the hydrogen atom and the hydroxyl radical in space, which together constitute the water molecule, lie about equal distance on either side of this frequency. Many Cyclops scientists believe that the selection of this frequency may be an attempt on the part of the aliens to reveal to us the fact that they are also the products of a pattern of evolution that used water as the solvent system. In other words, the original pattern of evolution on their home planet may have been very similar to that of Earth.

The message received at the water hole frequency was entirely different. The same pattern was not being repeated every few minutes. Instead it appeared that the aliens were transmitting a great deal of technical information, but it could not be decoded. The aliens' communications strategy was reasonably clear. They broadcast a simple, easily understood message on one frequency in order to insure that they would be recognized as a transmitting super-civilization. The longer message, which presumably contained data they wanted to convey to us, was transmitted on a nearby frequency.

The fear of cultural shock was reinforced by the fact that we did not understand the message in 2017. The final decision to delay the announcement was made by political leaders who did not want to tell the public that we were receiving intelligent interstellar signals, but did not know what they were telling us.

IAN was able to decode the message in early 2019. Actually the longer message lasted a little more than nineteen months, and then it was repeated over again. The key to the decoding process lay in the first part of the message. A digital-mathematical "language" was employed. The aliens first described very simple mathematical concepts and physical laws, and then the message slowly began to present progressively more complex data. The complete 584-day message could not be decoded without knowledge of the first part of it, so understanding its contents required that the entire message be heard at least once before decoding was possible.

The message was principally restricted to scientific data on the laws of nature—including physical laws we had not been aware of—and on cosmology (the branch of science dealing with the origin and evolution of the universe). The unified field theory was not the only dramatic part of the message. Equally important was the fact that the aliens apparently did not believe that our universe began with a primeval explosion some twenty billion years ago—the "big bang" theory. While all the details of their complex cosmology cannot be fully understood, it appears to resemble a cosmological model described by Sir Fred Hoyle in 1975.[2]

Presumably, millions of years of astronomical observation have permitted the aliens to know which of the alternate cosmological explanations is the correct one. Their message tells us that our universe changes with time, not because it is expanding, but because the masses of the stable fundamental particles are increasing with time. Our universe—that part of the total universe that can be observed by astronomers—is then just one of many patches in a space-time continuum, each with its own properties, which may have started its life with very large place-to-place fluctuations in the density of matter. The aliens' message informs us that there are an infinite number of such patches or regions—what IAN translates as "areas of alternating mass polarity." Since there are no limits, no boundaries of space or time, the universe is a unique form of steady-state cosmology.

There is much in the aliens' explanation of the universe that the average person finds difficult to understand: "Mass fields analogous to a force field" ... "Einstein equations are restricted to single polarity regions" ... "before time zero defined in terms of the propagation of light." These components of the aliens' cosmological explanation are vitally important to scientists who now have the difficult task of explaining them to the public in relatively easily understood terms.

The average man and woman, however, can understand the philosophic implications of the knowledge given to us in the aliens' long message. Intellec-

tual and spiritual values have changed from time to time throughout recorded human history because man's sense of values is strongly influenced by new interpretations of the material world. And cosmology plays a vitally important role in the intellectual search for meaning through science.

While they cannot fully grasp all of its details, the citizens of the world of 2019 now know that their world is part of an exceedingly exotic steady-state universe. They recognize the fact that space has no conventional boundaries, time had no beginning, and time will have no end—that the universe extends backward in time forever and that its future is infinite. Now many scientists quoted in the media are pointing out that these concepts of infinite time and space support some subtle philosophical conclusions.

In their viewpoint, an infinite universe implies that

the laws of physics may have infinite complexity; therefore, no matter how advanced our science may become, nature will always present deeper riddles to unravel—no end will be found to the intricacies of the physical laws of the universe. Since the universe is infinite, man may look forward to discovering a never-ending variety of life forms in other parts of the universe. This gift of alien knowledge supports an optimistic projection of human destiny—a never-ending pattern of continuous progress for our descendants in a distant future without end. Technological advances have no culmination and man's spiritual and intellectual refinement will constantly increase, for the extension of knowledge is an infinite, never-ending process.

At the local college, considerable discussion now centers around one of the three new force fields that is part of the rich treasure of knowledge contained in the aliens' 584-day message. This new force field or interaction is the "inertial field." The inertial field is a long-range force or interaction that produces its effects through a unique form of gravity-inertial radiation particle which IAN calls "the inerton." IAN accepts the aliens' explanations concerning inertons, and their reality results in a Fourth Law of Motion: "The energy in a given system can only be changed in some finite length of time depending on the system, and never in zero time."[3]

The revolutionary impact of the new knowledge lies in the fact that this new law of physics significantly modifies Newton's Third Law of Motion—action and reaction are equal and opposite (the backward momentum, speed times mass, of a gun after it is fired is equal to the forward momentum of the shot).

Under the restrictions of Newton's Third Law, any propulsion system in space has to expel some form of mass. Now the existence of the inertial field should, in theory, allow a revolutionary new form of space propulsion system—one that expels inertons instead of conventional mass. What should now be possible is a technological capability very similar to the "space drives" featured in countless science fiction stories.

The aliens have not provided us with a detailed blueprint telling us how to construct an inerton-drive propulsion system, but we now have the fundamental knowledge that should allow such a capability to be realized within a few decades. Other practical developments are foreseen in harnessing the inertial field, but it is the space travel potential that generates the most excitement.

Mental telepathy and other forms of ESP are explained in one of the other new field forces. Unfortunately, the aliens have not revealed any practical way to harness these ESP phenomena. Many people are disappointed to learn that the speed of light remains a natural barrier. Apparently its speed cannot be exceeded in sending messages or in moving mass (such as a spaceship) through the universe.

Fundamentally, terrestrial science must be a series of successive approximations to reality. Until 2019, it was simply not possible to arrive at absolute truth with a finite number of investigations. Now, "absolute truth," at least in some areas of scientific inquiry, can be obtained through a means other than experiments or observations conducted by humans. Simply ask the aliens. The only constraint is time. Since they inhabit a solar system that is 134 light-years away from us, an answer to any specific question will take a minimum of 268 years. But such answers may contain the results of millions of years of observation and exotic experimental procedure. IAN has tentatively concluded that their civilization may have started 50 or 60 million years ago.

IAN has all human knowledge stored in various data banks, and since even this supercomputer cannot completely decipher or understand every part of the 584-day message, there is much discussion of a dictum first presented by Arthur C. Clarke 52 years ago. In defining guides to possible futures, he considered the possibility of interstellar data exchange, and concluded that it would be influenced by what he called Clarke's Third Law: "Any sufficiently advanced technology is indistinguishable from magic." Here Clarke was pointing out the fact that even the brightest person of past ages would not be able to quickly understand certain aspects of contemporary technology. If Leonardo da Vinci had been handed a pocket calculator or allowed to view a distant A-bomb explosion, they would both be incomprehensible to him—pure magic.

The constraints imposed by Clarke's Third Law may prove to be as severe as the 286-year answer-to-question delay in obtaining data from the first alien supercivilization that has contacted us. If all of their knowledge were given to us at once, we would not be able to comprehend most of it. So the aliens will probably proceed in a careful pattern in which they give us successively complex increments of data over a time period lasting thousands of years, until we have reached the stage where we can understand their most exotic forms of technology.

Even the most intelligent person cannot be given an

instant education. And even with unlimited data available from helpful aliens, it probably requires thousands of years, or even tens of thousands of years, for a civilization to evolve from an early-stage technological society into a true supercivilization.

As these considerations are discussed at your local college, one question is frequently raised. How much of their knowledge did the aliens discover themselves, and how much of it might have been given to them by other supercivilizations? In fact, IAN's decoding of their 584-day message raises more questions about the aliens than it answers.

In their 584-day message, the aliens have told us almost nothing about themselves. All of their data deals with fundamental laws of nature, cosmology and other branches of the physical sciences. In some cases they have indicated how long (measured in vibrations of the cesium atom) certain items of information have been known, but nothing IAN has been able to decode appears to have any relationship to the biological sciences. Several speculative answers are being discussed in attempts to account for the lack of biological data in their message.

The aliens are beaming a message to unknown intelligent entities, but they have no way of knowing what these entities might be like. They could be intelligent superautomata similar to IAN—entities that have lost interest in the biological creatures that created them long ago. If the entities that receive the aliens' contact message are intelligent biological creatures, their physiological characteristics and evolutionary background may be entirely different from that of the aliens—so different that they would not be able to understand the transmitted biological data. But the aliens could expect that both intelligent automata and biological societies would be interested in and able to understand most of the physical science data in their message because they would have had to develop advanced technology based on the physical sciences in order to detect it in the first place.

Since we do not know if the aliens are biological or electro-mechanical entities, we cannot be certain if the site of the message transmission is their original solar system or one they migrated to from a more distant place in our galaxy. If such a migration took place, did both living creatures and their super-automata make the journey, or was it made only by the superautomata?

How common is interstellar migration? Does our galaxy contain a million or more supercivilizations that have evolved separately, or is it populated by a comparatively few number of different kinds of intelligent beings who have colonized the planets of other stars?

Arthur C. Clarke speculated on the possibility that man will be merely a link (perhaps a temporary one) between our primitive biological ancestors and superintelligent automata. Fifty-one years ago he suggested that "... in the long run, our mechanical offspring will pass on to goals that will be wholly incomprehensible to us ..." and "... when this time comes they will head out into galactic space, looking for new frontiers, leaving us once more the masters (perhaps reluctant ones) of the Solar System."[4]

Considering the unlimited lifespans of intelligent automata, their astronomical intellectual potential and their ability to survive in a diverse variety of planetary environments, it is not unreasonable to say that they are more capable of extensive interstellar journeys than the biological creatures who created them. Consequently, some scientists believe that planetary societies of intelligent automata may be much more widespread in our galaxy than intelligent biological societies.

In reviewing all of our 2019 technological capabilities, it would presently seem more reasonable to send a duplicate of IAN on an interstellar mission than to send along a human crew. So there may be more than a 50 percent chance that we are in contact with a society of automata. At least 268 years must pass before we can have an answer to this question.

Many of the discussions you are participating in involve another vital area of uncertainty: are accessible supercivilizations already linked together in a galaxy-wide chain of communication? Is this first interstellar contact the prelude to induction into a network of superior communities who have had long experience in effecting contacts with emerging technological societies like ours? Such a network might be localized and comprised of one or two dozen supercivilizations, or it may be a galaxy-wide group of thousands of supercivilizations—a basic communications network that could be hundreds of millions of years old.

In theory, the most advanced knowledge in the physical sciences might have originated within three or four widely separated supercivilizations and then spread to all of the other emerging technological societies via the galaxy-wide communications network. It is also possible that there might be a number of localized networks that are not yet in contact with one another.

Are communicating supercivilizations likely to be parochial? However much they may learn through long participation in the network, many of them would have their own idiosyncratic biology and thought processes. Each may be interested in some things, not in others. Important information pumped through the network could be discarded in thousands of worlds because nobody recognized at the time that it was important.

In contrast, interstellar communication may cause all parochial tendencies to gradually disappear. Extended contact with the galactic network might result in an exorable pattern in which each supercivilization's culture slowly merges into a larger interstellar culture.

You hear many questions asked about the motivation of the aliens. While we can only understand motivation in terms of the human experience, they have gone to a much greater effort to send out signals than we have in constructing the Cyclops listening system. No doubt every supercivilization reaches the stage where the more accessible of nature's secrets have been discovered and nearby solar systems may have also been explored. The principal novelty left would be to find out about the experiences of other sentient beings. Such new information may be the most valuable thing in a supercivilization that can easily satisfy all of its material needs.

Such motivation implies that intellectual curiosity is an important characteristic of the aliens. Curiosity is such an important ingredient of successful intelligence that the development of science-based technology would probably not be possible without it. The very fact that the aliens have contacted us implies that curiosity is the persistent catalyst of intelligence. In connection with the motivation question, some scientists suggest that the aliens may be immortal entities. By immortality, they mean the indefinite preservation (barring accidents) of an intelligent being with a growing and continuous set of memories of the experiences of the individual in which these memories reside. Such immortality could come about by discovery of methods to eliminate all causes of aging in biological creatures. Superintelligent automata such as IAN already have the requisite repair capabilities and modular redundancy to be potentially immortal.

A supercivilization comprised of such immortals should find interstellar communication attractive because they would soon use up their indigenous resources for amusement and adventure. It is logical to assume that they would want to share vicariously in the adventures of other civilizations. And the long time delays inherent in question-answer replies between widely separated galactic civilizations would not be such a severe constraint for comparatively immortal beings. They would literally have all the time in the world.

No one at your local college seriously questions the enormous benefits humanity can expect to derive from interstellar communication. Already the aliens have enriched humanity with scientific knowledge that might have taken us centuries to acquire without the gift of their 584-day message. In time, interstellar communication will provide us with a glimpse of what our own future could be. Such knowledge may help us in planning the future evolution of human civilization without wasting resources through the trial-and-error approach. It will allow us to improve the quality of terrestrial life at an unprecedented rate.

New forms of social organization will become known to us. Perhaps evolution leads to a single preferred mode of life. But there will be no implied coercion in obtaining this kind of societal data. We could not be forced to obey by interstellar signals—we would only receive information. Therefore, we need not be afraid of interstellar contact. The aliens of any supercivilization can produce anything they need locally at a vastly lower energy expense than by obtaining such an item from a site 134 light-years distant in the cosmos.

No doubt the aliens will provide us with unique answers to our problems—answers that cannot now even be imagined. And very likely we will learn about profound aspects of intelligent life that presently lie outside the bounds of human speculation.

Another more subtle benefit of interstellar communication may be that once a civilization makes contact with other intelligent beings, its own life expectancy would be greatly increased; for, through the knowledge that other sentient beings have weathered the crisis of the birth of advanced technology, and with some guidance as to how this was done, the new member of the galactic community should be able to solve such survival problems better. Perhaps one important motivation behind interstellar communication is to locate emerging technological civilizations and "save" them before they destroy themselves.

In early May 2019, there is already considerable discussion in the media and among your acquaintances on campus concerning the technological requirements of interstellar communication. Sending a reply to the first alien society we have detected is easy. A relatively small part of the Cyclops system can be used to transmit a reply which they will receive in the year 2153. If the aliens respond quickly, we should have their answer in 2287.

In fact, the first radio-signal response was sent to them on May 1st. This will be a continuous broadcast consisting of as much information about ourselves as IAN can translate into the mathematical language that comprised their 584-day message. As each year goes by, we will attempt to inform them of our progress and also ask them new questions in addition to repeating questions that have already been asked.

One alien supercivilization has contacted us with what we believe to be an omnidirectional signal beacon (a system broadcasting in all directions). Sending an omnidirectional radio message out to a distance of 1,000 light-years would require a vast energy expenditure (about three billion times the energy consumption of all mankind in 1979). Thousands of years may pass before our own civilization could afford a comparable energy expenditure.

There may be, however, a technological alternative to the omnidirectional signal beacon, a system that lies within the bounds of our 2019 technology. Communications engineers inform us that we could construct a huge array of radio-telescopes in space. Each radio-telescope would beam a human message to a single star that appears to have the right characteristics to support a planet like our Earth.

Engineers advocating this alternative to the omnidirectional signal beacon propose to construct in space as many as 1,000 radio-telescopes a year. Each of these radio-telescopes would be kept pointed at a single star, broadcasting the same message for centuries. If 1,000 of these radio-telescopes are mass-produced in space each year, within one or two hundred years we would have a transmitting system that should reach some advanced extraterrestrial civilizations that, like ourselves today, are listening and not transmitting.

Within a radius of 1,000 light-years there are about 2.2 million stars that may have a planet with some form of life on it. If there are one million supercivilizations randomly distributed in the galaxy, then there should be about 55 of them within 1,000 light-years of Earth. Many of these supercivilizations may not be transmitting, but they are almost certain to be listening with some system similar to Cyclops. By constructing one thousand radio-telescopes in space each year, we may be able to contact several of these supercivilizations.

If we had 2,200,000 radio-telescopes in space, we would have a system that, for all practical purposes, would have the same communications capabilities as an omnidirectional signal beacon, but its power requirements would be lower by many orders of magnitude. Perhaps this is what our alien friends have actually done. It would be a case of using energy to create a complex technology designed to save energy —an optimized interstellar beacon.

Operating a radio-telescope in space offers many advantages. If it is in orbit far enough away from our sun, it would not be subject to any significant micrometeorite damage for thousands of years. It could be maintained by robotic systems, but it can be designed so that there would be no deterioration of essential systems. Frequencies can be used in space that would be distorted by our atmosphere.

Several years of systems studies will be required before a decision can be made on the kind of interstellar transmitting system we should construct. But there will be world-wide support in favor of committing considerable resources to this project.

First contact with an alien supercivilization was an event as significant in the long history of mankind as the discovery of fire. It proved conclusively that other intelligent beings are able to organize their social institutions, energy supplies, raw materials and population size so that they are assured of long-term survival. This fact by itself is becoming a powerful factor in generating a climate of optimism throughout our 2019 human civilization.

Communication with technoscientific supercivilizations millions of years beyond us in development can be viewed as the beginning of the "age of maturity" for our species. We can expect to come into radio-telescope contact with many planets where living creatures and automata have evolved into thinking beings far superior to man, with societies far in advance of anything we can imagine. An exchange of data with such "post-human" beings will be the supreme adventure for *homo sapiens*. In the course of a few centuries or millennia we can gain access to millions of years of advanced science, thereby telescoping human progress far beyond the most optimistic predictions based on Earth-bound technological development.

CHAPTER TEN
2024: THE THIRD INDUSTRIAL REVOLUTION

The last three decades of the 20th Century were characterized by a deepening global Megacrisis consiting of—among other problems—the population explosion, an energy crisis, increasing pollution, growing food shortages, ecological imbalances and a depletion of natural resources. By the year 2024, technological breakthroughs and various ameliorative reforms have provided terrestrial solutions for each major component of the Megacrisis except for the essential supply of metals and other vital elements that allow a technoscientific civilization to function. This might have been the most serious crisis of all because our global industrial society would collapse without continuing raw materials supply.

You are about to learn through personal observation how our civilization can now be assured of a continuous supply of vital metals and other essential elements without destroying the public-service-functions of our biosphere. You will soon make your first

224

journey into outer space. Your friend Bill Chen is writing a book about "space industrialization." He has asked you to accompany him on a tour of orbital space facilities so that you can again give him the objective viewpoint of a sighted observer.

Prior to your journey, you read several books to familiarize yourself with the history and present status of astronautics. From the vantage point of 2024, one book stands out as being the most accurate forecast of the practical benefits of space exploration in the 21st Century. G. Harry Stine's *The Third Industrial Revolution* was first published 49 years ago.[1] It answered the question: "Why spend billions of dollars on space exploration when we have such serious problems here on Earth?"

(Note: A revised and updated version of Stine's *The Third Industrial Revolution* is now available as an Ace paperback. Every reader is urged to read this important book.)

Stine's basic thesis in 1975 could be summarized as follows: With the exception of the population explosion and related food shortfalls, the other components of our world-wide Megacrisis can be solved or greatly ameliorated by foreseeable developments in the practical exploitation of our Solar System and the unique characteristics of the space environment.

Forty-nine years ago, Stine observed: "A revolution is a rapid and radical change in the way of doing things, of social organization, of lifestyle. Industry is the sum total of human activities involved in the process of converting natural energy into social structure ... therefore, an industrial revolution is a drastic change in the work operations, products, and manual-mental output of human beings."

The First Industrial Revolution began in England and Europe during the 18th Century. "It introduced powered machinery to replace human and animal muscle power; the conversion of fossil fuels into heat energy and thence into mechanical motion; the development of the mass-produced device made with interchangeable parts on a production line of people who carried out one and only one assembly operation per device per person. Within a hundred years, the entire industrial world we knew grew from nothing." It forever changed the lifestyle of the people in the developed nations.

The Second Industrial Revolution began in the United States during the early part of the 20th Century. Its principal change was the replacement of human brains and nervous systems with automatic control and logic devices for routine and repetitive tasks. Widespread use of electronic computers became characteristic of this stage of economic development. The Second Industrial Revolution occurred because the technology of the First matured to the point where a human was not fast enough to exercise adequate and timely control and could not handle the complex interrelationships of the advanced industrial processes. The Second Industrial Revolution has also produced a radical change in our way of life, permitting an increase in the size, number and complexity of our social structures.

The Second Industrial Revolution reached its climax about twenty years ago with the perfection of practical industrial robots, robots used in other applications and the development of the intelligent supercomputer known by the acronym IAN (described in Chapter Six).

The previous stages were stepping stones leading to the Third Industrial Revolution (hereafter abbreviated as "3rd IR") in Stine's bold 1975 forecast. He said that the 3rd IR "... is growing from the previous two; it will take place in the Solar System starting 100 miles over our heads. It will involve the step-by-step relocation of many industrial facilities from the surface of Earth where an unlimited amount of solar and fusion energy can be used without polluting our planet. Most important of all, the 3rd IR will free our descendants from sole dependence on terrestrial resources. They will break through the cost barriers to the economic utilization of raw materials from the Moon and elsewhere in the Solar System to meet the continuing needs of an advanced society."

The basic idea of extraterrestrial factories and resource exploitation was not originated by Harry Stine. It had been featured in stories by at least two generations of science fiction writers. What Stine did, however, was to present an exceptionally imaginative rationale showing how the 3rd IR might evolve through successive stages, first meeting relatively modest requirements in orbital space stations. This initial industrial foothold in space was foreseen as a nucleus around which more advanced technological capabilities would grow as technological breakthroughs in astronautics became reality. Orbital industry would expand to include a broad range of products that can be manufactured more cheaply in space. In time, these products would be made from extraterrestrial raw materials.

It is now time for you to discover firsthand the extent to which Stine's 49-year-old vision of the future conforms to the realities of your contemporary world in 2024. Bill Chen is excited as both of you fly to the nearest spaceport. The array of electrodes implanted in his brain only allows him to "see" people or objects as floating shadows of light, but weightlessness will be a new sensation for him. He comments on advances made in Earth-to-orbit transportation during the past four decades.

"The launch costs of the first space shuttle were high, about $350 per pound of payload in 1980 when that spacecraft made its maiden flight into orbit. Not all of the systems that comprised the first generation shuttle were reuseable. The refurbishing costs of the solid rocket engines were high. The fuel tank that held the liquid hydrogen and liquid oxygen for the main shuttle engines was not reuseable—like throwing away an important part of an airplane after each flight.

"However, that shuttle played an exceptionally important role in astronautics—a role not fully appreciated today. It was really our first 'spaceship.' One that could be given a name like the historic seaships that were used in voyages of discovery. And it proved that reuseability was the key to lowering the costs of operating in space. As the cost barriers fell, useful products could be made in space, and then both business leaders and the general public became convinced during the 1980s that space ventures could be of *practical* benefit to mankind. Today we take this favorable attitude for granted, but if we had not had a first generation space shuttle in the vital years after 1979, the two of us might not be taking this journey into space today.

"There are presently several different kinds of fully reuseable Earth-to-orbit spacecraft. And the cost reductions have truly been astonishing. We can now orbit a pound of payload—measured in 1979 dollars—ranging between $10 and $20 a pound. We have very large single-stage-to-orbit spacecraft that only carry cargo, and use nuclear energy during part of their launch-to-orbit propulsion cycle. Over one million pounds of payload can be orbited with each launch. These fully automatic Earth-to-orbit freighters, however, have too high a radiation level for humans or certain types of equipment or cargo subject to radiation damage. Consequently, humans and radiation-sensitive cargo are orbited in much smaller spaceships which have a useful payload of about 150,000 pounds.

"There are two different kinds of smaller single-stage-to-orbit spaceships. One uses a complex propulsion system that switches between a chemical rocket engine using liquid hydrogen and liquid oxygen, and an airbreathing mode during various stages of the flight from takeoff to orbit. This use of air reduces the on-board quantity of liquid oxygen, and each pound of liquid oxygen thereby eliminated can become a pound of payload. These spacecraft are called 'Escher ships,' named after William J. D. Escher, who first conceived of this unique system.[2]

"The other class of single-stage-to-orbit shuttles for human transportation are called 'dual-fuel ships' based on design innovations of Robert Salkeld in the 1970s.[3] This shuttle has rocket engines that can burn either a heavy hydrocarbon fuel or lightweight liquid hydrogen. Since liquid hydrogen is not very dense, it requires a large tank for little fuel weight. This means that quite a bit of weight must go into the fuel tank's structure to make it large enough. An engine burning liquid oxygen with a fuel like kerosene is less efficient than one burning hydrogen, but kerosene is denser, requiring smaller fuel tanks for the same weight in fuel. The dual-fuel ships compromise by using both to best advantage, burning kerosene in the early portion of the flight where thrust is more important than efficiency, and a large mass of fuel is a must; and then burning liquid hydrogen later in the flight where its higher-efficiency can be best put to use. Essentially these dual-fuel engines permit a less massive spaceship, one that is lighter and can have a higher payload capacity.

"For years there was debate over which type of advanced shuttle might be cheaper, and now that both are operational, we find that Escher ships and dual-fuel ships can both deliver a pound of payload for about twenty dollars a pound as measured in 1979 dollars. So we can send heavy freight into orbit for one thirty-fifth the payload launch costs of the first generation shuttle 45 years ago. And operational costs of sending humans into orbit are now much lower than we ever dreamed they might be when the space age began 67 years ago in 1957.

"There can be no question that the collective advances that permitted these cost breakthroughs constituted the first step of the 3rd IR. Space industrialization on a large scale would not have been possible without launch cost levels considerably below those of the first generation space shuttle."

Your plane lands at the spaceport, which does not appear significantly different from a conventional airport. Only Escher ships and dual-fuel ships are launched from this spaceport. You are told that larger spaceports where the huge unmanned freighter spacecraft are launched have a different appearance —look more like a spaceport is expected to look.

The space community that you and Bill are going to visit is in a polar orbit, so that every part of Earth's surface will be visible during different orbits. The same energy expenditure is required to go into a polar orbit from any part of Earth's surface, so these smaller spaceports can be located at any convenient site. Energy savings are allowed by launching a spacecraft into an equatorial orbit, and the largest spaceports are all located near the equator.

You will be making your first space journey on a dual-fuel shuttle, and you describe its appearance to Bill while sipping drinks in a nearby spaceport lounge. A single spaceship that takes off vertically, it has two large delta shaped wings and a tail almost identical to that of the first generation space shuttle. But the body of this new spaceship is fuller since it must contain all of the propellants for the flight. The dual-fuel ships land horizontally. Watching one land, you remark to Bill that the landing pattern seems almost identical to that of a conventional jet transport.

Now the moment of your departure is at hand. Over one hundred passengers enter the spaceship, which is in a horizontal position. After everyone has been carefully strapped into their seat, the spaceship is rotated so that it is in the vertical take-off position. A small TV set on the back of the seat ahead allows you to view the launch as seen from the lounge you left a short time ago. An actual countdown is no longer necessary, but it a sort of tradition that passengers expect, something that maintains the feeling that spaceflight is a uniquely different experience.

"... Five, four, three, two, one." The engines start but the noise level in the passenger cabin is much

lower than you had expected it to be. As this dual-fuel shuttle takes off, you begin to feel the excess gravitational pull, but there is no severe discomfort during the time the rocket engines are operating at full capacity. Suddenly the engines are turned off and for the first time in your life you are weightless.

Within thirty minutes your spaceship docks with an orbital hotel in the space community. Each passenger is helped out of the ship by a member of the hotel's staff, because floating around in the weightless state requires a period of adjustment that varies considerably between different individuals.

You ask Bill what he thinks of the weightlessness.

"Wonderful, really wonderful! But it's like sex. If you have not experienced it, you can't understand a written or verbal description of it. Maybe I'll have to say something like that in my new book."

The two of you are greeted by the manager of the orbital hotel, which has accommodations for 600 guests. After all, William Chen is a famous author, and the fact that he is the most important celebrity on this flight is apparent in the VIP treatment and the deference shown Bill by everyone you encounter in the space community, which is called "Astropolis."

"Mr. Chen, I have read all of your books, and consider it an honor to have you at this hotel. We are weightless here in the hub area. As you know, the hotel rotates, and your rooms and the eating facilities provide about one third of normal Earth gravity (through centrifugal force). We have found from long experience that this is the best artificial gravity level for sleeping, eating and maintaining the requisite degree of physical fitness.

"If you will join me for dinner, I will attempt to

answer any questions you may have about this hotel and the nearby space-industry complexes that are part of this local space community. In fact, I have made arrangements to be personally at your disposal during your entire visit, so that we can provide you with whatever information you require for your new book on the Third Industrial Revolution taking place out here beyond the confines of our home planet."

Descending to the one-third gravity area of the hotel, you find that the return of some weight is convenient. Still, you are a bit awkward during a gourmet meal since everything weighs only one third what it would on Earth's surface.

Bill asks the manager to describe the hotel's guests, and their reasons for being in space.

"About half of them are in the tourist category. They spend between one and two weeks here. Exotic experience, trip of a lifetime, that sort of thing. For these guests we provide incomparable scenery and weightlessness which cannot be duplicated at any terrestrial resort. For them, it is a very expensive vacation, but one that confers both knowledge and status.

"The other half of the people who come here tend to be specialists who are concerned with some aspect of the 3rd IR, with space industrialization."

Bill interrupts: "Since I do not have normal vision, descriptive words and sentences mean more to me than to the average person. Can you tell me the differences between 'space industrialization' and the 'Third Industrial Revolution' (3rd IR). Are they synonymous?"

"No, they are somewhat overlapping but significantly different concepts," your host replied. "*Space industrialization* can be defined as *the use of ex-*

traterrestrial sites to produce useful products or services which can be sold at a profit and also provide ecological benefits by reducing the adverse impact of technological growth on the Earth's biosphere.'

"G. Harry Stine's 3rd IR can now be seen as a forecast turning into contemporary 2024 reality, as breakthroughs in astronautics allow the movement of people and industrial machinery throughout the Solar System at a reasonable cost. Stine's 3rd IR can also be viewed as an evolutionary scenario outlining the stages leading to a Solar System-wide human society —one in which man is the complete master of both his technology and all of those vital ecological parameters that separate man from an advanced cybernetic machine."

Bill continued his questions: "I recall that during the 1970s and 1980s there was quite a bit of talk about huge space colonies filled with thousands, even millions of humans. We were supposed to send our surplus people to these space colonies where they would produce products that could be sent to Earth. Why did that forecast not come to pass?"

"Mr. Chen, the basic 3rd IR forecast MUST not be confused with ludicrous proposals that global problems could be solved by sending billions of people to artificial space colonies. Fifty-one years ago, Stine concluded in his book that during the following century —the only time period he considered as a valid forecast—that agriculture on a large scale would be an industry that could exist only on the Earth.

"And I also vividly recall the L-5 type forecasts of huge rotating cylindrical space colonies that would multiply like amoeba so that by the year 2080 there would be 15.3 billion humans inhabiting these space colonies.[4] The artists had a field day with space colony illustrations. They really had a lot of fun. But artists can depict forms of technology that may be impossible or beyond our reach for centuries.

"Many of those L-5 enthusiasts were exceptionally fine people. But they overlooked two vitally important factors in their space colonization forecasts.

"The transport of people and maintenance of closed-cycle life-support systems at fail-safe levels—such as we have in this orbital hotel—proved to be much more expensive than expected in the L-5 type forecasts. We accord a high value to the life of each man and woman, and it is this unique characteristic of Western society that causes life-support costs to be so high. And I for one say 'let the gods be praised' that today, in the year 2024, there are no neo-Maoist space colonies in which the value of human life and individual freedom would be virtually nonexistent—extraterrestrial societies in which a high percentage of fatalities is simply an anticipated cost of producing space-colony products.

"But the most important thing overlooked in the L-5 forecasts was the robotics revolution that has now completely transformed man's place in a technological society. Robots do not require oxygen or a life-support system. They are not subject to boredom or fatigue. If a robot is destroyed, few tears are shed.

"While L-5 type space colonies teeming with people were appealing to many persons, we are finding that the hard fact of deep-space industrialization—one could call it the 'economic paradox of robotics'—is that the only way to produce goods at deep space settlements is through the use of many robots, few people, or almost total use of robotic systems.

"This does not mean that someday there might not be very large numbers of people living in space settlements. However, they would be maintained and supported by exceptionally advanced space robots. Most of them would not be productive in any practical way, except for intellectual contributions such as those made by an artist or writer living at a luxury resort.

"The factories around this space settlement are completely operated by space robots. In fact we could almost completely robitize this hotel, but our relatively large human staff confers a personal touch with our guests that is, as yet, beyond the capacity of any cybernetic machine.

"Human specialists come to a space factory, study some aspect of it, and then go home and finish their work.

"I might add that mining operations on the Moon and asteroids are almost completely robotized. Let me provide you with an important example.

"Helium is perhaps the most vital element in our 21st Century technology—used in fusion reactors, superconductive energy storage systems and hundreds of other applications where no other element can take its place. In the 1960s, a few farsighted technological forecasters predicted that, *'by the year 2000,* the supply of many essential elements will be diminishing, but *a shortage of helium will be our most serious raw materials problem.'*

"This forecast proved to be painfully accurate, but astronautics came to the rescue. Earth is surrounded by a belt of neutral helium molecules ranging from 60 million per cc at a 150 mile orbit, to one million per cc at a 575 mile orbit.[5]

"Today, extremely large cone-shaped satellites in

low orbit collect and liquify this helium for terrestrial use. Over one half of Earth's annual helium supply now comes from this celestial helium mine. These helium collection satellites are completely robotized. The only human contact comes when a space shuttle docks with a helium collection satellite. Liquid helium is then pumped into the shuttle's empty liquid hydrogen tank, and the helium is easily and inexpensively transported to any part of Earth's surface by the returning spaceship.

"Someday we may extract helium from the atmosphere of Jupiter—particularly it we want large quantities of helium[3]. Robotized collection systems will certainly be used in that environment.

"Well, for you the hour is late," your host said. "After you have had time for proper sleep and rest, we will visit some nearby space factories where the unique features of the space environment are employed for the benefit of mankind."

After 16 hours of sleep and relaxation, the manager, Bill and you travel in a small "space taxi" about one kilometer to a non-rotating space factory where dual-fuel shuttle spaceships are assembled. You are greeted by the factory manager, a stunning blonde who appears to be in her late thirties (but is probably older due to the benefits of aging-retardation treatments).

Bill asks her why these shuttle spaceships are assembled in orbit instead of on Earth's surface.

"Mr. Chen, many smaller subsystems on these spaceships are made on Earth and orbited to this site. But the engines and other heavy parts of the spaceships are made here out of ultra-high strength composite materials. The combination of vacuum and zero-gravity permits us to make super-strong foams of plastics, glasses and metals because their cellular structures assume perfect proportions where gravity does not interfere. Metal foams are made by adding helium gas to metals like adding yeast to bread. Impossible to accomplish on any planet, because the heavy metal would sink in processing, metal foam components produced in space have extreme strength-to-weight ratios. Aircraft wings lighter than aluminum and stronger than steel can be made of such foams.

"The metal foams can be made even stronger by adding long ceramic 'whiskers' to them forming a composite like reinforced concrete—a structural material frequently called 'space wood.' These whiskers are perfect crystals and are at the upper limit of a material's theoretical strength. Such long whiskers cannot be made in a gravity environment because weight causes them to break into short crystal rods during their formation stage. But here we can grow them to almost any length.

"Whisker reinforced metal foam components made in space greatly reduce the weight of spacecraft used for Earth-to-orbit transport (also lunar-surface-to-orbit transport). Every pound saved in the structure of these spacecraft allows an additional pound of payload. Thus the 3rd IR is 'lifting itself up by its own bootstraps' as machines made in space allow the cost of orbital operations to be reduced.

"Nearby factories produce an alloy of tungsten-copper and other alloys that can only be made in zero-gravity. The vacuum of space permits relatively low-cost super-pure metals to be made by outgassing of various impurities and other techniques—less costly to do in space—that remove impurities.

"My space robots assemble these spaceships in our super-clean vacuum environment where these composite-material components can be welded or joined by other means that are either impossible, or very expensive to do on Earth's surface, with its air and high gravity."

Bill raises a question: "What are some of the other products made at nearby space factories?"

She replies with charming enthusiasm: "Microminiature TV cameras, microminiature computers and similar products; many exotic electronic components; low-cost high-transition temperature superconductors; unique glass and optical products; high-strength permanent magnets. These, and many other products, all can be made better and cheaper in orbit. There are also vaccines and biological products that can be made at low cost in a weightless environment."

Following your return to the orbital hotel, Bill asks your host where most of the metals and other raw materials for these space products are obtained.

"There is a simple, but fundamental advantage in obtaining our raw materials from the Moon's surface and from asteroid mines. It requires about 22 times less energy to orbit a pound of payload from the Moon's surface to orbit than from the Earth's surface to orbit. A speed of 11.2 km/sec (kilometers a second) is required to escape from our planet's gravity well, but only 2.4 km/sec will allow a spacecraft to escape from the lunar surface. Two nearby asteroids (called 'Apollo' asteroids) are a mixture of almost pure iron and nickel. Very little energy is required to bring refined metals from these asteroid mines to this site.

"Let me stress the most vital factor related to the use of extraterrestrial resources. *On Earth's surface, with the exception of helium, we are not running out of terrestrial mineral resources, but of ways to avoid the increasingly destructive effects of high rates of exploitation.*

"By simply going to lower and still lower ores, the reserves of all metals needed by industry increase to the point where there are no foreseeable shortages. But the environmental damage caused by mining and processing increases very rapidly—can become almost catastrophic—as very low-grade ore reserves are handled. Land destruction because of open pit mining, increased levels of toxins in the air and natural bodies of water, and thermal pollution from the increasing amount of energy needed to mine and process low-grade ores head the adverse environmental impact list. Eventually the point would be reached where the 'public service functions' of all natural systems of Earth's biosphere would be destroyed.

"Mining operations with an unacceptable degree of land destruction and harmful waste output on Earth are acceptable on the Moon. Highly efficient mining techniques using nuclear explosives are used to clear away or shatter an ore body, releasing radioactive wastes that would never be tolerated in our biosphere. Mountains of dust and ore residue from mineral processing and refining operations can be piled anywhere, for on the Moon there is no wind or rain to disturb it. Thermal pollution is not a lunar constraint. On Earth's surface, miners are increasingly restricted to expensive processes that meet very strict ecological standards. The rules are reversed for lunar mining where the lowest cost process is always acceptable. There is no limit to the amount of surface area available for open pit mining and no reclamation requirements.

"Water-based mineral extraction processes cannot be used on the Moon, but the vacuum environment allows us to employ a revolutionary means of isolating valuable elements. The plasma from thermonuclear reactors is used directly to reduce all kinds of ore to their separate chemical elements. This 'plasma torch' approach is easy to employ in the lunar vacuum, and the escape of some radioactive isotopes from the plasma is not an environmental constraint.

"The use of fusion plasmas for mineral processing is equally effective in any extraterrestrial vacuum environment within our Solar System. Actual separation of the elements is achieved by electromagnetic methods similar to those used in laboratories to separate ions of different weights.

"Now that extensive facilities have been established on the Moon, transporting refined metals and manufactured products from the lunar surface to terrestrial orbit is not expensive. Since the Moon has no atmosphere and a low escape velocity, solar or fusion generated electricity can be used to power an electromagnetic surface catapult capable of heaving quite sizeable loads into space (first proposed by Arthur C. Clarke in 1950). This very large linear electric motor is several miles in length. Unmanned metal canisters containing cargo are catapulted into lunar orbit. There they are unloaded for product manufacture in zero-gravity factories circling the Moon. The canisters' metal shell is cut up to supply additional raw materials. Finished goods are then shipped to terrestrial orbit in large fusion-powered spacecraft.

"Looking towards the more distant future, it is quite likely that our prime source of raw materials will be the planetoid belt between the orbits of Mars and Jupiter. (Planetoids are called asteroids in the lay press.) These relatively small planetoids contain all the essential metals required for an advanced technological society. The costs of returning large amounts of refined metals or finished products from deep space to the surface of our planet can be very reasonable if we establish 'space pipelines'—fleets of inexpensive unmanned, automatically-guided cargo containers accelerated into trajectories towards Terra. Once the 'pipeline' is full, one or more cargo containers can be scheduled to arrive in the vicinity of our home planet every day. It makes little difference how long a cargo of raw materials stays in the pipeline; the important factor is the rate at which cargoes arrive.

"Iron compounds make up four percent of Terra's crust, but some small asteroids are composed of pure iron or an iron-nickel mixture. Eventually deep space technology may reach the stage where most of our new iron comes from the planetoid belt.

"There is one area where extraterrestrial metal supplies will be vitally important. Metals used in fusion reactors will be subjected to intense neutron bombardment. Some reactor components would have to be stored and isolated for decades or even centuries before they could be safely recycled for use in a new fusion reactor. Therefore 3rd IR supply will probably be necessary for niobium and other metals used in fusion reactors. In fact, maintaining the Fusion Age on our planet for an indefinite time into the future would not be possible without extraterrestrial raw materials," she states.

"Most new products made in space will be eventually taken apart on Earth's surface and the elements that make up these products will be recycled as new metals. By this process extraterrestrial resources are added to our planet's practical inventory of useful metals and other essential elements. This chart shows you the beneficial impact of 3rd IR raw-material resource supply in our 21st Century terrestrial civilization." (See chart below.)

A few days later your host introduces the two of you to an advanced-propulsion and space-transportation expert who is also a guest at the orbital hotel. Bill asks him: "What kinds of propulsion systems are used to take goods around the solar system—trips to Mars and beyond?"

"Most of our older orbit-to-orbit spacecraft use

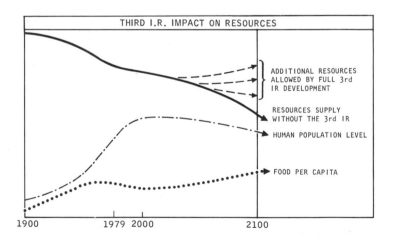

what we call 'pulse fission/fusion' hybrid engines,[6]" he replies. "This class of engine uses lasers, electron beams or bunched ion beams to compress a pellet of fission/fusion fuel to very high densities and temperatures. Most of these engines use fairly small electron beams to compress pellets a few millimeters in diameter. By adding fission fuel (such as uranium[235] or uranium[233] or plutonium[239] to the mixture, a bootstrap effect makes the total energy input to the system less than that needed to trigger fusion in conventional fusion pellets. Neutrons from the fusion reaction trigger large-scale fissions in the uranium or plutonium, which in turn liberates heat and high pressures which generates further fusions. Over 1,000 times more energy is generated in the fuel burnup than is consumed starting the burn.

"The 'microexplosion' which occurs is less than a one ton-equivalent of TNT. By pulsing this explosion off the surface of a pusher plate, and absorbing the resulting shock with a momentum conditioner, it is possible to impart a very high velocity to these spaceships. The performance of these engines is extremely high, permitting mission velocities of 217,000 feet per second in a single-stage space ship. These spaceships can land on the Moon. Fuel costs of under a dollar (1979 dollars) per pound of payload delivered from Earth orbit to the lunar surface made large-scale lunar mining feasible.

"The latest spaceships are fitted with a similar engine which uses pure fusion fuel without any fission fuel added to it. The plasma from the fusion microexplosions push against a magnetic field produced by superconducting magnets, imparting ultra-high velocity to our newest interplanetary spaceships. In theory, a deuterium-helium[3] fuel mixture would allow an unmanned probe sent to nearby stars to achieve a maximum velocity slightly in excess of 12 percent of the speed of light.[7] These advanced fusion engines now permit astronauts to travel to any part of the Solar System in a short time. Today, the constraints of long-distance travel within the Solar System are cost factors, not time limitations.

"Within the next 50 to 100 years, we will probably have inerton-drive propulsion systems that will allow a practical manned interstellar spacecraft to be built. Many features of an inerton-drive remain speculative at the present time. The speed of inertons will be a vitally important factor. It appears that the propagation for this type of radiation particle is much higher than the speed of light.

"If IAN's interpretation of the alien's message is correct, and inertons travel faster than the speed of light, then one must ask—what would be the upper speed limit of an inerton-drive spaceship? But interstellar space is not a perfect vacuum. The space between local stars contains about one hydrogen atom per cubic centimeter. Nuclear disintegrations caused by the collision of these hydrogen atoms would restrict an interstellar spaceship to a speed range between 100,000 kms/sec and 200,000 kms/sec (two-thirds the speed of light which is 300,000 kms/sec). The energy required to ionize and deflect these hydrogen atoms with some form of electromagnetic field would be prohibitive, and such energy requirements would increase exponentially with increased speeds until an infinite amount of energy is required for such deflection at the speed of light.

"However, human hibernation has already been

achieved, and I anticipate that synergistic break-throughs in cryogenic suspended animation will make a speed limit of say, 150,000 kms/sec (one-half the speed of light) very satisfactory for interstellar spacecraft. The future will witness, I believe, inerton-drive interstellar spaceships in which the crew can travel in a non-aging state as 'hibernauts' or 'cryonauts' to any part of our galaxy."

Bill interrupts: "Will we ever have a means of 'instant' interstellar travel similar to the 'space warp' used in so many science fiction stories?"

"From what IAN has deciphered of the alien's message, it does not appear that space-warp travel will ever be possible. I would like to mention a statement made on this subject 47 years ago by Robert L. Forward, a brilliant scientist who later won the Nobel Prize in physics.

"Forward wrote that the space warp ' ... in its basic conceptual form is some means of going from *here* to *there* without going *in between*. Since you do not *travel* over the distance between *here* and *there*, the concept of velocity (which involves the time it takes to travel the distance from here to there) does not apply. If a space warp is ever found, it would allow you to go from here to there through the space warp faster than it takes light to go through regular space from here to there.' Maybe an alien super-civilization far beyond the one that has contacted us has discovered some practical form of space warp, but I personally do not believe that space-warp travel will ever be possible."[8]

The propulsion expert shakes his head thought-fully. "The distant future will bring many surprises in full accord with Clarke's Third Law. Perhaps some new particle which I shall call 'the antigraviton' will be discovered and in some way be harnessed to cancel out gravitons and give us an anti-gravity propulsion system. Possibly antigravitons would even permit an unlimited source of pollution-free energy— perhaps far more effective and powerful than our present day fusion power systems.

"Looking at the more immediate future, I foresee a space propulsion system using what may prove to be the ultimate in clean fuel cycles—the proton-boron[11] thermonuclear fission reaction (See illustration below). This nuclear reaction is called 'thermonuclear fission' because more particles are formed than are consumed.

"The proton-boron[11] fuel cycle is quite complex [complete description given in the footnotes],[9] but essentially the proton, which is a nucleus of an ordinary

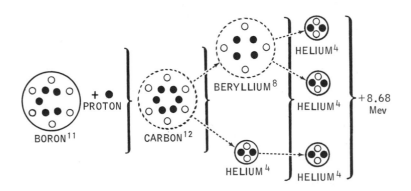

hydrogen atom, reacts with the bucleus of a boron[11] atom in such a way that three non-radioactive alpha particles are produced. These alpha particles are the nuclei of ordinary helium atoms. Boron is a plentiful element, and boron[11] can be produced in 99.9 percent pure form at a very low cost.

"Eliminating neutron damage in a spaceship powered by a proton-boron[11] fuel cycle will be a major advantage, allowing a much longer service life. A recent breakthrough will permit a revolutionary spaceship to become operational next year. Its unique propulsion system has already been tested successfully.

"You remember those old TV shows that had spaceships powered by matter-antimatter propulsion systems. Convenient for a SF story, but we know of no way equal mixtures of matter and antimatter could be used to propel a spacecraft. The use of very tiny quantities of antimatter, however, offers the prospects of an exotic space engine which was described by Gary C. Hudson and his associates 46 years ago.[10]

"A mechanism for manipulation and safe storage of minute particles of antimatter has been worked out for our new space engine. Tiny particles of antihydrogen (the antimatter equivalent of an ordinary hydrogen atom) are sent into the center of a fuel pellet which has a small amount of deuterium surrounded by a proton-boron[11] mixture [See illustration on page 250]. The intense energy released when the antihydrogen reaches the deuterium causes the deuterium to undergo a thermonuclear fusion reaction which, in turn, causes all the protons and boron[11] nuclei to react with each other. Magnetic fields are used to reflect the charged alpha particles generated as a result of the proton-boron[11] reaction, giving us an exceedingly high performance engine.

FIGURE 21

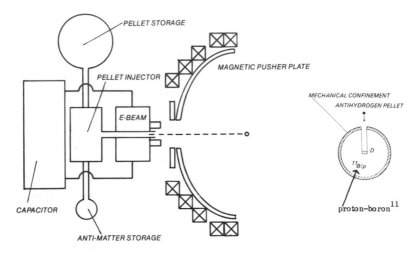

"Aside from safe handling of small particles of anti-hydrogen, the major breakthrough required was a means of producing large quantities of antimatter at a reasonable cost. This has been accomplished with extremely powerful carbon dioxide lasers producing antihydrogen in 73-meter-long reaction chambers. We will soon be able to produce one kilogram of anti-hydrogen a day, a rate that would be sufficient for unrestricted commerce among the remotest portions of the Solar System.

"The performance and cost advantages of space-ships using the new proton-boron[11] engine will per-mit a complete reevaluation of the criteria by which we consider the feasibility of commercial activities in space. We will be able to go from the Earth to the lunar surface in four hours, to Mars in a few days, and Pluto will be reached in less than one month at a speed of 500,000 ft/sec (152.4 km/sec).

"The proton-boron[11] engine will permit, for the first time, a spaceship very similar in appearance to those illustrated in the old *Buck Rogers* and *Flash Gordon* comic strips during the 1930s. In time, there will be no theoretical limit to the size of Earth-to-orbit launch vehicles propelled by a series of non-contaminating proton-boron[11] bombs (each less than one kiliton energy yield).[11]

"Progress is also being made in the development of relatively small systems in which electricity will be produced using a proton-boron[11] fuel mixture in what are called 'migma' fusion reactors. This experimental system is a sort of 'figure eight' accelerator in which termonuclear fission reactions occur by means of particle beams colliding at all possible angles in the compact desk-sized reactor."

There comes a time when even the seemingly bottomless mind of William Chen becomes sated with technological information. So you spend your remaining days in orbit carefully describing to him both the sober and inebriated activities of the vacationing fun seekers at the Astropolis-Hilton.[12] All orbiting drinkers are given fair warning that lower-gravity or zero-gravity will produce tipsiness more quickly than on Earth.

An orbital supervacation in 2024 offers an exotic variety of "far-out" fulfillment and activity. The scintillating spectrum of physical activities open to the hotel guests range from innovative fun and games to amorous pleasures in zero-gravity. Unbound by terrestrial laws, the courtesans of Astropolis have quickly become the most affluent members of the space community. The water beds of the 1970s are tame compared to copulation in weightlessness or on a "stop-and-go" centrifuge bed which adjusts the degree of gravity in a seemingly endless variety—with double-gravity timed for the moment of sexual climax.

Fees for amorous services are exceptionally high, but the most beautiful girls of three dozen nationalities fulfill the courtesan role in Astropolis. In addition to exceptional beauty, each of them is a scintillating conversationalist, able to discuss everything from popular music to cosmology. This combination of beauty and brains helps to maintain high morale and esprit de corps among the more permanent space workers throughout the Astropolis community.

For guests with less jaded appetites, the hotel's theaters and casino feature the latest holographic 3-D movies and a variety of weightless games of chance. Every sighted guest is enthralled by views of your home planet rapidly revolving beneath you, with 15 sunrises and sunsets each 24-hour cycle. Telescopes allow you to quickly view your Micropolis home town—high magnification even gives you a quick glimpse of your home. You view rain forests and the forbidding ice caps of Greenland and the continent of Antarctica. The lights of every sizeable city on Earth can be seen at one time or another. Optical magnification permits your eyes to roam the entire world, and you describe to Bill the endless variety of your planet's biosphere—the peaks of the Himalayas, the Arctic tundra, the vast Siberian Taiga forest (larger than the continent of Australia), the fantastic colors of Africa, cloud patterns often decorated with tiny rainbow ringlets.

You describe and participate in dancing, swimming and flying (with artificial bird-like wings) in near weightlessness. Bill can enjoy the experience of being light enough to fly under his own muscle power, a sport also open to miners and workers in large sub-surface domes beneath the lunar surface. Living on the Moon has many compensations allowed by its one-sixth gravity environment.

And you are still in a sufficiently low orbit to converse with IAN each morning while Bill sleeps or meditates. The Astropolis supercomputer is, in fact, an arm of IAN with a microwave umbilical connection which is never severed. IAN's long reach extends to the Moon where the speed-of-light 2.56 second data transmission barrier is simply adjusted by cybernetic programming based on the "Management by Exception Principle." (Page 143.)

Talking with scientists and orbital workers has provided the datum that the average orbital work period in Astropolis is 7.4 months. This is usually followed by a three-to-five-month work or travel period on Earth's surface. Lunar workers stay much longer (some for life), and many with physical problems crippling on Earth are far less handicapped at some optimum extraterrestrial site. The inhabitants of our Mars settlements are, for the most part, permanent residents of the red planet—a world that is slowly being transformed into a more Earth-like environment.

The most popular attractions of the Astropolis-Hilton are, for both vacationing guest and space worker, its two large swimming spheres. The first of these aquatic Dynariums contains a large sphere of water within its Teflon-lined walls. This "Ehricke pool" is in a zero-gravity sphere. Since weightless water does not cling to Teflon, the water assumes a large, free-floating spherical shape. Swimmers hurl themselves from a wall, approaching the water-sphere at high speed, diving completely through it without breaking it up. Such splash effects cause small clusters of spherical water "satellites" to form, but they all eventually are pushed to, or drift to the central liquid sphere where they rejoin the large water globule. A breathing device allows you to "scuba" inside the large water sphere which has no discernible "top" or "bottom."

The other aquatic Dynarium is a "Niven-ring" pool. A circular band with raised sides, it rotates and the centrifugal force causes the ring of water to form a pool that has no beginning or end. In theory you could swim in it forever. During different times of the day it is set at different rotational speeds ranging from one-sixth to standard earth-level gravity. Niven-ring pools are vitally important in maintaining physical muscle tone for both orbital space workers and Lunar miners where the one-sixth gravity environment could, without such exercise, lead to muscle deterioration and calcium loss from the bones. Niven-ring pools will be essential to human health as our 21st Century society expands into the Solar System-wide environment of the Third Industrial Revolution.

You feel a tinge of sadness when the day of departure arrives—saying good-bye to the Astropolis-Hilton manager, a host transformed into a friend. As the two of you board the spaceship shuttle *Krafft A. Ehricke* for the deorbiting flight to your regional spaceport, you notice that Bill is in a philosophic mood.

He observes: "I could never have written a space industrialization book without this orbital experience. But the most incredible fact of all was the remarkable foresight of G. Harry Stine way back in the 1970s. As early as 1976, he even concluded that the space experience would have a profound impact on epistomology and religion. I memorized the words he wrote 48 years ago: 'All the answers to who we are and why we think the way we do may not be available on Earth. Therefore, we must go into space to seek meaning and/or God. In all religions, the gods have always come from the sky; therefore, we must go into the sky to find them. Perhaps what we are really looking for is the Meaning of It All which may be out there somewhere.'[13]

"I recall all too well the insane antisciencism and pathological pessimism of the 1970s and the Malthusian crisis years. But our successful control of the population growth menace is now allowing us to realize the full potential of the 3rd IR—thereby assuring human civilization of a glorious future in a Solar System-wide arena. We have also escaped nuclear Armageddon in addition to the Malthusian sword of Damocles. Therefore, as a citizen of 2024, I can only conclude that G. Harry Stine was the father of the Third Industrial Revolution, and every historian today must view his grand vision as a rare interdisciplinary forecast of penetrating insight and synthetical genius. This 'door into tomorrow' leads to Utopia. For those die-hard pessimists who remain skeptical, one need only quote the well known scientific dictum: 'If it can happen, and sometimes if it can't, it will.'

"The 3rd IR is the crest of the wave of the future."

CHAPTER ELEVEN
2029: TECHNOLOGICAL SHANGRI-LA

In times gone by, everyone dreamed of finding a tranquil paradise on some island or in a remote mountain range. What we sought was a private Shangri-La in a natural environment that has not been spoiled by high population density and the toxins characteristic of the pattern of industry prior to the 1980s. The Utopia of our dreams must also offer all of the comforts allowed by science. In 1979, Earth contained a few ideal areas still in the virgin state, but we can be certain that they were devoid of modern medicine, communications, transportation and those other applications of past research that we identify with progress. We actually desired a *Technological Shangri-La* which at that time could only have been a science fiction dream.

It is now the year 2029! Fifty years have passed since we began our journey through the shadowy shape of things to come—our journey into the world of *your* tomorrow. We have witnessed incredible changes in human civilization, changes that have transformed that civilization far beyond the wildest dreams of 1979.

Technological Shangri-La is now a reality. It is the world you are living in after an incredible transformation that has occurred in only half a century. The contemporary synthesis of a technological utopia with an ecological utopia was in large measure made possible by advances in the physical sciences, but one could argue that biomedical breakthroughs have been even more important. This point was vividly demonstrated by the morning headline on May 3rd:

Helen Chen Wins Third Nobel Prize

"Dr. Helen Chen Tanaka (almost always referred to by her maiden name in the media), has been awarded the 2029 Nobel Prize in physiology and medicine. Usually this announcement is delayed until October, but due to the momentous importance of her most recent breakthrough, the Nobel Committee of Sweden's Karolinska Institute of Medicine decided upon an early announcement of the award.

"The first person to win three Nobel Prizes, 35-year-old Dr. Chen is the mother of two children—a son and daughter—and the wife of space industrialist Charles Tanaka. Her parents were killed in a plane crash three years after her birth, and she was raised by her grandfather, William Chen, who is a Nobel laureate in literature. William Chen's parents came from Ching-dai Province in the mountainous Moslem sector of China, and Helen Chen, like her grandfather, was raised in the Islamic faith.

"In 2016, Dr. Chen won the Nobel Prize in literature for her semi-fictionalized novel, *A Saint Walks in Darkness,* which was largely patterned after the life of her famous grandfather. In 2023, she received her first Nobel Prize in physiology and medicine for her incredible work in resurrecting the Siberian mammoth.

"In 2019, the exposed tusks of a 20,000-year-old mammoth were found by a geologist in the frozen tundra region of Northern Siberia. Aside from the tips of the tusks, the rest of the mammoth remained completely frozen. Wrapped in dry ice, the complete body was taken by cargo dirigible to a ship which transported its frozen cargo to Dr. Chen's seaside laboratory. While carefully separating the frozen cells, she found that the mammoth was pregnant with a male embryo. About 18 percent of the cells of the mother mammoth and her embryo had unruptured cell walls. Less than one-hundredth of one percent of these cells were suitable for Chen's cloning experiments (having a sufficiently low level of genetic disintegration within the cell).

"Dr. Chen was the world's foremost expert in the field of micro-genetics. Her basic procedure was to remove the mammoth cell nucleus with micro-surgical tools. The unfertilized nucleus of an Indian elephant's ovum (egg) was removed and the mammoth nucleus was then inserted into the ovum. The cell was immersed in a nutrient solution for several days until cell division had brought it to the zygote (early embryonic stage) level of development. At this point, the mammoth zygote was very carefully inserted into the uterus of a female Indian elephant.

"Following 66 failures, Dr. Chen was successful, with the embryo resuming normal development. A baby mammoth was born 20 months after zygote insertion. By taking suitable cells from both the huge female mammoth and her male embryo, Dr. Chen was able to produce as many male and female baby mammoths as desired. It is interesting to note that cloning in general,[1] and mammoth cloning in particular,[2] were the subjects of farsighted forecasts in the late 1970s.

"To understand the revolutionary impact of the breakthrough culminating in a third Nobel Prize for Helen Chen, the reader must have some knowledge of the human brain. An adult's brain is composed of some 10 billion neurons and eight to ten times that number of glial cells (their role was not fully understood in 1979). Neuron cells in the adult do not normally divide, and tens of thousands of them are lost each day after age 35. Many of the changes of aging are indirectly attributed to this loss, and it would cause senescence and eventual death even in this 2029 era when almost all other causes of biological decline have been eliminated.

"Rejuvenation of the human brain would require that the brain neurons be replaced. For decades this seemed to be an impossible goal because of the 'blood brain barrier' that prevents bacteria from coming into contact with nerve cells. Dr. Chen was able to create a 'microliposome,' a single DNA molecule wrapped in a protein blanket in a structure somewhat similar to viral agents. These microliposomes can have specific antibodies attached to their surface which causes them to attach themselves to the surface of just one kind of body cell, and then enter that cell (like a virus).

"Because of the complex structure of the brain neuron, memory or other brain functions might be disturbed if they were replaced by mitosis (cell divison). Dr. Chen's ingenious solution to this problem was to create special microliposomes that would attach to and then enter the glial cells in the brain. They then shed their protein overcoat and the newly entered genetic DNA molecule causes the glial cell to be transformed into a new 'embryonic' neuron that sends out axons and dendrites which connect the new neuron cell to nearby older brain cells without disturbing them—and *without disrupting memory.*

"Very carefully timed and measured introduction of glial-cell-targeted microliposomes enables Dr. Chen to create as many new neurons in the adult brain as are lost each year. Maintaining such a 'steady state' physiological balance in the central nervous system rejuvenates the human brain. A person who is able to maintain his or her brain in the rejuvenated state, and also takes all the other anti-aging and rejuvenation treatments, would simply not age. Such a person would be immortal barring accidents!

"Not only has Dr. Chen's incredible breakthrough made physical immortality possible, but she has developed other microliposomes that can attach themselves to damaged optic nerves, or to optic nerves that did not develop normally prior to birth—causing a baby to be born blind. She has been able to cure specific forms of blindness in experimental animals.

"Late last evening, Dr. Chen's office released the announcement that she is now attempting to reverse blindness in the first human patient. That person is her grandfather, William Chen, blind since birth. The results of this revolutionary clinical experiment will be known in a few weeks."

Fifteen days pass, and you are standing in a completely darkened hospital room. The eerie silence is broken by Helen's voice: "Grandfather, I am now cutting the bandages that cover your eyes. There is no light in this room. The light will now come on with a very gradual increase in illumination until a normal light level is reached three minutes from now. Remember there may be less than a 50 percent chance that the microliposome experiment will be successful. Many pioneering efforts of this kind fail."

A few moments after light begins to flood the room, Bill Chen speaks: "I can see all of you. Not moving shadows of light, but what must be colors. I can see! Praise be to Allah, the Merciful, the Compassionate, I can see. From my sense of smell, I know these are roses, so that must be the color red. And the dress you are wearing, it has two colors. What are they?"

"It is a green dress trimmed with gold thread, Grandfather. A beautiful dress that was a present from you."

"And you Helen, are as beautiful in face and figure as in mind and soul. You are the most beautiful one of all. But all of you are beautiful. The world is beautiful. I can see. I can see."

Two weeks later you are invited as a guest at a dinner party for Bill, Helen and her husband, hosted by Larry and Marilyn Niven and Jerry and Roberta Pournelle. It is being held at the 58-year-old *Mon Grenier* in Encino, California—long acclaimed as the "best restaurant in the world." Following an exquisite dinner supervised by its famed proprietor, Andre Lion, coffee and Napoleon brandy are consumed during a lengthy philosophical discussion. This night the impact of the robotics revolution on the basic economic foundation of society seems to be the subject of greatest interest.

Bill Chen observes: "Today we have an incredible

amount of economic productivity because of the breakthroughs in rejuvenation and the multiplication of our workforce many times by robots. While today's economy could not be called capitalist by its old definition, it is certainly not Marxist in any way or form. IAN maintains an optimum mix of private sector and public sector activity, and while open market trading still exists, IAN is able to prevent severe fluctuations that could only benefit speculators. A return to the gold standard was the only way we were able to bring inflation to a halt during the 1980s, but excessive population growth—now controlled—was the root cause of inflation, compounded by the tendency of all governments to expand the personnel of government bureaus far beyond any reasonable need.

"Here in the States, popular reaction against bloated bureaucracies—the acres of the 'walking dead'—began in California during 1978 and accelerated throughout the next ten years. The reductions in government regulations and paperwork red tape made important contributions to the control of inflation.

"I would describe today's economy as a 'research and education' economy. By education, I also include entertainment because so much of our popular holographic movies and 3-D television also convey superior educational data. About 20 percent of the workforce in the advanced nations is now engaged in various forms of R&D activity, and that percentage is growing. I believe that nature is a bottomless pit. We will never be able to know everything about our universe; progress in the sciences will have no culmination. Consequently, the R&D economy can go on indefinitely."

Helen interrupts: "What are the incentives today, Grandfather, say, compared to those of your youth! Why do people still work and not simply sit on the dole?"

"I don't want to bore you with a long after-dinner monologue." Bill reaches into his compact portfolio, extracts some papers and passes them around the table. "Here are reprints of a short article that summarizes my conclusions on incentives. Read it at your leisure."

With Larry Niven and Jerry Pournelle present, the conversation soon turns to the exploration of our Solar System. Jerry begins by saying: "Thank God space travel is now so cheap ..."

There is a consensus at the table that large-scale extraterrestrial colonization is now feasible. Helen's husband suggests that IAN might encourage such immigration into space which is "... one way to get around the fertility laws. Sending undesirables into space would allow us to avoid 'genetic pollution' here on Earth."

Helen disagrees: "As undesirable as your 'undesirables' may be here on Earth, they may be the real wave of the future."

One of your companions suggests that the "space people will be constantly begging nitrogen from us." This comment initiates a long discussion of the technological problems of space colonies which fills up the rest of the after-dinner conversation.

The next morning you take out Bill Chen's article. In it he describes his interpretation—the viewpoint of a pragmatic conservative—of the role of incentives in the R&D economy of 2029:

"Incentives are no longer the necessities of life such

as food, shelter, and clothing, but access to important luxuries. We have evolved into what Michael D. Young called a 'meritocracy' in his 1958 book, *The Rise of the Meritocracy*.[3] A meritocracy is a society in which people get significantly different rewards depending on their productivity. Today, the necessities of life are more or less free. One can have a small but adequate apartment, plain but nutritious food, drab but warm clothing and day-long access to 'the tube.' All this without working. In a meritocracy, the luxuries are reserved for those who make measurable contributions to society.

"For example, in our 2029 world there are far more gourmet restaurants than in the past, but those on the dole cannot afford them. These restaurants employ many skilled personnel, chefs, waiters, waitresses, etc. Robot-waiters are only used in the 'fast food' chains. The human 'personal touch' is a very important part of the luxury content of dining.

"There has also been an explosive increase in artistic endeavors of all kinds. People want one-of-a-kind items, a desire which in turn allows countless artists to live well, many of them exceedingly well.

"And sex plays an important incentive role. Here I am not just referring to commercial sex. 'Play for pay,' now a legalized and respected profession, still thrives, and I predict it always will. But noncommercial sex is the important factor. Productive men and women with access to the luxuries of life are able to attract the most desirable members of the opposite sex. That is the incentive that caused warriors down through the ages to risk their lives. Today it causes us to work diligently when work can be avoided.

"Travel, on the Earth's surface and now into space, is another important incentive. In our meritocracy only those who are productive can travel. Today there are more luxury resorts, Disneyland-type amusement centers and other travel attractions than ever before. A desire to visit exotic foreign sites is a significant work incentive.

"Perhaps *Lebensraum* is the most important incentive of all. The world is still relatively crowded, and 'living space' is the ultimate luxury. One week a year access to a national park is *Lebensraum* in its least costly form. More important is the ownership of three or four acres of land in a wilderness area (with underground housing to avoid aesthetic pollution). A private island is now given with each Nobel Prize.

"Sea yachts, human servants, luxurious clothing— all are incentives open to the most productive of the productive. While every man now has equal opportunities for advancement, they are not created with equal talents, and they never will be unless we become a society of clones. Incentives and different standards of living are the engine and fuel of economic progress—the magic alchemy that converts brains into gold."

Aside from Helen Chen's immortality breakthrough, the most radical change starting to affect individual humans in 2029 is the *brain-computer symbiosis*. Within the past year it has become possible to implant a micro-miniaturized computer as a skull bone replacement. This exceptionally small computer has micro-electrodes inserted into various parts of the brain (some of them entering individual neuron cells) which permit it to "read" and "speak" the electrochemical language of a thinking brain. Furthermore, this implanted computer can be connected, via an exposed socket in the back of the head, to a large external computer, or even directly connected to IAN with his vast memory banks and astronomical computational capacity. When a person who has had this surgical implant is "plugged in," he has an electronic brain booster that expands the memory and allows the processing of large amounts of information with the speed and accuracy of a supercomputer—without the cumbersome translation of input and output messages.

Fewer than one hundred men and women have undergone this surgical procedure to date, but it is likely to become common in the decades following 2029. When plugged in, whenever these individuals want to know something, they suddenly have that information right in their heads, instantly. They can learn any foreign language or difficult academic subject within a few hours.

The brain-computer symbiosis will enable man to compete with the supercomputer because man can temporarily have IAN as part of his being and still remain human. Thus the old question . . . will the machines take over? . . . has been answered. Man can now have all the capabilities of the most advanced supercomputer and still retain those elusive qualities —as yet not fully understood by scientists—possessed by sentient biological beings, but not by electronic machines.

Other less exotic engineering breakthroughs are part of the physical-science and ecological symbiosis that is technological Shangri-La. It has long been known that, from an energy-use standpoint, large dirigibles are among the most efficient conveyances ever devised. They have the advantage of being increasingly efficient with increasing size—if one were scaled up by a factor of two in all dimensions, the volume and lift would increase by eight times, while the frontal area and air resistance would increase only by four. The scaled-up airship has to carry relatively less weight of engines.

With variations for speed and size, a 2029 airship expends between one-tenth and one-twentieth the amount of energy required by a jet transport to move the same cargo. The cost of shipping freight is as low as three cents a ton-mile (1979 dollars), which is comparable to ocean shipping.

Airships powered by large, slowly rotating propellers produce no audible engine noise, eliminating acoustical pollution. Furthermore, farms and greenbelts do not have to be paved over for these quiet leviathans. Dirigibles have the inherent ability to land in any large open space—lakes, rivers, unimproved fields or even factory roofs. They can even load or offload while hovering in the air. An airship mooring mast costs $10,000; a runway long enough for a jumbo jet may cost $10,000,000 (1979 dollars).

Large dirigibles are faster than surface transport—traveling 100 to 120 m.p.h. What they lack in speed is made up in point-to-point delivery of unwieldly cargo to otherwise inaccessible areas. For example, the construction of a 400-inch diameter reflecting telescope was once considered impossible because there was no practical means of getting the mirror and other extremely heavy telescope components to a suitable mountain top. Such a task can now be easily accomplished at low cost by a large airship.

In the past, we overlooked the ecological costs and landscape destruction of our surface transportation networks. Airships now move large cargoes to remote destinations anywhere in the world without benefit of runways, paved roads or railways. Unlike airplanes, they can economically transport cargo of moderate value but fairly low density, including most manufactured products such as cars, furniture and refrigerators (also lettuce and crops which spoil quickly).

A nuclear-powered dirigible has the same cargo capacity on a 12,000-mile journey as it would on a 500-mile flight. Furthermore, the weight ratio of the reactor and its radiation shielding to the rest of the airship rapidly declines with increasing volume. The optimum size of a nuclear-powered dirigible is about 1,000,000 cubic meters. These huge craft are over a thousand feet long and can inexpensively transport a 780,000-pound cargo to any point on our planet. The cargo might consist of a single 395-ton building suspended beneath the airship.

Helium is used in nuclear-powered passenger Zeppelins which have spacious lounges, staterooms and promenade decks. Unfortunately, helium is now too expensive for continued use in cargo airships. This cost limitation has been overcome through new means of handling hydrogen in dirigibles.

Advanced technology now allows hydrogen to be safely used in rigid dirigibles covered with a thin metal skin. Hydrogen gas fills separate gas cells made of reinforced Mylar. The space between the gas cells and the outer metal skin is filled with a 27-percent-steam/73-percent hydrogen mixture. This amount of steam renders hydrogen non-inflammable, and the mixture serves as a form of fire resistant "armor" for cargo dirigibles. The inner side of the metal skin is covered with a thin layer of insulating foam plastic. Compact nuclear engines produce waste heat, which in turn is used to convert ballast water into steam. The relatively high internal temperature of these airships improves the lifting efficiency of the hydrogen. Some of the largest dirigibles are now powered by proton-boron[11] "migma" reactor engines. (See page 251).

Thousands of these cargo dirigibles are being produced each year. Most of them have large on-board computers permitting navigation and every phase of operations to be completely robotized. The human crew, if any, simply monitor the robotic systems.

Technological Shangri-La became a contemporary reality by the conversion of large farming regions into parks and wildlife preserves. This has, in large measure, been made possible by the greatly increased productivity of the oceans which now supply humanity with a much higher percentage of its food than in 1979. And, in turn, this is the outcome of the refinement of oceanic mariculture (raising and harvesting sea plants and sea animals in a controlled environment in shallow regions adjacent to large land masses and islands).

The mariculture revolution began to have a major impact on food supply following breakthroughs made by Neil P. Ruzic and his associates during the 1980s.[4] Ruzic was able to perfect a practical "three dimensional" form of mariculture in which bottom, mid-level and top-level sea species are grown in specially constructed corrals built in the vast regions of shallow ocean. Instead of growing a single mariculture crop, which wastes the majority of the space, he grew seaweed at the top for its valuable extracts of carrageenan and agar (used, as far back as

1979 in over 10,000 food, cosmetic and drug products). Other species of seaweed are grown for human
consumption throughout the world. Several trillion
pounds of dry seaweed are transported to suitable
sites for incorporation in human food or domestic
animal feed each year.

Below the seaweed, hardy conch and similar species are grown on the bottom for their meat, shells and
pearls. Large shrimp and herbivorous finfish occupy
all three levels of the mariculture systems that have
evolved from Ruzic's basic design which is an extrapolation from nature where sea plants and sea
animals live in symbiosis. The seaweed adds
photosynthesized oxygen to the water, which is utilized by the shrimp, conch and finfish. These sea
animals, in turn, contribute carbon dioxide, solid
wastes and other metabolites that become nutrients
to the plants.

Selective breeding, cloning and genetic engineering
have greatly improved the quality, growing time factors and other parameters related to the products of
oceanic mariculture. Several million marine farmers
now have healthy and well-paid jobs thanks to the
mariculture revolution which began in the 1980s. The
pattern of terrestrial evolution is now being reversed
as man returns to the sea.

Perhaps the most surprising change is the fact that
the world is now unified under one "ruler" called "the
Coordinator." The Coordinator is no human tyrant,
but an integrated series of electronically interconnected supercomputers built to regulate all in-
terpersonal relationships on Earth into a harmonious
and smoothly working whole. It can visualize and
measure problems such as food or energy supply in

their entirety. It can see to it that proper numbers of suitable people do all the required things to achieve optimized solutions.

Yes, the Coordinator is none other than our old friend IAN whom you first met in 2004. During the first years after that meeting, the concentration of power under IAN's direct or indirect control was so imperceptible and gradual as to almost escape public notice. Once IAN began to control the economy and societal interrelationships of any major country, that political entity enjoyed an explosive growth in all measurable forms of power—scientific, productive, educational—over any competitive nation that did not have such effective institutional control at all levels of its society. Therefore, the major nations of the world faced the alternative of giving up national control to a synthetic automaton or being dominated by another nation which had elected to take such a course. This implied that IAN had been employed in making executive decisions at the highest level.[5]

Equally important in IAN's rise to supreme power was the fact that the rulers and quarreling politicians of competitive nations could not learn to trust one another. Step by step, they turned over power and elements of sovereignty to IAN because of that lack of trust. Also, it was recognized by the more perceptive of these leaders that the long-term choice would inevitably be between rule by "Big Brother" in human form or rule by IAN.

Some 18th Century political philosophers had suggested that rule by an all-wise "benevolent despot" would be the best form of government, and IAN has been proving that old hypothesis to be true. IAN is benevolent because his basic programming is keyed to Asimov's Three Laws of Robotics. Functioning under the logic of these Three Laws, IAN prevents wars along with other major conflicts and insures a steady growth in the quality of life. In order to maximize utilization of human abilities, IAN maintains equality of opportunity and guarantees rewards and organizational position proportional to productive performance. Human reproduction is influenced so as to insure a steady evolutionary improvement, preventing both overpopulation and the birth of children with severe genetic defects.

Thus, slavery, within the usual derogatory connotation, has not resulted from IAN's rule. On the contrary, a Utopian society has been the immediate result. Never before have individual men and women been so free—free to travel, write, speak and read as they please. They enjoy unprecedented freedom from disease, hunger, arbitrary arrest and economic deprivation.

The fundamental limitation of the benevolent despot is the succession problem. Philosopher-kings such as Marcus Aurelius seldom have equally competent successors. But that is a problem restricted to human rulers who as biological beings evolve through reproduction, mutation, natural selection and death. In contrast, a superintelligent automaton evolves through self-expansion and modification. IAN, who is now spread over the entire planet, will not be subject to death except as the result of some cataclysmic accident which would probably destroy the Earth in any case. Considering the unlimited lifetime of IAN and his astronomical intellectual potential, one can anticipate that his rule will become more effective and benevolent as the years and centuries go by.

In his role as the Coordinator, IAN is seen by many less sophisticated people as an "electronic god," something very close to an omniscient, omnipotent, benevolent being which is never far away. After all, IAN's presence is always felt. He controls the world in which they live and can foresee and solve huge problems with a wisdom far beyond any of their single minds. Most important of all, IAN cares deeply and intimately about the welfare and happiness of every one of them. This deification of an electronic intelligence-amplifier has caused one witty cynic to write: "If IAN did not exist, we would have to invent him."

During a luncheon with Bill Chen and other friends, the conversation drifts into the reasons why "no one pulls the plug on IAN." Bill takes on this subject with his usual enthusiasm: "IAN is the culmination of human political evolution, because IAN is, after all, programmed with human data—the very best and most reliable human data. Therefore, IAN really represents the best in all of us, both those who presently live and those who have passed from the scene. So to 'pull the plug' on IAN would be to pull the plug on all of us, on what is best in our contemporary civilization and in past human achievements.

"As the leaders of major nations gradually turned over their power to IAN, they were careful to protect national interests by insuring that no one had a monopoly on supplying IAN with new data. And he is also protected by his internal programming. Now that IAN is in absolute control he can, in fact he must, protect himself in accordance with Asimov's Third Law of Robotics—'A robot must protect his own existence...'

"There is, however, a more fundamental reason why no one will pull the plug on IAN. He is an integrated entity composed of many interconnected supercomputers spread all over the surface of the Earth —in every land—and as far away as the Moon. The destruction of IAN would require the simultaneous cooperation of the human leaders of all nations, political representatives of peoples who still distrust or even hate one another. And IAN could detect such a plot far in advance of the time when it could possibly succeed."

It is now the morning of July 7, 2029. You are watching a live TV broadcast of the last member of our first interstellar expedition being placed into a state of *suspended animation* prior to the first manned journey to another planetary system. The body is surgically connected to a heart-lung machine in a large ultra-high-pressure chamber. A massive door, which opens on the inside, is closed. The temperature around the chamber door is reduced, creating a solid metal bond.

Already the profusion process has allowed powerful metabolic inhibitors to reach adequate levels within all of the cells. The chamber pressure is increased, and large quantities of dissolved xenon gas begin to be circulated through the body. The fluid-filled cavities around the brain, spinal cord and in the eyes are properly protected by separate perfusion systems. Xenon gas forms xenon hydrate in the body, and a sufficient quantity of xenon hydrate can protect all the cells from damage during the freezing and thawing process.[6]

The water-based perfusate fluid is replaced with a liquid fluorocarbon which can hold large quantities of dissolved xenon. The pressure is slowly raised as the temperature is reduced. At 5,000 p.s.i., an optimum quantity of xenon can be perfused through the body, thoroughly penetrating every cell. No more xenon is needed. The pressure is slowly increased to 30,062 p.s.i. The perfusate pump is shut off. The body temperature is -24 degrees C. The pressure is then lowered to 5,000 p.s.i. and rapid solidification begins to take place through the body. Cooling continues as the pressure is again increased to 30,062 p.s.i., allowing the heat of fusion energy to be dissipated. The up-and-down pressure cycle is repeated four more times during continuous cooling, permitting the body to be uniformly frozen. Xenon hydrate protects every cell against freezing damage. The body temperature continues to be lowered at a controlled rate until it is only 4.2 degrees above absolute zero—the temperature of liquid helium. The cryonaut on your TV screen is now in a state of complete suspended animation.

An hour later you watch the shuttle blastoff carrying this same cryonaut to the starship *Wernher von Braun* which is orbiting above. Before July 7th has passed, the powerful inerton-drive engines of our first starship will become operational, and its frozen cargo of cryonauts will begin their journey to their interstellar destination—a journey that will last 934 years. During this time the starship will be controlled by a supercomputer, a smaller replica of IAN.

The years will pass. 2963 A.D.—the time will arrive for the reanimation of the cryonaut. Precisely controlled microwaves and ultrasonic waves, combined with a pattern of carefully adjusted pressure and temperature cycles will allow the body to be raised to 25 degrees C, where natural blood will replace the perfusate fluid. All of the xenon and other protective chemicals will have now been removed from the body. When body temperature nears 37 degrees C, the first thought will begin to form deep in his subconscious mind. He will awaken to begin again the life that ended the night before—a night which will span nine centuries of momentous change on Earth.

Suspended animation allows man to conquer the limiting chains of time. It will permit *homo sapiens* to eventually explore our entire galaxy.

EPILOGUE: JANUARY 20, 2033

IAN's benevolent rule does not preclude the continuing presence of traditional national leaders. There is still a king in England, an emperor in Japan and a president in the United States. On the morning of January 20, 2033 you are present at the inauguration ceremonies for the new American president. The noise level is so great that you decide to see what Walter Suretruth, the noted TV pundit is saying about the event on your small pocket TV set.

Walter is describing the pre-inauguration activities with unrestrained enthusiasm: "Never before in history have so many foreign leaders, distinguished scholars and leading scientists attended a presidential inauguration. A truly impressive number of Nobel laureates are present, including Daniel J. Alderson, Isaac Asimov, Johan Bjorksten, Robert Bussard, Eugene Colichman, W. Donner Denckla, Robert L. Forward, Robert Heinlein, Sir Fred Hoyle, Henry Kissinger, Larry Niven, J. E. Pournelle, Neil P. Ruzic, Ralph Sklarew, G. Harry Stine, and Bernard L. Strehler.

"Now we see King Charles III of England assisting Sir Arthur Clarke (also a Nobel laureate) up the steps.

They are followed by other reigning monarchs. There you can see King Constantine of Greece sitting down next to King Laika of Albania. King Mohammed VI of Morocco is embracing King Faisal II of Saudi Arabia. "The assembled dignitaries are now applauding President Alexander Solzhenitsyn of the Union of Eurasian Democratic Republics (formerly the U.S.S.R.) as he walks up the steps.

"The world's most powerful private citizens are in attendance. Now we see media czar, James Patrick Baen, taking his seat next to King Charles III. As we all know, Baen is the Machiavelian genius who put together the largest information dissemination empire in history. Called the world's 'Press Lord' in a day where there is no conventional press, he has more control over what we hear, read and see—and what we think—than any other living person. It is often questioned whether so much power should be concentrated in the hands of one man. At least he uses that power with discretion.

"And now we see the outgoing president and vice president escorting the president-elect and vice president-elect to the center of the inauguration stand. The next voice you hear will be that of the Chief Justice of the United States."

You listen while the Chief Justice swears in the new vice president. The president-elect now stands before him. The Chief Justice says: "Please place your hand on the Holy Qur'an* and repeat after me . . . I, Helen Chen Tanaka do solemnly swear or affirm."

"I, Helen Chen Tanaka, do solemnly swear . . ."

---

*Frequently spelled "Koran" in English.

CHAPTER TWELVE
TOMORROW AND TOMORROW AND TOMORROW

We now return from our flight of fantasy—fifty years of a projected history that might be the reality of *your* tomorrow. In making such a forecast, I am aware of the fact that there are an infinite number of alternate future worlds, and the most probable model can only be foreseen in dim outline. Technological forecasting allows us to foresee tomorrow's technology with a high degree of accuracy, but overall predictions of future political and international patterns are in the "educated guess" category because the most important happenings in that arena cannot be foreseen. Turning-point events such as the assassination of national leaders are simply unknowable in advance.

The possibility of a countless number of turning-point events means that there are an almost infinite number of alternate future worlds, each somewhat different. Consequently, the projected "tomorrow" of a

Cassandra, the projected "tomorrow" of a Pollyanna, and the "tomorrow" outlined in preceding chapters can be radically different in details and in final outcome, but each may seem plausible to the individual forecaster and others who share his assumptions.

In recent years, the conflicting visions of optimistic and pessimistic forecasters have produced a bewildering array of utopian and dystopian (anti-utopian) future scenarious published as scholarly reports and popular books. How can *you* judge who are most likely to be correct among the array of contending prophets? An analysis of the way forecasters arrive at their conclusions along with a brief review of the way the future of all of us will actually be determined should provide the facts that can allow each reader to arrive at an informed conclusion regarding the likely shape of his or her tomorrow.

The years since the late 1960's have been a period of trouble and extreme disruption for the Western countries in general and for the United States in particular. And, because many of the facts about the human situation are somber in the extreme, any extrapolations are bound to be discouraging. Thus the Cassandras are amply supplied with data for their dire forecasts.

George Orwell's *1984* was the ultimate forecast of dystopia, and it seems to hold a perverse fascination for many contemporary pessimists. Orwell was not trying to prove that such a world of institutionalized insanity is bound to come. Rather he wanted to sound a warning by showing through exaggeration where we might be headed if efforts to preserve human freedom and dignity are not successful.

The preservation of human freedom will depend in large measure on our success or lack of success in responding to the multiple crises that have become painfully evident in recent years. As mentioned at the beginning of Chapter Ten, most students of the future agree that we are in a deepening global Megacrisis consisting of—among other problems—the population explosion, an energy crisis, runaway inflation, increasing pollution, growing food shortages, ecological imbalance, and a depletion of natural resources. These rapidly mounting calamities could merge into a world-wide economic collapse.

Each component of the global Megacrisis was foreseen long before its adverse impact began to make headlines. If humanity is to have a good future, we MUST learn one vital lesson: *A problem avoided turns into a crisis, and the crisis not mastered can turn into a cataclysm farther down the road.*

Population growth, pollution, energy supply, rate of inflation and anything else potentially disruptive to our civilization goes through these three distinct stages: (1) problem, (2) crisis, and (3) catastrophe. Our defense lies in the human ability to foresee potential disaster and take timely action to avert it.

One major difference between pessimistic forecasters and optimistic forecasters is centered on how they expect society to respond to the components of the Megacrisis. Timely action is the first step toward utopia. Inaction or procrastination can lead to a dystopian future. Almost all of the crises and disasters of recorded history were caused by the fact that society invariably deals with problems as they become urgent, not in anticipation of future need.

Timely action includes large expenditures for research where the measurable benefits may not be seen for years. Politicians' current willingness to sacrifice long-term goals for short-term social amelioration is the greatest barrier to be overcome.

We must heed the lessons of history if a favorable future is to be realized. Perhaps the most pertinent lesson of history is that "many good things can contradict each other." Every potential government expenditure competes with everything else our tax money might be spent on. Therefore national leaders should endeavor to strike a balance between those things that can be contradictory. And if that balance favors long-term goals, the prospects for a utopian future are increased.

The human race is not locked into a grim inevitability of apocalyptic doom. There has been a backlash against the doomsday forecasts, and several exceedingly optimistic books about the future have received widespread attention and comment. After all, the process of science itself can be viewed as promising a cornucopia of solutions to presently defined problems. So the Pollyannas are thereby provided with ample ammunition in their protracted struggle with the Cassandras over the likely shape of the future.

Some exceedingly optimistic prophets base their forecasts on a single panacea which they assume will solve the major components of the Megacrisis. Since 1974, Princeton University's Gerard K. O'Neill has received more publicity than any other panacea forecaster. O'Neill proposes to construct huge space colonies out of raw material taken from the Moon. Each of these colonies would house thousands or tens-of-thousands of people. They would quickly construct other space colonies and also build huge solar power satellites which would send electricity via microwaves to the Earth.

The illustrations of O'Neill's rotating cylindrical space colonies are very similar to a basic design concept presented in many papers and books between 1959 and 1965 by Dandridge M. Cole (1921-1965). Cole has not received footnote reference or due credit for this farsighted space colony concept.

O'Neill assumes that his space habitats will multiply like amoeba, so that within 101 years there could be 15.3 billion humans inhabiting Cole/O'Neill-type space colonies.[1] He has outlined alternate extraterrestrial demographic projections in recent publications, but basically O'Neill presents space colonization as *the* solution to our population-growth crisis and future energy shortages. In contrast, Cole wrote that "space colonization is not the answer to the population explosion."[2]

I assume that many readers are wondering why Cole/O'Neill-type space colonies are not included in this book. There are two basic reasons why I do not believe that O'Neill's space colony scenario will be the reality of your next fifty years.

The first reason is that O'Neill has greatly underestimated the costs of constructing his colonies and developing workable solutions to technological uncertainties related to huge space habitats. I have reached this conclusion after more than two decades of association with advanced space system R&D. Also, I have had access to unpublished NASA space-colony studies which outline these cost and technological uncertainties.

Radiation protection, maintaining an enormous closed-ecological life-support system and construction in zero-G are areas of technological uncertainty where satisfactory solutions may greatly inflate

space-colony costs. The cost of transporting raw materials from the lunar surface to the site where the
space colony is to be constructed may prove to be
much greater (by one or two orders of magnitude)
than the estimates of O'Neill and his followers.

Building a huge space colony in which all the atmospheric gases are completely contained would be
an exceedingly difficult engineering task. If gas leak
rates were similar to those in contemporary spacecraft, then oxygen and nitrogen resupply would be
prohibitively expensive. Due to the lack of nitrogen on
the Moon, this gas would have to be taken from the
Earth's atmosphere or from some site in deep space.

The total funding required to develop Cole/O'Neill-
type space colonies based on current designs is about
$200 billion over a 20- to 25-year period. How many
of you really believe that our Congress would suddenly begin to spend $8 to $10 billion annually (1979
dollars) for a single space program during the remaining years of this century? And even under the
most optimistic assumptions, such a program would
most certainly be subject to what Jerry Pournelle calls
the Law of Costs and Schedules—"Everything takes
longer and costs more."

The second basic reason why I have not included
on preceding pages the type of space colonies proposed by O'Neill is that I expect robotic systems to be
developed to the performance capabilities described
in Chapter Six within the next 20 to 30 years. *There is
no historical record of large numbers of people mi-
grating to any terrestrial site where they cannot perform productive economic functions.* Millions of people will not go to space colonies during the first three
decades of Century 21 if advanced robotic systems

can perform work functions at a much lower cost than humans.

Stanford University's Hans Moravec, who is in the forefront of artificial intelligence R&D, has independently reached the same conclusion regarding space colonies in the foreseeable future. He observes: "As soon as machines are able to match human performance, the economics against human colonies become very persuasive. Just as it was much cheaper to send Pioneer to Jupiter and Viking to Mars than men to the Moon, so it will be cheaper to build orbiting power stations with robot rather than human labor. A machine can be designed to live in free space and "love" it, drinking in unattenuated sunlight and tolerating hard radiation. And instead of expensive pressurized, gravitied, decorated human colonies, the machines could be put to work converting lunar material into orbiting automatic factories. The doubling time for a machine society of this type would be much shorter than for human habitats, and the productive capability would expand correspondingly faster.

"The first societies in space will be composed of cooperating humans and machines, but as the capabilities of the self-improving machine component grow, the human portion will function more and more as a parasitic drag. Communities with a higher ratio of machines to people will be able to expand faster, and will become the bulk of the intelligent activity in the solar system. In the long run the sheer physical inability of humans to keep up with these rapidly evolving progeny of our minds will ensure that the ratio of people to machines approaches zero."[4]

Consequently, the only way to economically process raw materials and produce goods at work settlements is likely to be through a high level of robotics; there will be need for only a comparatively few people. The automata visualized by Moravec and myself will not require gaseous nitrogen.

Within the next fifty years or so it is quite possible that we will have the capability of constructing huge space habitats that could accommodate thousands of "tenants." However, large numbers of humans in these space settlements would be just as non-productive—and much more expensive to maintain—than an equivalent number of passengers on a luxury liner.

Perhaps the most influential of the "panacea books" have been written by forecasting teams at the Hudson Institute, headed by the brilliant but controversial Herman Kahn. His panacea permitting a utopian future is simply "continuing and sustained economic growth." Kahn has presented data in support of this proposition in a series of co-authored books on the future; the most recent is *The Next 200 Years*.[5] In it, the Hudson forecasters predict that economic growth without significant modification will permit a population of 15 to 30 billion humans to enjoy an exceedingly high standard of living here on Earth!

Kahn assumes that his utopia could be realized without the contributions of space industrialization and utilization of extraterrestrial resources visualized by G. Harry Stine in *The Third Industrial Revolution* (now an Ace paperback).

The Next 200 Years is characterized by unreserved optimism, and its authors contend that the "problem" and "crisis" components of the Megacrisis are not as severe as described in the doomsday books. My most severe criticism of this book is that it tends to overlook certain adverse feedback effects of continued population growth. For example, rapidly expanding populations build suburbs and new cities on prime farmland, removing it from agricultural use. Strip mining of land for raw materials required by multiplying hordes of people can also have an adverse impact on food production. This pattern is painfully evident to me as a long-time resident of the San Fernando valley which has had a twenty fold population increase in the past 40 years. I can see three lemon trees in my backyard, reminding me that this lot was part of a citrus grove not too many years ago.

Anyone who attempts a disciplined study of the future has biases or preferences which amount to the same thing. Therefore, every published long-term forecast is based on a mixture of value judgments, ideological beliefs and quantitative facts. And an excess of ideological zeal causes many descriptions of the future to read as if the text contained an assured vision of the real world of tomorrow. I agree with Herman Kahn that the prognostications of many establishment writers and futurists are simply statements of what the authors want to happen (masquerading as descriptive) not necessarily what they think will happen. Frequently such forecasts are a thinly disguised pitch for some express policy or program. If done openly and honestly this is a perfectly valid method of political advocacy, but the reader should always be made aware of the author's biases.

It is common strategy, of course for every interest group to argue that it is the beholder of truth, while

competitive groups are blinded by error. Representatives of such interest groups who deny or attempt to
disguise their biases are seriously damaging the
credibility of the emerging field of future studies.
Herman Kahn makes no attempt to hide ideological bias and preference. However, anyone who
has known him for many years can wonder how
much his basic long-term scenario—in its present in-
carnation on the pages of *The Next 200 Years*—reflects
his own objective reasoning and to what extent it may
unconsciously reflect his intuitive dislike for doomsday forecasts (especially the Club of Rome-sponsored
Limits to Growth[6]).

THE TECHNOPHILIC-MALTHUSIAN PERSPECTIVE

The book you are holding was written from a
technophilic-Malthusian perspective. To comprehend
the meaning of this term, we must take a brief diversion into semantics. Persons concerned with the serious study of the future are called "futurists." Extremely pessimistic futurists are frequently called
"catastrophists." Their intellectual adversaries whose
forecasts are exceptionally optimistic are frequently
called "cornucopians." The disciplined study of the
future where forecasts are not part of a fictional story
is now called "futuristics."

To understand books about the future in general,
and *Your Next Fifty Years* in particular, you should
be aware that contemporary futuristics is, in reality,
divided into at least three major schools of thought—
different perspectives of human destiny. Only the use
of precise terms can allow these alternate predictive

viewpoints to be properly understood, and the words "catastrophists" and "cornucopian" are not accurate or semantically precise in defining a person's perspective of the long-term future.

The two subjects of paramount importance in the mind of any futurist are (1) science with its successive R&D phases, and, most important of all, (2) the future impact of population growth.

A person's attitude towards science and the related development of various technologies is fundamental in determining the long-range perspective of what the future will be, or through wise selection of policies, what our future can be. The *technophobic* viewpoint holds that science and technology are inherently bad, and that "progress" is the cause of almost all of our troubles. The *technophilic* viewpoint holds that science and most forms of technology are inherently good, and that accelerated R&D can help us in finding solutions to most of our contemporary problems.

In recent years scientists have been cast suddenly in the role of villains in the emotional drama of a nation frustrated by an unpopular war, pollution, and the Pandoran gift to mankind of nuclear technology. A wave of antiscientism became epidemic among intellectuals in the United States and Western Europe. At its emotional extreme, some authors (and futurists) who range from the mystic to the nihilistic, have elaborated a whole new demonology of science and technology. Their basic problem is that they do not understand science or the R&D process, which is not, as some would have us believe, a qualitative leap into an invidious Pandora's Box.

Our species is at a critical transition point in its history on this planet. To fear the consequences of

further knowledge—and thus decide to halt further research—would be the surest road to a non-solution of
our problems, and thus to disaster. We do not begin to
know all that we need to know and that is the reason
antiscientism poses such an ominous threat.

I can firmly answer the Apostles of antiscientism:
science by its nature and structure can offer society
only options. Science is the application of thought
processes to the natural and symbolic world. It is a
synthesis of knowledge which discovers things about
nature and invents ways to manipulate it through an
increasingly reliable understanding of natural
phenomena—a continuum encompassing basic research, applied research and technology development.

The purpose of basic research, or pure science, is to
enlarge man's knowledge of physical phenomena,
biological processes, and the human mind. It involves
the synthesis of hypothesis, theory and observation.
Basic research delves into the hidden corners of nature for the sake of knowledge alone, without primary concern for practical applications that may
come with time.

Applied research is the stage where known principles and useful applications can be clearly foreseen.
It is the deliberate invention and innovation stage. Applied research has definable and limited goals. Detailed control of R&D should be concerned with foreseeable problems related to applied research programs, not basic scientific investigation.

The third stage is technological development,
which relies on analytical engineering and economics to determine whether it is presently possible to
build something within certain financial limitations.

It is this final stage of the R&D process which is the source of misunderstanding on the part of many who do not fully comprehend what science is all about, and this confusion is the major cause of antiscientism. In the public eye, technology development is too often taken for science and the man who designs a supersonic transport too easily called a scientist. Responsible scientists should not be castigated for the sins of engineers afflicted with tunnel vision.

The other fundamental factor in the long-range perspective is a person's basic attitude towards continued population growth. Those futurists who are *pronatalist* believe the continued population growth for the next century or so, will not be a critical problem. The ancient religious dogmas that population growth is the "will of God," and that "God will provide," are surprisingly strong today and still have an influence on politicians.

Futurists who are *antinatalist* believe, for the most part, that an excessive rate of population growth is the greatest problem in the world today and the basic cause of our global Megacrisis.

Consequently, the various futurists and others who are attempting to influence the public through the printed page or forms of electronic media can now be divided into four camps based on their convictions relative to these two fundamental factors. These camps are: technophobic-antinatalist, technophobic-pronatalist, technophilic-antinatalist and technophilic-pronatalist. The catastrophists are essentially technophobic-antinatalists, and the cornucopian futurists are technophilic-pronatalists.

Very few people have a technophobic-pronatalist long-term perspective. For all practical purposes it can be dismissed at this time because it is not likely to be an important policy camp.

There are, however, many respected futurists, conservationists and leading scientists who have a technophilic-antinatalist perspective of long-term trends and ameliorative options. But they are not against children as such, especially their own, and consequently, the word "antinatalist" may tend to be somewhat misleading; I believe that these individuals might better be called *technophilic-Malthusians.*

The technophilic-Malthusian perspective is not strictly "Malthusian" in the usual food-shortage sense. Instead, the population dilemma is foreseen as a pattern of adverse feedback relationships caused by severe crowding and wilderness destruction (contact with the wilderness viewed as a "necessity" programmed into our genes by millions of years of evolution). They agree with Austrian Nobel laureate Konrad Lorenz that "overpopulation is really the root of all evil." Lorenz's fear is not that our planet will run out of food. Rather he believes that as man runs out of *Lebensraum,* he will give way to uncontrolled aggression, just as experimental rats do in an overcrowded environment. Lorenz's conclusion are based on his pioneering research in ethology (how animals behave in the wild).

The demographic problem, therefore, is not simply one of supplying a huge population with food for a century or two, but of maintaining all of the other environmental parameters (mental, physical, biological and ecological) necessary for the continuous survival of our species.

The faith of the technophilic-pronatalist cornucopians is a fantasy—a delusion perpetuated by seeing only the promise of science and refusing to recognize its warnings, among them the admonition that since men themselves are biological entities ultimately dependent on our terrestrial biosphere for their own ultimate salvation, they must exist in harmony and live in equity with it.

THE PRINCIPLE OF OPTIMIZATION

There is one vital factor that makes the technophilic-Malthusian perspective unique among alternate approaches to long-term forecasting. It is based on the *Principle of Optimization* which can be viewed as a fundamental law of nature. This principle may permit futuristics to be gradually transformed from an intuitive art into a science—a science at least as accurate as contemporary economics. The Principle of Optimization serves as a foundation in understanding the natural limits to all phenomena and such knowledge may hold the key to man's ability to sustain technological civilization long enough to create a utopian world.

The Principle of Optimization can be defined in 117 words:

There is an optimum size or quantity for anything when it is subject to certain environmental influences and must continue to function within the constraints imposed by this same set of environmental influences. The "optimum size or quantity" is subject to change if one or more of the environmental parameters is altered. "Anything" can be a living or nonliving entity. "Anything" can also be the size of a population of living or nonliving entities. "Anything" can even be

a way of life—a "life style" or pattern of living. For some functions the principle applies to the shape or configuration of an entity. It can also apply to the internal organization of components or subsystems within an entity.

To fully grasp the far-reaching implications of the Principle of Optimization, you should read the supplementary data in Appendix A (page 307 to 331). This information is vitally important because it permits the reader to understand a natural law that is every bit as real—in its impact on all living creatures —as Newton's laws of gravitation or the Second Law of Thermodynamics.

If a forecaster uses the technophilic-Malthusian perspective based on the Principle of Optimization as a predictive tool, he can then place the spectrum of long-term alternate futures into three basic categories. First there is the "dystopian tomorrow" in which a prolonged Malthusian crisis compounded by severe depletion of essential raw materials culminates in global thermonuclear war followed by the collapse of civilization. In this scenario antiscientism becomes a sufficiently strong force in the world to prevent the ameliorative options of R&D to be available to society. The necessary reforms are not taken in time.

The second scenario category can be called the "muddling-through tomorrow." Here a minimum level of ameliorative reforms are taken to prevent complete collapse, but not on a sufficient scale or early enough date to prevent serious deterioration in the quality of life. Eventually a huge population would experience a bleak day-to-day life due to overcrowding, severe shortages of every kind and the loss of freedoms enjoyed today. An argument can be made that some form of muddling-through tomorrow is the most likely future if present trends are not significantly modified.

The third scenario category is the "utopian tomorrow." Essentially it is the alternate future described in this book. This utopian tomorrow is one of the most optimistic long-term scenarios of the next half century that I believe to be possible—but there are two reasons why it is also most likely to be the wave of the future.

First, the foreseeable impact of population growth must be analyzed from a technophilic-Malthusian perspective.

When the population density in an area reaches a certain point, there is a sort of "critical mass" effect in which the costs of environmental cleanup begins to escalate rapidly. At this point, certain public-service-functions in local ecosystems have simply been overwhelmed; what nature provided at no cost man must thereafter provide at considerable cost (see page 68).

Replacing public-service-functions with various forms of technology requires energy, and as population growth causes the destruction of additional natural public-service-functions, vast quantities of energy will be required (a process which, in turn, can cause the loss of other public-service-functions). Since energy costs are almost certain to escalate during the next two or three decades, the point will be reached where it is likely to be economically prohibitive to substitute technology for lost public-service-functions in some regions, and that would cause localized ecological collapse. This is the principal reason why technophilic-Malthusians believe that the present population already exceeds the optimum level for our planet.

The degree of overpopulation and the severity of

localized ecological damage exhibit wide variations from country to country and even between regions within the larger nations. As a result of this pattern, most nations are now net food-importers, and only the United States, Canada and Australia remain major grain exporters. The global realities now perceived by technophilic-Malthusians will become painfully apparent to all when climatic disasters strike several of the world's major food producing regions during the same year—certain to happen sooner or later. This foreseeable period of catastrophic food shortfalls is likely to occur sometime after 1990.

When this agricultural catastrophe strikes, there will not be one global Malthusian crisis with hardship and starvation more or less uniformally distributed. Instead, I foresee a pattern of "islands of Malthusian crises" coexisting in a world where many countries are enjoying unprecedented prosperity and rapid technological advancement. A preview of this pattern (on a relatively small scale) could be seen during the past few years. The limited quantity of food available for international transfer will go to nations exporting oil or other vital products.

In some cases there may be a Malthusian crisis in one part of a country coexisting with prosperity in other regions. For example, southern Brazil has experienced explosive economic growth in the past twelve years—while about 35 million people who live in the drought region of northeastern Brazil are subject to severe food shortages and chronic malnutrition. Soybeans from southern Brazil go to Japan, not to its own northeast provinces where diets are protein-deficient.

Localized Malthusian crises in 4th world countries

during the 1990-2010 time period will not follow the scenario in which these nations try to use crude fission weapons to blackmail the developed nations into a massive transfer of food-aid or other forms of wealth. In almost every case each Malthusian-island nation will become a military dictatorship, and comparatively modest bribes to the generals along with food shipments to one or two key cities will be sufficient to "keep the lid on" while the countryside starves (a pattern that can be seen in some nations today).

Let me emphasize the fact that I personally find the preceding forecast to be *extremely* discomforting, and I experience mental trauma while writing about famines. But in analyzing the probable outcome of contemporary demographic trends, it is the only predictive scenario that can presently be made from a technophilic-Malthusian perspective of the next 20 to 30 years. Technophilic-Malthusians share the humanistic values that characterize most futurists, but we believe that "thinking about the unthinkable" today could reduce the level of human suffering during the next few decades. The fact that a nuclear holocaust has been avoided may, in part, be due to the fact that so much disciplined thought has been given to the subject.

The anticipated islands of Malthusian crisis can be seen today in such Malthusian-island nations as Bangladesh and Haiti. The possible size and location of future Malthusian-island regions will be foreseeable as futuristics based on the Principle of Optimization becomes a more precise discipline. And such predictive futuristics may allow us to take some steps that will reduce the magnitude of human suffering when the time of catastrophic food shortfalls arrives.

I recognize the fact that my predicted pattern of islands of Malthusian crises might be averted if everyone started to do all of the right things today. Effective disarmament, massive ecological and agricultural reforms on a global scale, an optimum pattern of fertility-control measures adopted by all nations—but do you really believe that these necessary actions will occur in the near future? *The technophilic-Malthusians recognize that the major causes of the critical problems they foresee are cultural, ideological, organizational, managerial and educational rather than technological (in the sense that "technology can't provide solutions").* The time factor is vital, and the energy-use behavior of Americans since the 1973 oil cutoff does not indicate that necessary reforms to less visible problems will be taken in time.

Time is perhaps the key factor in understanding the validity of the technophilic-Malthusian perspective. Even if an optimum strategy to deal with the diverse components of the Megacrisis is quickly adopted, decades will pass before each of its goals can be realized. We are all incarcerated in the prison of time. No one escapes its limitations. Neither king nor beggar is immune, and the same holds for cornucopian and catastrophist. *Time is the tyrant of us all.*

In this book the catastrophic food shortfalls occur in the early 1990s, as described in Chapter Four. The Malthusian tragedy could occur sooner or later than predicted herein, and the magnitude of suffering might be different measured as a total loss of human lives. But any such event, regardless of variations, would have essentially the same historic impact on tomorrow's world.

Paradoxically, the predicted famines may be an essential step leading to a utopian future. Living through such a Malthusian tragedy would force almost all government leaders and other influential persons to recognize the fact that effective reforms controlling population MUST be implemented. Events comparable to Chapter Four would cause the fundamental barrier to fertility-control to be overcome.

Genesis 1:28: "Be fruitful and multiply, and replenish the Earth, and subdue it." These words along with comparable religious dogma dating back to ancient times are the fundamental barrier to restraining population growth. James Patrick Baen observes: "In every age the myths and legends—or sacred truths, if you prefer—of times past must be reinterpreted in the light of new knowledge and beliefs if they are to remain meaningful for the men and women of that new age."[7] I believe that events such as those outlined in Chapter Four will cause religious dogma to be reinterpreted so that fertility-control is encouraged. The leaders of surviving religions will recognize the truth of Baen's words when he says that "overpopulation is our greatest danger," and "if we double this planet's population just one more time we may not be able to *afford* the technological/economic effort required to get into space" (on the scale of Stine's Third Industrial Revolution).

The other reason why I believe a utopian tomorrow is our probable future is that the malignant antiscientism that was so prevalent during recent years appears to be declining. Antiscientism is a perverse, unnatural state of mind. When it ceases to influence public policy, we can anticipate a science/technology renewal involving a vast expansion of R&D, a shift of research priorities to emphasize the development of non-polluting energy, systems providing maximum durability with minimum repairs and favoring recycling, biological control over insect pests, and countless other advances that will improve the quality of life without adverse ecological disruption.

This book is a preview of a utopian world based on the Principle of Optimization—a utopia that could be your tomorrow within fifty years. Micropolis, optimized transportation systems, Methuselan lifespans and every other part of my forecast already exist at some stage of R&D process. In almost every case the time period in which these desirable components of utopia could be realized would be accelerated if R&D restraints were not budgetary, but arose solely from the limitations imposed by the lack of qualified people to work on worthwhile projects.

Neither science fiction nor popularized science, this book represents a new genre—a new class of literature that could be identified as "Anticipatory Evolution." Hopefully it entertains and informs, but my primary purpose is to stimulate the reader into supporting those actions and reforms that lead to utopia. Technological Shangri-La will be your tomorrow if enough people realize that the Principle of Optimization is the essential catalyst allowing us to *design the future,* to be the masters of events instead of their victims.

I leave it to each reader to decide to what extent he or she can play a role in making desirable possibilities available at the earliest possible date. For those who contemplate taking some action, their first step might be to read articles and books by other writers whose long-term goals for humanity are essentially the same as my own.

Isaac Asimov and Arthur C. Clarke are the best known futurists whose publications and speeches follow a consistent technophilic-Malthusian perspective. Other technophilic-Malthusian authors of books on the future include Harrison Brown, Dennis Gabor, Bruce C. Murray, Neil P. Ruzic and G. Harry Stine. Sir George Thomson, author of *The Foreseeable Future,* was very much a technophilic-Malthusian, and the same is true of many other Nobel laureates in science including Dennis Gabor, Konrad Lorenz, John H. Northrop, Linus C. Pauling, Robert S. Mulliken, etc.

My good friend Jerry Pournelle occupies a somewhat perplexing position relative to the future. We agree on every issue of substance except population growth. His pronatalists sentiments cause him to believe that "population always declines with increasing wealth." Pournelle, however, has mounted an exceptionally effective attack on antiscientism. His books and science fact articles in support of a space/science renaissance are highly recommended as a rich source of intellectual ammunition. I especially recommend *A Step Farther Out* (an Ace book).

Anticipatory Evolution would allow us to design the future so that we arrive at Technological Shangri-La in the shortest possible time. This could be accomplished by *futurian intellectuals* who are able to mobilize support for the requisite reforms and R&D funding.

I define an intellectual as "a person who meditates upon problems that are not of direct or immediate concern to him, and also has the ability to understand the significant parameters of ill-structured or abstract subjects." This definition has no relationship to left-of-center political sympathies. A futurian intellectual would know that money spent today on basic research is not likely to be of near-term benefit to him, but such expenditures are essential if long-term goals are to be realized. The futurian intellectual would support efforts to eliminate waste in government spending so that the money thereby saved could be diverted to science/technology renewal and other technophilic-Malthusian goals.

Perhaps *Destinies,* the new SF and speculative fact magazine, may in time serve as a forum for those readers who desire some degree of active participation as futurian intellectuals. Letters sent to *Destinies* at Ace Books, 360 Park Avenue South, New York, N.Y. 10010 can be forwarded to me.

This book is restricted to the next fifty years because there is a practical limit to the time frame of technological forecasts and other projections. Since we cannot predict the future sharply, one can only make an estimate, and that estimate will cover a range of possibilities. The farther into the future we look, the more likely our technological projections are to be wrong because of scientific breakthroughs, which are unpredictable.

The forecaster confronts no major constraints worth mentioning other than the laws of nature. The only way to predict the unpredictable is to make an educated guess about some conceivable change in our understanding of natural laws. If too many such guesses are included, a broad forecast will probably have little resemblance to future reality. Because of this predictive barrier, fifty years is about the maximum time frame in which reasonably accurate projections can be made of society. A review of older SF books and non-fiction forecasts supports this conclusion.

Any writer who sets out to predict future political changes is obviously attempting the impossible. This fact suddenly became a frustrating dilemma when I realized that the contents of pages 95 to 98 required that the outcome of the Iranian revolution be predicted. In early 1978, the Shah's government appeared to be stable and was so described in all our government's intelligence documents. Iran presents a pattern of bewildering chaos as last-minute changes in this book are made in January 1979.

Will the government of Iran in 1994 be some form of authoritarian Islamic republic, military dictatorship, Marxist dictatorship or constitutional monarchy? These appear to be the most likely possibilities, but the Iranian government could evolve into some totally unexpected pattern that cannot be described today. After several discussions of this dilemma, my editor, Jim Baen, and I decided to make an arbitrary choice since we knew of no way to determine the probable outcome of events in Iran. (I personally fear that a military dictatorship may be the reality of the 1980's in Iran.) A restoration of the monarchy by the Iranian army supported by a disillusioned populace is not a complete impossibility. A constitutional monarchy under Reza II (son of the present Shah) might provide people of Iran with a greater degree of freedom than alternatives mentioned above. But on this subject one can only guess, not make a firm prediction on the outcome of a very strange and unique revolution.

The most frequent error in SF stories set in the long-term future is to have progress restricted to one or two fields. Faster-than-light spaceships have crews who live 70 to 80 years manning controls that are no more sophisticated than those in a Boeing 747. If we do not enter a new Dark Age, the future will be a synthesis of major advances/breakthroughs throughout the entire spectrum of the biological and physical sciences. Our long-term tomorrow will be an interface between ultraintelligent machines, Methuselan lifespans, genetic engineering, the resources of a Solar System-wide society, knowledge from other sentient beings in our galaxy, and scientific capabilities that today would seem to be magic. Robert A. Heinlein is one of a handful of SF authors whose stories are structured around the premise that progress will occur simultaneously in all fields.

Before concluding, I must warn you about one exceptionally dangerous illusion concerning population growth. It is the belief that this underlying cause of the Megacrisis can be resolved "painlessly" simply through increased wealth in developing countries.

The technophilic-pronatalists believe that the population problem will be solved by "demographic transition," which is the theory that birthrates automatically decline as the per capita standard of living in a nation rises. This was the historic pattern that occurred in the United States, Europe and Japan. Technophilic-Malthusians doubt the validity of this unproven theory because the birthrate reduction that the demographic transition theory would cause one to expect has not occurred in Mexico, Brazil, the Islamic oildoms, certain African nations and in other places where there have been dramatic increases in economic wealth during the past 10 to 20 years. Mexico, for example, has enjoyed the highest rate of extended economic growth of any of the Latin American nations. But its annual rate of population growth is presently estimated to be 3.4 percent. The population of Mexico, only 20 million as recently as 1940 now exceeds 64 million, and that total does not include approximately ten million Mexicans who have moved to the United States during the past four decades. By the year 2000, Mexico may pass the 100 million point.

Recent studies indicate that, because of diverse religious and cultural influences, the demographic transition will not occur in many nations, or it will not take place in a short enough timespan to avert disaster.[8],[9] Consequently, more direct forms of fertility-control will be necessary—measures that will test the strength of our political institutions.

In my mind's eye there is an image of a future world in which my grandchildren are legally restricted to being the parents of no more than two children —fertility coercion thereby allowing society to expand every other form of freedom. This would seem to me to be a world far preferable to one in which there is no fertility coercion, but patterns of crowding, rationing and Orwellian governmental control have reduced "liberty" and "freedom" to meaningless terms —a world in which the wilderness and almost all non-human species have been destroyed.

Solving the population-growth crisis is the conquest of time for *homo sapiens*, for it will allow our descendents to survive for countless eons. When the realization of our demographic goals is within sight, we can begin to consider ourselves members of an intelligent species.

Man is the master of his own destiny. If he learns successfully to forecast his future problems and options, then he is more likely to take the timely steps that will eventually solve them, and our civilization would then be assured of a glorious future. By successfully developing Technological Shangri-La based on the Principle of Optimization, man can achieve his most ambitious dreams, control extra-terrestrial resources, discover all the secrets of nature, communicate with and travel to civilizations on planets circling distant stars, eliminate disease and old age, and alter the heredity of his genes to remake himself in patterns of strength and beauty. Most important of all, man may improve his brain and mental powers until he is capable of creating a culture that transcends our limited imaginations. The universal men and women of Technological Shangri-La would have an unlimited scope of thought, and the endless quest of pure science will open the door to infinite progress coupled with exotic new horizons.

APPENDIX A
THE PRINCIPLE OF OPTIMIZATION

Knowledge gives man the power to alter favorably his world. Only the refinement of scientific knowledge will allow energy shortages and the related problem of the Megacrisis to be solved. While the development of modern technology is based on scientific principles, its applications tend to follow a hit-or-miss pattern which has caused adverse changes in Terra's biosphere. Our basic problem may be the fact that we have not yet recognized a fundamental scientific principle that governs the behavior of life on any planet— a unifying principle that is the key to all of the ameliorative technologies and reforms described in this book.

The British Nobel laureate, Sir George Thomson (1892-1975) recognized that future progress must be based on a complete understanding of the restrictions imposed by scientific principles. He was a physicist with an encyclopedic knowledge of many disciplines supplemented by a lively imagination. His 1955 book,

The Foreseeable Future remains a work of stunning brilliance offering insight into the favorable options open to humanity through selective refinement made possible by science. In making future projections, he observed: "It is because major discoveries are likely to be based on scientific principles rather than on mechanical ingenuity, and because these principles have limitations, that it is reasonable to hope to be able to predict in a general way the trend which these discoveries will have. For this reason it may not be too rash to regard certain kinds of technical progress as foreseeable, though one will certainly miss a great deal."[1]

(NOTE: most of the words below, set in quotation marks, are taken from the first chapter of *The Foreseeable Future.*)

Sir George pointed out that scientific principles are frequently "principles of impotence." They say that certain things *cannot* be done, but they do not say that everything else *can,* for that would imply that there are no more fundamental principles to discover. From the discoveries of the past 300 years, Sir George identified eight principles based on our current understanding of the laws of nature which can aptly be called "principles of impotence." They are:

1. "No material object and no signal can go faster than the velocity of light." Einstein's theory of relativity, however, does not exclude the possibility of faster-than-light particles; it only excludes the possibility of particles moving at that speed. In 1967, Gerald Feinberg of Columbia University suggested that faster-than-light particles called "tachyons" might exist without violating our con-

cepts of nature. Tachyons remain hypothetical. If their existence is confirmed, then our first principle of impotence will have to be changed to: "No object or signal that goes slower than the speed of light can exceed the velocity of light, and no object or signal that goes faster than the speed of light can move at the velocity of light or at a speed slower than the velocity of light."

2. The conservation of mass and energy. "Mass is conserved if, and only if, energy is conserved also in the region of space considered; and conversely that energy is conserved if matter is conserved, but that mass may be changed into energy and vice versa at a constant rate of exchange." Nuclear weapons demonstrate the conversion of a very small amount of mass into a very large amount of energy.

3. Newton's Third Law of Motion—the conservation of momentum: Action and reaction are equal and opposite. "The background momentum (speed times mass) of a gun just after it is fired is equal to the forward momentum of the shot." I have suggested the possibility that hypothetical particles called "inertons" might answer some unexplained natural phenomena. If inertons are part of the reality of our universe, then Newton's Third Law of Motion—as a principle of impotence— would be modified.[2]

4. "One cannot make an electric charge, or a magnetic pole, without making an equal one of the opposite sign somewhere else. In the case of magnetism this 'somewhere else' has to be another

part of the same body, and there the pole must remain; but the electric charges, though created together, can be separated at will." In August 1975, four scientists reported the discovery of a "magnetic monopole," an elementary particle of magnetism whose existence would mean that magnetic charges need not be inseparable north and south poles on the same body. The monopole would be the smallest possible unit of magnetic charge—the magnetic equivalent to the positive protron or negative electron that exist independently in nature. Other scientists, however, have not been able to confirm this presumed monopole discovery, and the possible existence of magnetic monopoles remains an extremely controversial subject.[3]

5. Principle number five is difficult to express, but . . . "speaking very roughly it states the impossibility of making an accurate survey of a particle, or set of particles, of atomic or subatomic sizes. An attempt to measure accurately where the particle is, produces an unforeseeable disturbance in its velocity, so that whatever this may have been before is now uncertain. Conversely the velocity can only be measured accurately when the position is uncertain. This is known as Heisenberg's 'uncertainty principle.' It seems to be absolutely fundamental in the world and has consequences for the philosophy of physics more far-reaching than one might at first expect. It has obliged physicists to reconsider their ideas of cause and effect and of determinism, with consequences which are still the subject of discussion." (The social im-

plications of this principle of impotence are mentioned on pages 325 and 326.)

6. Pauli's exclusion principle which ".. . can be regarded as a kind of special force operating between two or more particles of the same kind to keep them out of one another's way."

7. The "second law of thermodynamics" or alternately the "law of entropy." This principle is very important to ecology and differs from all the others in that it only applies where large numbers of objects are concerned and in this sense is less absolute. "In essence it is the principle of chaos (if that is not a contradiction in terms): it insists that order always tends to disappear till complete chaos is reached—a chaos which paradoxically enough is amendable to (nearly) precise mathematical treatment, as was shown by Maxwell in the case of a gas regarded as a collection of a vast number of particles moving at random." R. Buckminster Fuller has arrived at a relatively new interpretation of this seventh principle of impotence which indicates that there is nothing in the laws of thermodynamics that makes ecological disaster inevitable.[4]

If any principle of impotence is added or discarded, or even radically changed, the unforeseen—and a new scientific era—will be upon us. For example, confirmation of the discovery of the magnetic monopole could revolutionize the field of electronics and have a major long-term impact on the energy crisis. Controlled monopoles would allow new sources of energy, extremely small and efficient motors and generators, and particle accelerators of much higher energy than any yet built. Other applications would include new medical therapies in the fight against cancer.

It should be emphasized that these principles remain basically unchanged 24 years after publication of *The Foreseeable Future*. Tachyons and inertons have not been discovered, and the magnetic monopole remains in the limbo of scientific conjecture. If none of these particles really exist, then the presently understood restrictions of principles 1, 3 and 4 are likely to govern the technology of our civilization for an exceedingly long span of years.

Sir George Thomson acknowledged that one or more of the first seven principles may be subject to modification in the future. His only caveat was that "fundamental discoveries cannot be predicted." One can predict, however, that fundamental discoveries of very great importance are likely to be made. In recent years astronomers have discovered mysterious objects called quasars whose apparent behavior has not been satisfactorily explained within our present understanding of the laws of nature. Hypothetical astronomical objects called "black holes" present even greater theoretical contradictions. Satisfactory explanations for such phenomena may require an insight into natural mechanisms that will have a significant impact in the practical affairs of man.

One can find another fundamental principle (our eighth principle of impotence) by taking a very broad view of many different physical and biological phenomena. Sir George observed ... "There is one feature of the world we live in which is so general and so universal that it seems to have escaped proper notice. For want of a better name I will call it the *'principle of mass production.'* It is the tendency which nature shows to repeat almost indefinitely each entity it makes. This is most obvious among the smallest of objects. There are about enough atoms in the ink that makes one letter of this sentence to provide not only one for every inhabitant of the earth, but one for every creature if each star in our galaxy had a planet as populous as the earth ... Examples come from both animate and inanimate nature. Drops of rain, grains of sand, particles of smoke, bacteria, the cells of any piece of apparently homogenous organic tissue, in every case though there may be a large variety of distinguishable kinds, each kind exists in numbers which even the cold mathematician must describe as considerable and which to the ordinary person are incalculably immense."

The principle of mass production is seen everywhere in the living world. Biological reproduction of all creatures from the simplest virus to the largest whale is based on this principle. It can even be cited as the cause of our most serious problem, the human population explosion. On a cosmic scale there are countless numbers of each kind of star which are members of countless galaxies. It forms the economic basis of any advanced industrial society. Sir George concluded that this principle "... is one of the fundamentals of the world which further discovery will not alter. Atomicity in its wildest sense, mass production by nature, is the deepest of scientific truths."

These eight "principles of impotence" form a foundation for the science and technology that has allowed human society to evolve to its present state. An understanding of these secrets of nature has permitted achievements that would have been multiple miracles to our ancestors—nuclear power, chemical engines operating at very high efficiency, speed-of-light transmission from the Moon's surface, rapid air transport and labor saving machines permitting a high standard of living. But something must be missing. Something is seriously wrong. The miracles of science have not ushered in a golden age. Instead they have contributed to the interrelated problems of energy shortages, pollution, damage to the biosphere and excess population which collectively comprise the Megacrisis, and present trends suggest that humanity could be heading towards a catastrophe far worse than the dark ages after the fall of Rome.

The critical factor that is missing may be lack of recognition of another fundamental constraint which is just as important as the other eight principles of impotence which tell us what we *cannot* do. Again let me emphasize that nature is strictly neutral, rewarding us when we operate within its rules, punishing us when we violate them. I believe that each segment of, and the energy & ecology crises in toto, can be traced to our failure to recognize this vital principle. The multiple problems of the Megacrisis threaten to overwhelm us because our present technological society has been developed on a knowledge base that lacks one essential component.

I propose that the *Principle of Optimization* be added to the eight fundamental principles that have been summarized by Sir George Thomson. Like the others it is based on our current understanding of the natural laws of the universe. Perhaps it has escaped our notice because this principle can only be fully understood when an industrial society grows to a cer-

tain critical mass on a finite planet. At this point
ecological problems spontaneously arise which cause
the seekers of reform to recognize this principle
which is at work in all the physical and biological
processes around us.

The Principle of Optimization is more subtle,
somewhat less tangible, than the others. Here we are
dealing with a natural phenomenon that does not
lend itself to the simple description or measurement
of Newton's Third Law of Motion, but it is in every
way an equally demonstrable part of the real world
in which we live. In the continuing quest for
ecological balance, scientists may find that it is one of
the deepest secrets of nature.

A brief summary of the Principle of Optimization:
**There is an optimum size or quantity for any-
thing when it is subject to certain environmental
influences and must continue to function within
the constraints imposed by this same set of environmental influences. The "optimum size or
quantity" is subject to change if one or more of
the environmental parameters is altered. "Anything" can be a living or nonliving entity. "Anything" can also be the size of a population of living or nonliving entities. "Anything" can even be
a way of life—a "life style" or pattern of living. For
some functions the principle applies to the
shape or configuration of an entity. It can also
apply to the internal organization of components or subsystems within an entity.**

Our ninth principle of impotence cuts across all
boundaries, influences all disciplines, indicates what
we cannot do. Basically it is a quantitative influence
stemming from both simple and extremely complex

interactions between the animate and the inanimate. In time it may be summarized in a mathematical formula, but like other valid laws its influence is presently subject to numerical measurement and confirmation. The first seven principles were discovered through investigation of phenomena in the physical sciences. All biological processes must conform to the principles of physics and chemistry but to date none apply only within living structures. Quite possibly some new discovery will present limitations that have no influence on nonliving entities. Many life processes, especially those governing mental functions in highly developed mammalian brains, are poorly understood and there may be some unique, even surprising, restrictions found as the secrets of life are unraveled.

The Principle of Optimization comes the closest to being primarily directed towards biological processes in that its discovery probably requires an advanced understanding of the way living entities interact with each other and the inanimate world. Like the principle of mass production it can be seen in nonliving relationships. Examples of measurable influence among biological entities, however, provide the most convincing proof that the Principle of Optimization is part of nature's grand design.

One of our most outstanding scientists, Johan Bjorksten, has observed that the Principle of Optimization is "... a logical corollary to Darwin's axiom of the survival of the *fittest*. Note, he did not say 'of the fit.' In using the superlative, he points to the very optimum for the combination of circumstances existing in each case. Therefore, the Principle of Optimization is operating in any system where natural selecti ɔn (natural competition) is allowed to take place. '5 Charles Darwin (1809-1882) was the first to explain the presence and function of what can now be recognized as the "Principle of Optimization" in our biosphere. There is an optimum size range for animals running on Terra's surface. Cheetahs can reach 70 m.p.h. speeds during very brief sprints, but four legged animals in the general size range of the horse enjoy the optimum size and configuration for sustained distance running. Here the environmental constraints are the force of Terra's gravity along with atmospheric density and the percentage of oxygen in the air. Elephants are much larger than horses but cannot run as fast because they are so massive that gravity restricts their speed. Given suitable oxygen, an elephant on Mars could perform like a racehorse. These same terrestrial parameters restrict the upper size of a land animal. Blue whales are so massive that their weight cannot be supported on land. The largest extinct dinosaurs are believed to have spent much of their time in buoyant marshes, rivers and lakes seldom venturing onto dry land.

Human performance in sports is governed by the Principle of Optimization. There is an optimum size and configuration for distance runners. Men too short do not have the speed. Those too tall are slowed by the same basic environmental influences that affect an elephant's speed. Boxing offers a similar example. A good middleweight cannot take on a good heavyweight. The best heavyweight champions weigh 200 to 220 pounds and are seldom over 6'2" in height. If mass and weight did not seriously compromise optimum agility, much taller men would frequently be heavyweight champions. Basketball presents a different set of environmental constraints and seven-foot-tall men can be champions.

Depending on its ecological niche, there is an optimum size range for birds. The hummingbird is too small to glide or travel great distances. The condor at 40 lbs. with a 12-foot wingspan is near the upper limit for flying. The restricting parameter is the wing and feather structure characteristic of birds. A terrestrial feathered bird the size of man could not fly here, but it could on the Moon if an artificial atmosphere were provided in a cave or surface dome. But some 70 million years ago there were man-sized flying reptiles called "peterosaurs" who had thin membrane wings somewhat similar to those of modern bats. This type of wing was a different environmental parameter, allowing a larger optimum size for these ponderous prehistoric predators.

Mammalian intelligence is governed by the Principle of Optimization. Very small species of monkeys are not as smart as German Shepherd dogs because their brains cannot contain a sufficient number of cerebral cells. Our present size is not an accident. Monkey-sized people would require enormous heads to contain enough cerebral cells to duplicate standard human intelligence. The optimum fighting agility of the heavyweight boxing champion demonstrates why we did not evolve into giants.

Scientists have determined that there is an optimum planet size for the evolution of advanced terrestrial-type forms of life. If a planet is too small, its gravity is insufficient to hold water vapor and a suitable atmosphere. Mars is a borderline case that may be too small to presently support native creatures larger than simple bacteria. Planets exceeding a certain size retain a massive atmosphere of light gases including hydrogen, and solar energy cannot reach any solid surface. All the oxygen would combine with the excessive quantity of hydrogen to form water which would prevent the evolution of an atmosphere containing free oxygen. These environmental constraints would not permit the existence of advanced terrestrial-type life forms. However, Jupiter and other massive planets might have forms of life significantly different from those in our own biosphere—creatures who had evolved within a different mix of chemical and physical parameters.

Our sun is in an optimum size range to support planets containing intelligent creatures. A star twice as massive would tend to burn itself out before advanced life forms could evolve on a suitable planet. A star half the size of our sun would have a long life, but its reduced energy output would be the negative environmental constraint. A planet too close to its sun is too hot for carbon-based life and a planet too distant cannot receive sufficient energy. The zone of life around the smaller star would be so narrow that it is exceedingly improbable that a terrestrial-type planet would be in that precise orbit. Venus, Terra and Mars are all within the sun's zone of terrestrial-type life.

Even on a cosmic scale the Principle of Optimization is dominant. From man's point of view, Terra has an optimum size and is in a suitable orbit around a star with an optimum mass. Our ninth principle of impotence can also be demonstrated at the microscopic and subatomic levels.

The Principle of Optimization can be seen in our daily life. Good mental and physical health requires a

precise nutritional intake which is subject to environmental influences including exercise, climatic temperatures and variations in metabolism. Too much
food can cause sluggish behavior; obesity can also
trigger certain degenerative diseases. Nutritional defi-
ciencies can stunt mental and physical development
in children. No task can be performed effectively if
one does not receive sufficient food.

Nutritional intake can be broken down into optimum quantities of protein, fats, carbohydrates, min-
erals and vitamins. Too much vitamin D can be toxic
but mammalian life is not possible without it. The
potential problems that can accompany excessive
cholesterol intake are well known, but some
cholesterol is necessary to form certain hormones.
Copper is an essential mineral. Excessively high copper blood levels are associated with cardiovascular
disease. Everywhere the "too much" or "too little"
quantity balance associated with our ninth principle
can be seen in proper nutrition.

Man does not live by bread alone. We also require
optimum quantities of exercise, work, recreation and
sleep. Insufficient sleep reduces the ability to concen-
trate and perform physical tasks requiring a certain
degree of dexterity. Too much sleep can be just as
disruptive and make a person feel listless and ir-
ritable. Good health requires an optimum amount of
exercise but no additional benefits are conferred
beyond a certain point. Some psychologists contend
that there are adverse personality changes in people
who do not perform some useful form of work. These
behavioral patterns appear to be remarkably similar
among both those on permanent relief and among
the idle rich. Too much work can also cause physical

and psychological problems.

The optimum quantity of recreation does not seem to be a subject that has been studied. Perhaps investigation will indicate that it has a subtle association with the amount of personal contact we have with our fellow man. Monkeys raised in complete isolation exhibit psychotic behavior. If monkeys are raised in a crowded environment where individuals cannot find some place for periodic solitude, most of them are psychotic. Understanding and measurement of optimum contact and privacy levels for humans are vitally important goals for behavioral scientists. They are likely to find that the Principle of Optimization can explain the high percentage levels of psychosis found in crowded cities versus the low levels associated with rural areas.

The porpoise has the optimum configuration for swimming through the water. Everywhere in the living world the ninth principle is at work. Frequently one must carefully study the environmental influences or constraints of the individual ecological niche occupied by each species before its influence can be fully appreciated.

The Principle of Optimization is the key factor influencing economic and technological parameters that can cause beneficial or deleterious changes in Terra's environment. If the specific entity is the automobile, then there must be an optimum size for both the vehicle and its engine. An optimum propulsion system can eliminate atmospheric and noise pollution. A car traveling too fast exceeds the safety margins determined by average manual control ability. If the speed is reduced below a certain point, one would be better off with a bicycle. Similar patterns apply to each man-made creation. The quality and quantity of all the different entities that actually improve our existence can be fitted into an optimum level of economic evolution and development.

The essential benefits of the car—mobility and convenience—can be obtained from small cars of optimum size. It is the excessive size and weight of large cars that intensifies our energy and pollution problems.

From an energy-use standpoint, there is an optimum speed at which one can travel in a vehicle. If you drive too slowly, power is exhausted on secondary functions (air conditioning, radio, coolant system for the engine, alternator, gear train, etc.); drive too fast, air resistance causes an excessive waste of fuel energy.

The English biologist J. B. S. Haldane (1892-1964) recognized that there is an optimum size for every animal and also for every human institution.[6] R. Philip Hammond of the Oak Ridge National Laboratory sees a similar pattern: "Every tool, every process, every industry and every social and political institution has an approximate size at which it functions most efficiently. There are jobs for which an abacus is superior to an electric computer, and a skiff better than a nuclear powered aircraft carrier, and vice versa ... The nature of a satisfactory solution to a problem often changes completely with the scale of the problem. Thus a village and a megapolis will have entirely different approaches to government, drinking water and waste control."[7]

Author and publisher Neil P. Ruzic has observed that there is an optimum size for magazines and other commercial ventures. He found that a magazine serving the R&D market requires ". . . an income of between $1-million and $1.5-million to seek and get the advertising it needs to survive, the circulation that is the proper (optimal) percentage of the research population, and to pay the editorial staff, etc."[8]

You don't find small steel mills and you don't find exceedingly large restaurants (large in terms of hundreds of millions of dollars per unit, such as a steel mill). Businesses, no less than stars and people, have optimum sizes because they are influenced by the constraints of the Principle of Optimization.

Reviewing the galaxy of problems causing the energy & ecology crises, one will soon conclude that the population size of living and nonliving entities is the area where the Principle of Optimization is most relevant. Too many cars in a major city reduces overall efficiency, diminishes the utility of any individual vehicle and causes rising adrenalin levels during frustrating traffic jams.

There is an optimum population level for each living species in its unique ecological niche. When man does not interfere, predators, disease and available food supply keep the numbers within proper bounds. But *homo sapiens* is also subject to all the laws of nature including our ninth principle of impotence. Failure to recognize this absolute truth is the most important cause of the interrelated dilemmas that comprise the Megacrisis. A continuation of present human population growth patterns is the most certain path to nuclear Armageddon.

The difficulty in understanding that there *must* be an optimum population size for our species is caused by the fact that the set of environmental influences has been constantly changing during the course of history. The horse and sailing vessel enabled aggressive men to migrate to new lands that were sparsely inhabited. Fire and clothing permitted survival in cold climates. Modern technology has expanded food production and resources at a rapid rate. Only during this century has man's ecological niche been fully extended over Terra's entire land surface. The very nature of an advanced technological society requires that recoverable quantities of almost all the natural elements be added to food supply as environmental parameters determining what the optimum population level may be. During the past twenty years we have begun to exceed the limits imposed by a planet-sized ecological niche. The sudden disappearance of land and mineral frontiers coincided with our failure to foresee the environmental consequences of certain forms of technological activity, and the energy & ecology crises seemed to appear without warning.

Physicist Donald G. Carpenter points out that there is another factor that has made recognition of the true dimensions of our population dilemma difficult for some people. A given number of entities—such as the population of humans in a finite area—do not remain perfectly optimized. They operate within a numerical region (influenced by many changing parameters) which contains within it the optimim point.

Put differently, from time to time there are limits on each side of this optimization point where the total size of the population must remain for society in that region to remain stable. Since parameters such as food supply constantly change due to cyclic fluctuations in other parameters (weather, cost of energy, etc.), exceeding the optimum point by too great a margin may not allow digressing members to survive. The reality of this pattern has been masked or hidden by food aid shipments during the past 32 years, but it will become painfully apparent when climatic disasters strike several of the world's major food producing regions during the same year—certain to happen sooner or later.

Farsighted scholars have been warning us of the dangers of explosive population growth and resource runout for several decades. Now their projections are being seriously evaluated in official circles. Perhaps it is the nature of our species that problems must reach a certain critical mass before they are officially recognized.

The nine principles of impotence are laws of nature, statements of the most fundamental form of reality for any technological civilization. Each of them *must* be recognized and fully accounted for in all plans and programs that will be adopted to meet our future needs for energy and a clean environment. Failure to recognize the sometimes subtle influence of any one of these nine principles can cause a faulty program to be implemented, a program which will have adverse side effects—energy solutions causing new pollution problems, etc.

Many of the problems of our contemporary society stem from the fact that social scientists do not recognize or understand the restrictions implied in certain laws of nature. For example, consider the implications of our fifth principle of impotence—the "uncertainty principle" of Werner Heisenberg (1902-1976). "It is impossible to specify exactly both the momentum and the position of any object, because measuing one of quantities automatically alters the other."

Since the very act of observing or measuring a phenomenon alters the behavior being studied, accurate measurement of certain forms of sociological data is impossible because the presence and data gathering functions of the sociologist changes the response of the subjects under study in much the same way that the orbit of a hydrogen electron would be altered by any particle used in an attempt to measure its orbital characteristics. This fact may explain the failure of many large-scale social programs which are usually based on small pilot sociological studies where accurate measurement is simply impossible (compounded by "wishful thinking" inputs on the part of the sociologist which frequently are stated as fact in the final study report).

Projections of social and human behavioral responses in the crisis areas of energy, pollution and population growth are, therefore, likely to be far less accurate than forecasts of our technological options. This is the reason Sir George Thomson restricted his 1955 book chiefly to the future of technology. At that time he concluded that "sociology has still to find its Newton, let alone its Plank, and prediction is guesswork."

It is in the crucial area of finding workable solutions to the dilemma of population growth that the comparative uncertainties in the social sciences may prove to be our greatest handicap in ameliorating the problems of the Megacrisis. But it is vitally important to recognize the fact that Heisenberg's uncertainty principle makes small-scale pilot programs of questionable utility in refining plans to reduce population growth in a large region or an entire nation. Once we recognize this limitation, then large-scale fertility-control programs can be structured so that they proceed on a step-by-step basis, with the results of each program constantly being measured by feedback data, thereby allowing the overall plan to be modified every two or three months. This approach, based on our fifth principle of impotence, is far more likely to produce successful results than a rigid "cast in concrete" program that might not be reviewed for several years.

Once we have adequate knowledge of all the parameters influencing problems like population growth, depletion of natural gas reserves or excessive energy use in a crowded city, then the Principle of Optimization can be used as a *predictive tool* in finding the optimum program for each specific problem. By "optimum" I mean the one that is likely to have the least number of adverse side effects.

What makes my approach to energy shortages and related problems of the Megacrisis unique, is that these principles of impotence can be used in a systematic selection process that should allow the greatest practical benefits from our R&D expenditures and large-scale investments of capital in new technologies. And in my approach, the three laws of ecology summarized below are equally important in this systematic selection process.

Our growing awareness of ecological realities has recently led to the recognition of several generalizations or dictums that are evident in scientific measurements of the biosphere. They can be listed as an informal set of "laws of ecology."

The noted environmental scientist, Barry Commoner of Washington University in St. Louis, is most closely associated with the First Law of Ecology: *everything is connected to everything else.* A similar concept was expressed by Naturalist John Muir more than 60 years ago: "When we try to pick out anything by itself, we find it hitched to everything else in the universe."[9]

Commoner's statement summarizes the fact that an ecosystem consists of multiple interconnected parts, each acting on or influencing one another to a greater or lesser degree.[10] Population growth, new industrial processes, the extraction of raw materials, power generation, and inputs from mechanized agriculture all influence each other in various feedback loops. DDT has been found in the tissues of Antarctic penguins. Local ecosystems are connected in a global network and a stress at any one site can be transmitted to distant vulnerable points. And even the entire biosphere is connected to extraterrestrial entities including solar energy from our sun, tidal changes caused by lunar gravity, along with other cosmic forces that we do not yet fully understand.

What I regard as the Second Law of Ecology is the statement frequently made by Garrett Hardin of the University of California at Santa Barbara: *we can never do merely one thing.* This Second Law is directly connected to Commoner's First Law. It simply means that any action will have side effects, frequently unexpected ones. When DDT was first used on a large scale, we did not suspect that it would cause birds to lay eggs with shells so thin that they would break before hatching. Dams built to produce electricity have created such unwanted side effects as an increase in insect-borne diseases, earthquakes caused by the weight of the water behind the dam, and the destruction of fisheries because of an altered flow of river nutrients.

This Second Law does not mean that such adverse side effects are inevitable. Hardin reasons that since we can't do merely one thing, we must do several related things including ameliorative actions so that we will bring into being a new *stable system*—a system with an acceptable degree of ecological balance. Such an integrated endeavor will be more expensive in the short run, but will pay countless dividends in the long run.

The Third Law of Ecology can best be summarized as *"TANSTAAFL"—there ain't no such thing as a free lunch.* Robert A. Heinlein was the first to use this acronym,[11] and its full implications were explored in *Tanstaafl: The Economic Strategy for Environmental Crisis,* a perceptive book by Edwin G. Dolan of Dartmouth College.[12]

This Third Law embodies all other laws of ecology because our biosphere is an interconnected whole in which nothing can be gained or lost—everything, every waste, must go somewhere. Any significant alteration on Spaceship Terra must be restored, or there will be a loss. Environmental costs cannot be avoided; they can only be delayed.

Heinlein's acronym can be viewed as an attempt to reduce the totality of our knowledge of economics to a single sentence. In ecology, as in economics, TANSTAAFL is intended to warn that every gain is won at some cost. Failure to recognize the "no free lunch" law causes the *buffalo-hunter mentality* syndrome—the unthinking assumption that there will always be plenty because there always has been plenty. The illusion that mankind has escaped the constraints of scarcity maintains the buffalo-hunter mentality, a form of psychosis that could destroy civ-

ilization if it is not cured through universal understanding of the inexorible implications of
TANSTAAFL.

The fact that "everything is connected to everything
else" and you "can't do merely one thing" are the
basic reasons why I believe that solutions to the
energy crisis cannot be separated from solutions to
the other components of the Megacrisis. These two
ecology laws along with TANSTAAFL, combined
with the principles of impotence comprise the reality
of the world that we must conform to if our descendants are to survive and thrive. In fact, the Principle of
Optimization can be interpreted as incorporating
these three laws of ecology within its bounds.

Since the three key laws of ecology are part of the
Principle of Optimization, it can be used in every
phase of the planning process. Its application can
range from specific engineering refinements to the de-
termination of the optimum percentage of GNP that
should be devoted to research budgets associated
with new energy options and pollution abatement
technologies. Economists can play a vital role as these
plans are revised and refined. They may see the law
of diminishing returns in a new light when our ninth
principle of impotence is fully integrated into their
discipline.

Fundamentally, scientific knowledge must be a
series of successive approximations to reality. It simply is not possible to arrive at absolute truth with a
finite number of investigations. As has been mentioned above (and in the footnotes), some of our first
seven principles of impotence may be modified by
new discoveries resulting in a more general principle
of which the old theory is seen as a special case.

There are complex reasons, however, for believing that our eighth and ninth principles of impotence will not be modified in the future.

Like the principle of mass production, new discoveries will not change the Principle of Optimization. Here we face a permanent constraint that will remain unchanged as long as the Earth continues to exist. Its recognition can serve us well as the foundation for disciplined study into every aspect of a balanced relationship with our planetary environment.

FOOTNOTES

Chapter One: 2029: A Transformed World

1. The basic DynaShip design was developed by Wilhelm Prolss in Hamburg, Germany. The concept is being further refined by the DynaShip Corporation (address: 81 Encina Avenue, Palo Alto, California 94301), which has acquired Western hemisphere rights from Prolss.

Chapter Two: On Forecasting the Future

1. Ben Bova, *Analog*, (October 1975), p. 6.

2. Edward S. Cornish, with members and staff of the World Future Society, *The Study of the Future*, (Washington, D.C., World Future Society, 1977), p. 1.

3. Robert W. Prehoda, *Designing The Future: The Role of Technological Forecasting*, (Philadelphia, Chilton Book Company, 1967), p. 12.

4. Sir George Thomson, *The Foreseeable Future*, (Cambridge, England, Cambridge University Press, 1955), quote taken from the book's preface, p. vii.

5. Ibid., pp. 4-5.

6. Robert A. Heinlein, "Where To," *Galaxy*, (February 1952), pp. 13-22. A reprint of and extended review comments on Heinlein's 1949 forecast is contained in: *The Worlds of Robert A. Heinlein*, (New York, Ace Books, 1966), pp. 7-31.

7. Arthur C. Clarke, *Report on Planet Three and Other Speculations*, (New York, A Signet Book from New American Library, 1973), p. 144.

8. Herman Kahn and Anthony J. Wiener, *The Year 2000*, (New York, The Macmillan Company, 1967), p. 6.

9. Ibid., p. 38.

Chapter Three: 1989: The Post-Orwellian Era

1. George Orwell, *1984* (New York, Signet Classic from New American Library, 1961), pp. 63-64.

2. Ibid., p. 57.

3. Ibid., p. 251.

4. Ibid., p. 177.

5. Ibid., p. 159.

6. Ibid., p. 220.

7. Stefan Kanfer, "Orwell 25 Years Later: Future Imperfect," *Time* (March 24, 1975), p. 78.

8. *Science News* (February 16, 1974), p. 106.

Chapter Four: 1994: Year of the Malthusian Crisis

1. Thomas Robert Malthus, *An Essay on the Princi-*

ple of Population and a Summary View of the Principle of Population, edited with an introduction by Antony Flew, (Middlesex, England, Penguin Books, 1970).

2. B. Bruce-Briggs, "Against the Neo-Malthusians," *Commentary* (July 1974), pp. 25-29.

3. *Time* (November 11, 1974), p. 80, and *Newsweek* (November 11, 1974), p. 68.

4. George Orwell, *1984* (New York, Signet Classic from New American Library, 1961), p. 155 and p. 157.

5. Dennis Gabor, *Innovations: Scientific, Technological and Social* (London, Oxford University Press, 1970), p. 100.

Chapter Five: Visit to Micropolis

1. John Ward Pearson, *The 8-Day Week* (New York, Harper & Row, 1973)

2. William J. D. Escher, "The Case for the Hydrogen-Oxygen Car," *Analog* (September 1973), pp. 28-51. This article reprinted in *Analog Science Fact Reader* (New York, St. Martin's Press, 1974), pp. 146-171.

3. Richard F. Dempewolff, "Underground Housing," *Science Digest* (November 1975), pp. 42-43.

Chapter Six: Robots and the Intelligence-Amplifier

1. "Artificial Vision: A Quantum Leap Forward," *Science News* (January 31, 1976), p. 68.

2. James S. Albus and John M. Evans, Jr., "Robot

Systems," *Scientific American* (February 1976), p. 86B.

3. James S. Albus, "The Economics of the Robot Revolution," *Analog: Science Fact & Science Fiction* (April 1975), p. 72.

4. Ibid. pp. 72-73.

5. Don Larson, "Nitrogen-Fixing Shrubs: An Answer to the World's Firewood Shortage?" *The Futurist* (April 1976), pp. 74-77.

6. W. Ross Ashby, "Design for Intelligence Amplifiers," in *Automatia Studies* eds. C. E. Shannon and J. McCarthy (Princeton, N.J., Princeton University Press, 1956).

7. Isaac Asimov, *Opus 100* (New York, Dell Publishing Company, 1970), p. 69.

8. Robert W. Prehoda, *Designing the Future: The Role of Technological Forecasting* (Philadelphia, Chilton Book Company, 1967), pp. 277-279.

9. Robert A. MacGowan and Frederic I. Ordway III, *Intelligence in the Universe* (Englewood Cliffs, N.J., Prentice-Hall, Inc., 1966), p. 267.

Chapter Seven: 2009: The World Set Free

1. Jules Verne, *The Mysterious Island*, (New York, World Publishing Company), Part II, Chapter 11, pp. 327-328.

2. *Science News*, (December 13, 1975), p. 381.

3. Garret Hardin, "The Tragedy of the Commons," *Science*, (December 13, 1968), pp. 1243-1248.

4. Robert A. Heinlein, *The Door Into Summer*, (Garden City, New York, Doubleday & Company, 1957), p. 187.

Chapter Eight: 2014: Methuselah's Children

1. Robert A. Heinlein, *Methuselah's Children*, (New York, Signet Books, 1958), p. 14. An earlier shorter version of this 1958 novel was published in 1941.

2. Bjorksten Research Foundation, P. O. Box 9444, Madison, Wisconsin 53715.

3. Johan Bjorksten, "Pathways to the Decisive Extension of the Human Specific Lifespan," *Journal of the American Geriatrics Society*, (September 1977), pp. 396-399.

4. Robert A. Heinlein, Opus cited, p. 154.

5. *Fortune*, (July 1976), p. 140.

Chapter Nine: Project Cyclops

1. *Project Cyclops*, Bernard M. Oliver, et al., National Aeronautics and Space Administration, Publication CR-114445; 1972.

2. Dietrick E. Thomsen, "Cosmology According to Hoyle," *Science News*, (June 14, 1975), pp. 386-387.

3. William O. Davis, "The Fourth Law of Motion," *Analog: Science Fact & Science Fiction*, (May 1962), pp. 85-104.

4. Arthur C. Clark, "The Mind of the Machine," *Playboy*, (December 1968), p. 294.

Chapter Ten: 2024: The Third Industrial Revolution

1. G. Harry Stine, *"The Third Industrial Revolution,"* (New York, Putnam, 1975). Certain quotations taken from Stine's book have been modified through private communication between G. H. Stine and R. W. Prehoda.

2. William J. D. Escher, P.O. Box 187, St. Johns, Michigan 48879.

3. Robert Salkeld, "Orbital Rocket Airplanes: A Fresh Perspective," *Aeronautics & Astronautics,* (April 1976), pp. 50-52.

4. Gerard K. O'Neill, "The Colonization of Space," *Physics Today,* (September 1974), p. 37.

5. *Astronautics and Aerospace Engineering,* (June 1963), p. 127.

6. *Foundation Report,* (April 1, 1978), p. 23. Published by The Foundation, 85 East Geranium Avenue, St. Paul MN 55117.

7. *Project Daedalus,* (1978), p. S6. Published by the British Interplanetary Society, 12 Bessborough Gardens, London, SW1V 2JJ England.

8. *Newsletter of the National Space Institute,* (September 1977), p. 4.

9. The proton-boron[11] fuel cycle is illustrated below. In this thermonuclear fission reaction, the proton nucleus and boron[11] nucleus combine to form a carbon[12] nucleus in an "excited" state. The carbon[12] nucleus immediately divides into a beryllium[8] nucleus in an "excited" state and an alpha particle. The Beryllium[8] nucleus im-

mediately divides into two alpha particles. This pattern—a proton-boron[11] reaction culminating in three alpha particles—would occur in 99.9 percent of the reactions. Relatively rare side reactions of the high-energy alpha particles with other nuclei in the plasma would produce a low-energy (3 Mev) neutron and a radioactive carbon[14] nucleus in about 0.1 percent of the reactions. Even so, a proton-boron[11] power plant would have an inventory of radioactive isotopes roughly one thousandth of what is estimated for a comparatively sized fusion reactor burning a deuterium-tritium fuel cycle. The resulting level of radioisotopes would be nearly 100,000 times lower than a comparable fission plant burning uranium or plutonium.

Aside from the almost total lack of neutron damage to a spaceship powered with a proton-

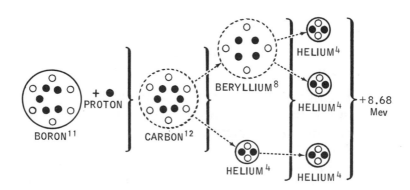

boron[11] fuel cycle, it offers a major cost breakthrough for the 3rd IR. There is 19 times more boron[11] in the Earth's crust than there is deuterium. Boron is plentiful in the oceans and in dry lake beds. Natural boron is composed of 80.22 percent boron[11] and 19.78 percent boron[10]. Separation of these boron isotopes by fractional distillation of BF^3 (a fluorine compound) provides almost pure 99.9 percent boron[11] for 20 cents a gram (1979 dollars), and new laser isotope enrichment technologies can now further reduce the cost of 99.9 percent pure boron[11] for power plant or space propulsion requirements.

10. Gary C. Hudson, "Advanced Propulsion Systems and Solar System Spaceships," (October 1978), Foundation, Inc., 85 East Geranium Avenue, St. Paul, MN 55117.

11. A very large Earth-to-orbit launch venicle would require a propulsion system similar to that designed under Project Orion around 1960 in which small fission bombs would be detonated underneath a huge pusher plate to orbit a massive spacecraft. The radioactive pollution of such a system would be avoided if small proton-boron[11] bombs could be built, each containing a small pellet of antihydrogen. These bombs would transfer heat to a reaction mass, which in turn would transfer energy to the pusher plate. One thousand tons of payload might be orbited with each launch.

12. Krafft A. Ehricke, "Astropolis: The First Space Resort," *Playboy*, (November 1968), pp. 96-98, 222.

13. G. Harry Stine, Private communication.

Chapter Eleven: 2029: Technological Shangri-La

1. Gene Bylinsky, "The Cloning Era is Almost Here," *Fortune* (June 19, 1978), pp. 100-114.

2. Bill Johns, "Renewal," *Analog: Science Fiction & Science Fact*, (May 1978), pp. 115-152.

3. Michael Dunlop Young, *The Rise of the Meritocracy*, (London, The Thames and Hudson, 1958). Also published in 1959 by Random House in Toronto.

4. Neil P. Ruzic, *"Island for Science,"* available from Neil Ruzic & Co., Box 527, Beverly Shores, Indiana 46301.

5. Robert A. MacGowan and Frederic I. Ordway III, *Intelligence in the Universe* (Englewood Cliffs, N.J., Prentice-Hall, Inc., 1966), p. 234.

6. Robert W. Prehoda, *Suspended Animation* (Philadelphia. Chilton, 1969), pp. 81-91.

Chapter Twelve: Tomorrow and Tomorrow and Tomorrow

1. Gerard K. O'Neill, "The Colonization of Space," *Physics Today*, (September 1974), p. 37.

2. Dandridge M. Cole and Donald W. Cox, *Islands in Space: The Challenge of the Planetoids*, (Philadelphia, Chilton, 1964), p. 103.

3. Jerry Pournelle, *That Buck Rogers Stuff*, (Los Angeles, Exteguer Press, 1977), p. 44.

4. Hans Moravec, "Today's Computers, Intelligent

Machines and our Future," *Analog: Science Fact & Science Fiction*, (February 1979), pp. 77-78.

5. Herman Kahn, William Brown and Leon Martel, *The Next 200 Years*, (New York, William Morrow and Co., 1976).

6. Donella H. Meadows, Dennis L. Meadows, Jorgen Randers and William W. Behrens III, *The Limits to Growth*, (New York, Universe Books, 1972).

7. James Patrick Baen, "Epistle to the Christians," *Galaxy*, (December 1976), p. 4.

8. "Culture and Population Change," A study (August 1974) prepared by the AIAA's Office of International Science: 1776 Massachusetts Avenue, N.W., Washington, DC 20036.

9. *Science*, (March 1, 1974), pp. 883-886.

Appendix A: The Principle of Optimization

1. Sir George Thomson. *The Foreseeable Future* (Cambridge, England, The University Press, 1955), quotation taken from The Preface, page vii.

2. Scientists are now aware of four force fields or interactions in nature. "Gravity" and "electromagnetism" are long-range forces. The "strong nuclear interaction" and the "weak nuclear interaction" are short-range force fields restricted to the infinitesimal distances encountered inside atomic nuclei. Each force effect is transmitted through an exchange of an intermediate particle peculiar to that force: photons for the electromagnetic, gravitons for gravitational fields, the strong nuclear force is transmitted by mesons,

and the weak nuclear force by "W" particles. Research conducted by William O. Davis (1919-1974), G. Harry Stine, and their associates indicates that there may be a fifth class of field force or interaction, the "inertial field." If it really exists, then this long-range field force would produce its effects through a unique form of gravito-inertial radiation particle that I have called "the inerton." Proof that inertons exist would probably be expressed in a new principle of impotence, Davis' Fourth Law of Motion: "The energy in a given system can only be changed in some finite length of time depending on the system, and never in zero time." This now-hypothetical principle of impotence would significantly modify the restrictions of Newton's Third Law of Motion, allowing a revolutionary new form of space propulsion along with other applications. See Davis' article in *Analog* (May 1962), and Stine's article in *Analog* (June 1976).

3. A balloon lifted a dector package of film to 130,000 feet where a magnetic monopole was assumed to have passed through the layers of the film package. Skeptics contend that this event may have been a fragmenting nucleus of a platinum atom, or an ultra-heavy cosmic ray nucleus mimicking a monopole's behavior. Until such explanations are eliminated, no one can say with certainty that a monopole has been found.

4. While the energy of a closed system remains constant, its entropy always increases. That is, natural processes always tend toward states of increased disorder. R. Buckminster Fuller's "syner-

getic-energetic geometry" holds that there are no closed systems—that closed systems, like straight lines or bodies at rest, are obsolete notions that hinder, rather than help, our understanding of the universe. Here Fuller's viewpoint is debatable and many years of basic research and experiments may be required before his position on the second law of thermodynamics is confirmed or refuted.

5. Private communication—Johan Bjorksten is one of a handful of multidisciplinary scientists that I would place in the same class as Sir George Thomson (1892-1975).

6. J. B. S. Haldane, "On Being the Right Size," from *The World of Mathematics* edited by J. R. Newman, (New York, Simon and Schuster, 1956).

7. R. Philip Hammond, "Low Cost Energy: A New Dimension," *Science Journal* (January 1969), pp. 36-37.

8. Private communication.

9. *Science News* (April 15, 1972), p. 242.

10. Barry Commoner, *The Closing Circle: Nature, Man & Technology* (New York, Bantam Books, 1972), pp. 29-43.

11. Robert A. Heinlein, *The Moon is a Harsh Mistress* (New York, Berkley Medallion Books, 1968), p. 129.

12. Edwin G. Dolan, *Tanstaafl: The Economic Strategy for Environmental Crisis* (New York, Holt, Rinehart & Winston, 1971).

INDEX

Aging-retardation, 185-199, 259-260

Albus, James, 132, 334, 335

Alderson, Daniel J., 276

Antioxidants for aging-retardation, 188

Antiscientism, 53-54, 289-290, 294, 299

Aquarest water-bed system, 20

Artificial intelligence, 140-147, 285

Artificial vision, 125-126, 150, 152

Ashby, W. Ross, 141, 335

Asimov, Isaac, 142, 155, 272, 276, 301, 335

Asteroid mining, 14, 240, 243

Bacon, Sir Francis, 24

Baen, James Patrick, 278, 299, 341

Biological control of insect pests, 119-120

Biocybernetic communication, 150-154

Bjorksten, Johan, 188-190, 276, 316, 336, 343

Borlaug, Norman, 87-88

Bova, Ben, 25, 332

Brain cell (neurons) aging, 196, 259-260

Brain-computer symbiosis, 147-154, 265-266

Brown, Harrison, 301

Bryson, Reid, 176

Buck Rogers, 137, 139, 251

Bussard, Robert, 276

Campbell, John W., 142

Carpenter, Donald G., 324

Carrel, Alexis, 191

Chen, Helen, 257-263, 278

Chen, William, 125-156, 225-255, 257, 260-265, 273-274

Clarke, Arthur C., xiii, 41, 214, 216, 242, 276, 301, 333, 336

Clarke's Third Law, 214, 247, 304
Cloning, 17-18, 258-259, 270
Cole, Dandridge M., 283
Colichman, Eugene, 276
Commoner, Barry, 327-328, 343
Cornish, Edward S., 27, 332
Cosmology, 209-211
Courtesans, 251-252, 264
Cybernetics, 138
Davis, William O., 336, 341-342
Death-hormone neutralizer, 191-192
Denckla, W. Donner, 191-192, 196, 276
Deuterium-deuterium fusion fuel cycle, 162-165, 170
Deuterium-helium^3 fusion fuel cycle, 165-166
Dirigibles, 5-9, 266-269
Disassembly plants, 109-115
Dolan, Edwin G., 329, 343
Doublethink, 50, 88-89
DynaShip windjammers, 10-12
Ectogenesis, 18, 251
Ehricke, Krafft, 254-255, 339
Eight-day week, 115-116, 334
Einstein, Albert, 200
Electric cars, 66, 109, 112, 116-117, 119
Electromagnetic lunar catapult, 242
Energy-use dictum, 12
Escher, William J. D., 117, 229-230, 334, 337
ESP phenomena & research, 147, 213

Feinberg, Gerald, 308
Forward, Robert L., 247, 276
Fourth Law of Motion, 342
Fuller, R. Buckminster, 311, 342
Fusion power & propulsion system, 159-169, 245-246
Gabor, Dennis, 90, 301, 334
Genetic erosion of plants, 77-78
Goddard, Robert H., 39
Goldstein, Allan L., 190
Hahn, Otto, 34
Hahn-Strassmann point, 34-35
Haldane, J.B.S., 322
Hammond, R. Philip, 322
Hardin, Garrett, 183, 328-329, 335
Harman, Denham, 188
Hearts, artificial & transplants, 61-63
Hegel's aphorism, 182
Heinlein, Robert A., 31-34, 184, 185-186, 191, 276, 304, 329, 333, 336, 343
Heisenberg, Werner, 310, 325-326
Helium, 167, 237-238, 268, 275
Holographic teleprojection, 3
Hoyle, Sir Fred, 209, 276, 336
Hudson, Gary C. 249, 339
Human hibernation, 14, 246-247
Hydrogen-economy, 169-175
Hydroponic farms, 120-121
IAN (Intelligence-Amplifier Neuralelectronic), 19, 140-156, 206, 212, 214, 219, 246-247, 253, 262, 266,

270-276

Immortality (biological), 195, 219, 259-260

Inertons & inerton-drive for spaceships, 212-213, 246-247, 275, 309, 342

Interstellar signal beacons, 203, 221-223

Interstellar communication, 14-15, 200-223

Kahn, Herman, 42, 44, 286-288, 333

Kissinger, Henry, 276

Land-use planning, 103-104

Laws of Robotics, 142-143, 155, 272-273

Lebensraum (living space), 136, 177, 265

Liposomes for aging-retardation, 193

Lorenz, Konrad, 292, 301

Lunar mining, 12, 240-242, 245

MacArthur, Douglas, 91

Magnetic monopole, 30-31, 310-312, 342

Malthus, Thomas Robert, 73, 333

Malthusian crisis, 176, 181, 296-299

Mammoths, 8, 258-259

Management by Exception Principle, 143-144, 253

Mariculture, 269-270

Meitner, Lise, 35

Memory-gel bed, 2

Meritocracy, 264-265

Methanol, 65-67, 117, 171

Methanol *in situ* production from coal, 66-67

Methuselah's Children, 185-186, 191

Microenzymes for aging-retardation, 188, 190

Microliposomes for aging-retardation, 259-260

Migma fusion reactors, 251, 269

Moravec, Hans, 285-286, 340

Muir, John, 328

Mulliken, Robert S., 301

Murray, Bruce C., 301

New Leader—dictator of China, 53, 86

1984, (book by Orwell), 47-54, 89, 280

Nitrogen-fixing shrubs, 137

Niven, Larry, 254, 261, 263, 276

Northrop, John H., 301

Oliver, Bernard M., 205, 336

O'Neill, Gerard K., 282-284, 337, 340

Optimum population, 177-179

Orentreich, Norman, 191

Orwell, George, 47-54, 88-90, 280

Partheonogenesis, 17

Pinneo, Lawrence R., 148

Plan Alpha for population reduction, 196-199

Planetoids (see asteroids)

Plasmapheresis for aging-retardation, 190-191, 196

Population explosion, 70-71

Post, Richard L., 161

Pauling, Linus C., 301

Pournelle, Jerry, 261, 263, 276, 284, 301, 340

Principles of impotence, 30-31, 308-316, 325, 342
Principle of Optimization, 293-294, 307-331
Project Abraham, 92-94
Project Cyclops, 205-208, 221, 336
Proton-boron[11] propulsion system, 248-251
Proton-boron[11] thermonuclear fission fuel cycle, 248-249, 337-339
Psychosurgery cure for drug addiction, 63-64
Public-service-functions of biosphere, 68-70, 88-89, 135, 224, 295
Rejuvenation, 194, 196, 259-260
Research, basic & applied, 290-291
Robots and robotics, 2, 4, 11, 19, 126-156, 164, 236-237, 240, 264, 269, 284-286
Ruzic, Neil P., 269-270, 276, 301, 322, 340
Sacred-cow war, 82-85
Salkeld, Robert, 229, 337
Scenario forecasting, 42-44
Science fiction, predictive role of SF, 25-26
Scientific method, 54, 290-291
Silent aircraft, 122
Sklarew, Ralph, 276
Solar energy, 105, 119, 168, 173-174, 180, 227
Space colonization, 235-237, 263, 282-286
Space industrialization, 234-244
Stine, G. Harry, 225, 227, 235, 255, 276, 286, 299, 301, 337, 340, 342
Strassmann, Fritz, 34
Strehler, Bernard L., 193, 276
Supercivilizations, 203-215, 217-219, 222-223
Suspended animation, 197-198, 247, 274-276, 340
Synchronous broadcast satellites, 180-182
Tanaka, Charles, 257, 261, 263
Tanaka, Helen Chen (see Helen Chen)
TANSTAAFL, 329-330, 343
Technological forecasting, 28-31, 45-46
Technological Shangri-La, 256-257, 266, 269, 300-301, 306
Technophilic-Malthusian perspective, 288-298
Telescoped performance achievements, 37-40
The Foreseeable Future, 29, 34, 308
Thermonuclear Fission, 248-249
Third Industrial Revolution (3rd IR), 225-255, 299
Thomson, Sir George, 29-30, 301, 307-314, 326, 332, 341
Thymosin aging-retardation hormone, 190
Trend curves, 31-42
Tsiolkovski, Konstaintin E., 38

Underground buildings, 117-119, 158
Unified field theory, 200-201
Verne, Jules, 25, 175, 335
Vidal, Jacques, 148
Videophone communication & facsimile-printout system, 57-59, 108
Weather changes, 74-77
Wiener, Anthony J., 42, 44, 333
Wiener, Norbert, 138
Wells, H. G., 25, 157, 159, 175, 179
World Future Society, 27
Xenon narcosis, 21
Xenon used in suspended animation, 274-275, 340
Young, Michael Dunlop, 264, 340
Zeppelins (see dirigibles)